An Introduction for Airmen

As an expeditionary Airman you must stay ready to deploy anywhere in the world on short notice. This manual doesn't contain everything you must know. It doesn't focus on the integrated joint or multinational nature of combat operations. It doesn't replace regulations or local procedures you'll need to follow. This manual does, however, cover basic warfighting skills and points of knowledge with the intent to help you successfully complete the mission. The tasks outlined in this manual apply at both deployed and home station locations. Keep the Airman's Manual close to you; use it while training and exercising for contingencies and deployments. Refer to it often... you'll need it.

Fly, Fight, and Win!

THE AIRMAN'S CREED

I AM AN AMERICAN AIRMAN.
I AM A WARRIOR.
I HAVE ANSWERED MY NATION'S CALL.

I AM AN AMERICAN AIRMAN.
MY MISSION IS TO FLY, FIGHT, AND WIN.
I AM FAITHFUL TO A PROUD HERITAGE,
A TRADITION OF HONOR,
AND A LEGACY OF VALOR.

I AM AN AMERICAN AIRMAN,
GUARDIAN OF FREEDOM AND JUSTICE,
MY NATION'S SWORD AND SHIELD,
ITS SENTRY AND AVENGER.
I DEFEND MY COUNTRY WITH MY LIFE.

I AM AN AMERICAN AIRMAN:
WINGMAN, LEADER, WARRIOR.
I WILL NEVER LEAVE AN AIRMAN BEHIND,
I WILL NEVER FALTER,
AND I WILL NOT FAIL.

Table of Contents

An Introduction for Airmen i
Airman's Creed ii
Table of Contents iii

Section 1
Staying Ready

Personal Affairs 2
Predeployment Maintenance Checklist 4
Personal Bag 5
Host Nation Sensitivities 6

Section 2
Deploy

Prepare for Deployment 8
Team Integrity and Accountability 9
Rules of Engagement (ROE) 10
Law of Armed Conflict (LOAC) 11
Handling News Media 13
OCONUS Legal Concerns 16
Force Protection Conditions (FPCON) 17
Attack Warning Signals for Chemical, Biological, Radiological, Nuclear, and high-yield Explosives in High Threat Areas 18
Individual Protective Equipment (IPE) 19
Chemical Protective Overgarment (CPO) ... 20
Mission Oriented Protective Posture (MOPP) 23
MOPP Options 29
Split-MOPP Concept 30
Lifting and Carrying Safety 32

Section 3
Employment

Arrival at Deployment Location 34
Arrival Actions 36
Improvised Explosive Device (IED) Threat 38
Health Concerns During Deployment 42
Other Concerns 44
Mental Health 46
Fire Safety 47
Expedient Firefighting 48
Waste Control 50
Contaminated Waste Control and Disposal 51
Food Consumption 53
Resources Protection and Crime Prevention 54
Passive Defense 55
Expedient Hardening 57
Camouflage, Concealment, and Blackout 58
Defensive Fighting Position (DFP's) 60
Contamination Avoidance and CBRN Pre-Attack Preparation 62
Command and Control 65
Field Communications 67
Anti-Terrorism Force Protection Measures .. 68
Be Suspicious 69
Terrorist Threats and Vehicles 71
Pre-Attack Actions 73
Additional Attack Preparations Under Alarm Yellow 76

Section 4
Fight

Integrated Base Defense (IBD)	78
Security Procedures	80
Challenging Intruders	81
Challenge and Password	84
Handling Prisoners and Defectors	85
Audible and Visual Warnings	87
Attack Warning	89
Reporting an Attack	91
S-A-L-U-T-E	91
Reactions to Flares	93
Vehicle and Equipment Protection, Marking, and Decon	94
Convoy Procedures	96
Convoy Attack Procedures	96
Weapons Skills–Rifle	98
Care and Cleaning of Small Arms M4, M9, M16	111
Weapons Decontamination	113
Weapons Skills–Pistol/M9	115

Section 5
Survive

Alarm Black–Attack Is Over, Initiate Base Recovery	124
Post-Attack Reconnaissance	124
Unexploded Ordnance (UXO)	126
Reporting Unexploded Ordnance	129
Contamination Control	131
M8 Chemical Agent Detection Paper	133
M9 Chemical Agent Detection Paper (Tape)	136
Nuclear Attack/Radioactive Individual Protective Actions	137
Nuclear and Biological Protection	138
Operational Differences Between Chemical and Biological Warfare Agents	143
Chemical Agent Individual Protective Actions - Nerve Agents	144
Nerve Agent Antidote Injectors	145
Chemical Agent Individual Protective Actions - Blister Agents	147
Toxic Industrial Material (TIM)	148
Shelter-In-Place	149
MCU-2 Series Protective Mask	152
M45 Land Warrior Chemical-Biological Mask	158
Canisters and Filters	163
Mask Second Skin	164
M50 Joint Service General Purpose Field Mask	166
Drinking Through the Mask	168
Levels of Chemical Decontamination	170
M291 Skin Decontamination Kit	171
M295 Individual Equipment Decontamination Kit	172
Casualty Collection	173
Casualty Care in an CBRN Contaminated Environment	174
Basic Lifesaving Steps	174
Common Injuries	178
Combating Heat Illness and Cold Injury	180
Dehydration	181
Heat Exhaustion	181
Heat Stroke	183
Heat Injuries	184
Cold Injuries	185
Emergency Life-Saving Equipment	186
Handling Human Remains	187

Rights as a Prisoner of War 188
Code of Conduct 191

Section 6
Quick Reference

Phonetic Alphabet/Numbers 194
Radio Communications
   Procedure Words (PROWORDS) 195
Wind Chill Chart 197
Ground Crew Layout
   Contamination Control Area 198
Air Crew Layout
   Contamination Control Area 199
Nuclear, Biological, and Chemical (NBC) and
   Unexploded Ordnance (UXO)
   Hazard Markers 200
Nuclear, Biological, Chemical, and
   Conventional (NBCC)
   Hazard Markers 201
IED Reporting and Evacuation 202
Serviceable Tag-Materiel,
   DD Form 1574 203
MCU-2 Series Mask Inspection 204
M45 Mask Inspection 206
M50 Mask Inspection 210
Chemical Protective Overgarment (CPO)
   Accessory Checklist 214
Quick MOPP 215
Work Rest Cycles and Fluid
   Replacement Guidelines 216
Square Grid Matrix 217
Reading a Grid Map 218
Chemical Agent General Information 219
Acronyms and Definitions 220
Index 223

EXTRA FEATURE:
Open back cover for access to critical items

Critical Information Checklist

Post Attack Actions 1
UXO Survey 2
USAF Unexploded Ordnance (UXO)
   Recognition and Reporting Chart ... 3
Nuclear Attack Radioactive
   Individual Protective Actions 8
Nerve Agent Poisoning and Antidote 10
Shelter In-Place Actions 13
Lifesaving Steps 17
Control Bleeding 18
Tourniquet 19
Shock 20
Abdominal Wound 21
Common Injury Treatment 22
Spinal/Neck/Head Injury 22
Eye Injury 23
Chest Wound 23
Fracture 24
M16 Jammed 25
M9 Jammed 26
Important Phone Numbers
   and Quick Reference 27

Section 1
Staying Ready

Personal Affairs

Ref: 10 United States Code (USC), Sec 1044; AFI 51-504

The military is a dangerous profession. You must keep your personal affairs in order at all times. Avoid problems later by effectively managing your personal matters BEFORE you deploy.

Finance

- Obtain a myPay Personal Identification Number to access your military pay account (Leave and Earning Statement, Pay Changes, Taxes, Thrift Savings Plan) via the Defense Finance and Accounting Service myPay website at https://mypay.dfas.mil
- Settle any Government Travel Card bills
- Upon notice of deployment consider establishing "accrual travel payments" to help you pay your travel expenses while deployed.

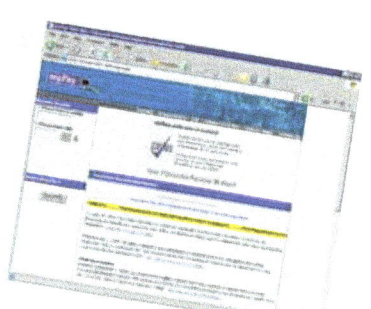

Legal

Periodically review your legal documents and keep them up-to-date. Marriage, divorce, births, deaths, and changes in personal assets are significant events that affect your legal interests.

Will—Legal instrument everyone should have that allows you to:
- Declare who should carry out (or "execute") the provisions of your will
- Dispose of your property after death
- Name guardians to raise your minor children and manage any property you leave to them

Life Insurance—Your life insurance policy, including Servicemembers' Group Life Insurance, pays money to named beneficiaries upon your death. It's a contract between you and your insurer. Because of that, the provisions of your will generally do not impact insurance payouts. You should discuss with legal assistance providers the risks/dangers of designating "by law" distribution of insurance proceeds, compared with specifically naming individuals. Make sure your policy is the correct type and the value you need.

Power of Attorney (POA)–Lets you designate someone else to perform one or more legal acts on your behalf for a set period of time. POAs are powerful documents. Make sure the people you choose to execute your POA are trustworthy, have good common sense, and clearly understand what you desire concerning the matters you ask them to conduct. No company or agency is required to accept or honor any POA. Prior to deployment, check with the company/agency with which your designee will be doing business, and ensure the POA meets its needs. Three types of POAs are:

- General–a designee may do virtually anything you can legally do. This is an extremely powerful document
- Special–a designee may carry out only a specific matter such as sell a vehicle, buy or sell real estate, or ship/store household goods
- Health Care–a designee may make health care decisions if you're unable to do so because of injury, illness, or the effects of medication

Uniformed Services Employment and Re-employment Rights Act (USERRA)–This law assists anyone, particularly reservists and guardsmen, to get their jobs back after deployment. USERRA also addresses issues such as seniority, leave, pension plans, and continuing health care coverage for members and dependents while deployed.

Soldiers and Sailors Civil Relief Act (SSCRA)–A comprehensive law that provides protection of many different types to members while on active duty, from capping interest rates on pre-service loans to postponing civil court cases.

Taxes–Your activation and deployment to certain areas of the world may greatly impact your federal and/or state income tax filing and refund. You may be able to exclude your income earned during a deployment or you may be entitled to an extension of the filing deadline.

Predeployment Maintenance Checklist

General
- ☐ Chaplain and religious concerns
- ☐ Family Support Center
- ☐ Child Care Center
- ☐ Family Care Certification (AF Form 357)
- ☐ Emergency contact information
- ☐ Emergency Data Card (DD Form 93)
- ☐ Real estate/rent
- ☐ Vehicle
- ☐ Pets
- ☐ Education
- ☐ Voter registration
- ☐ Safe deposit box
- ☐ Restricted area badge
- ☐ Weapons qualification (AF Form 522)
- ☐ Government and flightline drivers license
- ☐ Passport

Legal
- ☐ Will / Living will
- ☐ Life Insurance:
    - Servicemembers' Group Life Insurance
    - Private policy
- ☐ Power of Attorney:
    - General
    - Medical/Special

Health Care
- ☐ Prescription medicine
- ☐ Dental care
- ☐ Corrective lenses:
    - Clear
    - Sunglasses
    - Protective mask
- ☐ Immunizations
- ☐ Preventive/predeployment health assessment
- ☐ Force Health Managment (Public Health)

Finance
- ☐ Installment loans
- ☐ Allotments
- ☐ Automatic payments
- ☐ Investment portfolios
- ☐ Tax and accounting
- ☐ Government Travel Card
- ☐ Keep a supply of extra personal checks on hand

Use as a reference to help you stay prepared.

Personal Bag

Along with mobility bags, you must prepare a personal bag that contains mission essential items you must take based on the most probable deployment scenario. Since a Tactical Field Exchange may not be operational at your deployed site, you should pack a 30 to 45 day supply of personal consumable items to help you through your initial stay.

Here are some things your unit will require you to pack and some additional items you may wish to take when they're authorized. Follow your unit deployment checklist for mandatory items and quantities.

Prepare a personal bag.

- Uniform sets
- Civilian clothing
- Athletic clothing
- Cold/Wet weather gear
- Undergarments and socks
- Clothes hangers
- Waterproof bags
- Sunblock, lip balm, lotions, insect repellent
- Towels, washcloths, premoistened towelettes
- Mirror, comb/brush, toothpaste, toothbrush, floss, toothpicks, shampoo, soap, razor, tissues, hygiene products
- Snacks, gum, candy, antacids, vitamins, aspirin, prescription medicines
- Extra prescription glasses and sunglasses
- Radio, audio player, alarm clock, wristwatch, flashlight, spare batteries, camera, film
- Zipper bag with powdered laundry detergent
- Religious material, magazines, crossword puzzles, photos, paperbacks, study guides, stationery kit, address book
- Some emergency cash, a checkbook, and a credit card (Transport aircraft can be diverted or break down en route... be prepared!)

Host Nation Sensitivities

Where you're deploying to may be profoundly different than what you're accustomed to in the United States. Don't be surprised if you learn that some of your rights, freedoms, and customs aren't recognized or are altogether unacceptable in some global regions. You have a lot of things to remember, so when you study the deployment region, consider these important issues.

- Religion—not all countries guarantee religious freedom. Displaying certain religious icons or symbols may be offensive to our hosts and, in some cases, may violate host nation laws
- Dress and Appearance—what might seem acceptable in the US may be offensive or even illegal somewhere else
- Literature—beware of anything that might be construed as pornographic material or illegal in certain regions
- Food Items—many countries stringently control what you can and can't bring in, especially tobacco and alcohol
- Gender Specific Laws and Customs—women and men may not be granted equal rights where you're going
- Social Customs—learn the do's and don'ts of the host nation

● Example deployment regions.

Section 2
Deploy

Prepare for Deployment

There are many things you can do to prepare for a deployment days, weeks, and months before you may be tasked to depart. Don't wait until the final moment to prepare. Here are a few of those actions you can do early:

C-17.

Home Station or Prior to Deployment
- Review
  - Force Protection Condition (FPCON) actions
  - Deployment actions such as medical preparations, mobility bag issue, and personal requirements
  - Attack Warning Signals
  - Alarm Conditions
  - Mission Oriented Protective Postures (MOPP)
  - Individual protective actions
  - Self-aid and buddy care actions
  - Unit pre-conflict and attack actions checklists
- Carry or have immediate access to this manual
- Inspect your Individual Protective Equipment (IPE), paying particular attention to the mask. If you have questions on mask serviceability, contact your local CE Readiness and Emergency Management Flight
- Verify you have your eyeglasses and protective mask inserts
- Carry several permanent black markers in your IPE
- Complete protective mask fit test and mask assessment for the mask you're issued

Here are some tips to follow once you're en route:
- Determine FPCON, Alarm Condition, and MOPP at each en route stop
- Carry your IPE on the aircraft or vessel if you're deploying to a CBRNE medium or high threat area
- Keep your IPE at hand during en route stops (when directed)
- Review this manual

Team Integrity and Accountability

Ref: AFI 10-403; AFI 10-215

Nearly every Air Force member may be tasked to deploy with very little notice to support all types of contingency operations around the globe. Depending on the operational need, you may be tasked to deploy with your unit, in a small group, or alone.

If you deploy in a group, you'll form up in deployment chalks that are traditionally associated with an aircraft mission number. Usually, you'll first assemble at your unit then shuttle with your group to a Personnel Deployment Function (PDF.) PDFs offer you one last-chance opportunity to ensure you have your affairs in order and your medical needs met before you depart. Most PDFs provide representatives from finance, legal, family support, medical, personnel, and the chaplain's office to assist you. During processing, AFOSI, medical, and weather will also brief you on the latest information for your destination. Before leaving the PDF, a troop commander (officer or enlisted) will be assigned to your chalk (this could be you). It's the troop commander's responsibility to hand carry a personnel and equipment accountability kit for that chalk to the deployed location.

Personnel deployment function briefing.

Rules of Engagement (ROE)

Ref: CJCSI 3121.01B: (www.dtic.mil)
Command authorities issue ROE that describe the circumstances and limitations under which we can start, execute, or expand military operations. You'll find ROE incorporated in almost every operations plan and operational order.

ROE tailored for each mission.

Commanders use ROE to ensure operations follow national policy goals, mission requirements, and the rule of law. You must understand, remember, and apply the Law of Armed Conflict (LOAC) and ROE while performing your duties.

In armed conflict, ROE specifically tailored for each mission or area of responsibility and LOAC provide guidance on the use of force.

> Unless otherwise directed by a unit commander, military members may exercise individual self-defense in response to a hostile act or demonstrated hostile intent.

The purpose of the US standing ROE is to implement guidance on the application of force for mission accomplishment and the exercise of the inherent right and obligation of self-defense.

Unit self-defense is an inherent right and obligation of the commander.

Understand that:
- ROE questions and concerns should be properly elevated up the chain of command for resolution
- Failure to comply with ROE may be punishable under the Uniform Code of Military Justice

Law of Armed Conflict (LOAC)

Ref: CJSI 3121.01B; AFI 51-401; DOD Directive 2311.01E

Every military member must follow LOAC.

Every military member must obey and follow the LOAC. The fundamental purposes of LOAC are to prevent unnecessary suffering, safeguard persons who fall into enemy hands, and maintain a well-disciplined military force. LOAC includes the Geneva and Hague Conventions, other treaties, and customary international law. LOAC must be followed during all military operations. Failure to comply may be punishable under the Uniform Code of Military Justice. Here are some things to remember:

Use amount of force required.

Do...
- Use the minimum amount of force necessary to complete your mission, and counter hostile acts or hostile intent
- Fight those combatants who are declared hostile. An enemy combatant is a person engaged in hostilities against the US or its coalition partners during an armed conflict
- **Pull the trigger when required... many people are counting on you!**

Do Not...
- Harm enemy personnel who surrender
- Kill or torture Enemy Prisoners of War (EPW)
- Attack civilians or noncombatants, including the sick and wounded, medical personnel, EPW, and chaplains
- Attack diplomatic, religious, and medical facilities or equipment
- Attack persons, vehicles, or buildings marked with a Red Cross, Red Crescent, Red Star of David, or other protected symbols
- Misuse a protected symbol

Do not attack medical facilities.

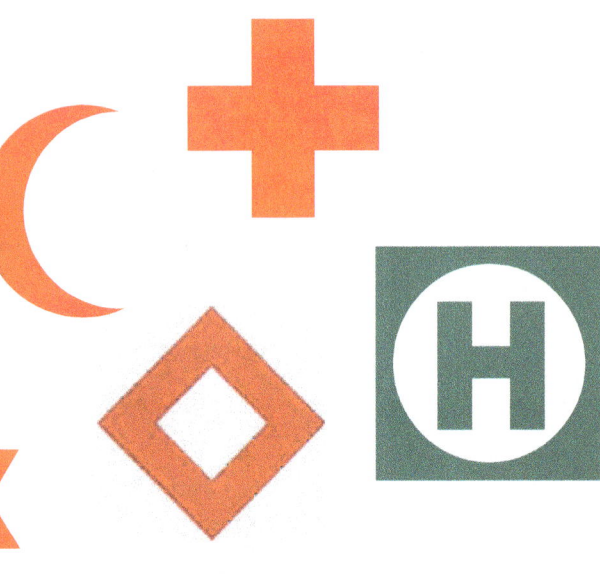

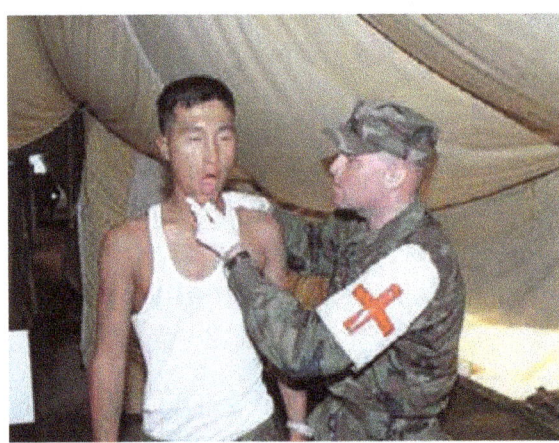

Treat EPWs humanely.

Always...
- Collect and care for all wounded
- Treat civilians and EPWs humanely and with respect
- Respect private property and possessions
- Report actual or suspected LOAC violations to your commander, JA, and/or OSI - **it's your duty!**

Handling News Media

Ref: AFI 35-101; Joint Pub 3-61; AFDD 2-5.3; AFI 71-101, Vol 1

Role of the Media

Access to information is critical for a healthy democratic system. The role the media plays in this process is far too important to ignore. Senior AF leaders recognize the need for public trust and support in all facets of military operations. The military is accountable and responsible to the public for performing its national defense mission. The news media are the principal means of communicating information about the military to the general public. Remember:

Public opinion of a military operation is fragile.
Media reports can shape public opinion.
News stories shape the public agenda on issues.

Media Embeds
- The DOD embedded nearly 500 journalists during Operation IRAQI FREEDOM

- Media provided a vital role in reporting the war in Iraq and helped distinguish between Iraqi misinformation and what was actually happening
- Media embeds have become a routine part of military operations

Contact with Foreign Nationals and Foreign Media

Refer foreign news media to Public Affairs.

If you should ever have contact with any host nation local or third country national and they attempt to gather information about military operations or an organizational unit, immediately report the incident to the AFOSI. If a local AFOSI detachment isn't available, report the incident up through your chain of command. If you're contacted by foreign news media, refer them to your public affairs representative.

Public Affairs (PA) Role
- Inform people on USAF capabilities and current issues
- PA professionals will most likely deploy with or precede your unit and help you prepare for an interview that reflects your professionalism, knowledge, and enthusiasm

Member's Role
- Learn to be proactive with the press, don't fear or avoid them, and don't perceive them as an obstacle
- Contact PA if you don't feel comfortable answering media questions
- Never forget operations security (OPSEC) guidelines and the need to protect classified information

Be proactive with the press.

The Interviewer and Audience
- Learn as much as you can about your interviewer and the intended audience
- Tailor your message accordingly

The Record—always consider yourself "on the record." Never say anything you wouldn't want printed or broadcasted.

Language—speak the public's language. Avoid acronyms, jargon, or technical terms.

Arguments—never become a passive participant, and never argue with a reporter. Stay calm and stick to your talking points and your message.

Protect the Record
- Be sure to protect and, if necessary, correct the record
- Avoid repeating any false data or negative statements

Honesty—always answer honestly.
- Don't use the cliché "no comment"
- If you don't know the answer to a question, tell them
- If the answer is classified, say so

Don't use the cliché "no comment."

Before you meet with a reporter, evaluate and plan each aspect of your media encounter with your public affairs advisor.

- Who will interview you, and is this interviewer a military correspondent or local reporter?
- Who's the audience?
- Will other guests be present?
- What's the subject?
- What are you expected to address?
- What else on this issue is in the news?
- When is the interview?
- When should you arrive?
- When will it be published or aired?
- Where will the interview take place?
- Where should you sit?
- Where should you look?
- Why do they want you?
- Why are they interested in the subject?
- How will the interview be conducted?
- How long will it last and is it live or taped?

OCONUS Legal Concerns

Ref: Uniform Code of Military Justice

Be a good US ambassador while serving in foreign countries. Learn pertinent host country laws and customs to avoid potential trouble and misunderstanding.

The **Uniform Code of Military Justice** (UCMJ)–applies **wherever** US military members are serving.

Government Regulations–apply regardless of where you are stationed or deployed.

US Laws–certain US laws have force outside of the United States. Some of these include the LOAC, fiscal and tax laws, and various criminal laws.

Learn host country laws and customs.

Status of Forces Agreement (SOFA)–are negotiated between the US government and foreign governments regarding US military forces present in the foreign country.

Host Nation Laws
- Apply for local matters
- May be very different from US laws and customs
- Include tax and criminal laws
- May still apply to US military members even when a SOFA exists

The UCMJ applies wherever you serve.

Consult your legal office for information concerning SOFA rights and responsibilities and the application of host nation law.

Force Protection Condition (FPCON)

Ref: AFI 10-245

FPCONs describe progressive levels of terrorist threats and initiate pre-planned defensive or mitigation actions. FPCON declarations are normally provided through your chain-of-command, public address system, and other available resources.

Base alert warning system.

Condition	Application	Considerations
FPCON NORMAL	Applies when a general global threat of possible terrorist activity exists.	Warrants a routine security posture.
FPCON ALPHA	Applies when there is an increased general threat of possible terrorist activity against personnel or facilities, the nature, and extent of which are unpredictable.	ALPHA measures must be capable of being maintained indefinitely.
FPCON BRAVO	Applies when an increased or more predictable threat of terrorist activity exists.	Sustaining BRAVO measures for a prolonged period may affect operational capability and relations with local authorities.
FPCON CHARLIE	Applies when an incident occurs or intelligence is received indicating some form of terrorist action or targeting against personnel or facilities is likely.	Implementation of CHARLIE measures will create hardship and affect the activities of the unit and its personnel.
FPCON DELTA	Applies in the immediate area where a terrorist attack has occurred or when intelligence has been received that terrorist action against a specific location or person is imminent.	Normally, this FPCON is declared as a localized condition. FPCON DELTA measures are not intended to be sustained for substantial periods.

Attack Warning Signals for Chemical, Biological, Radiological, Nuclear, and high-yield Explosives in High Threat Areas

Ref: AFI 10-2501; AFMAN 10-2602; CONUS AFVA 10-2510; AFVA 10-2511

Standardized attack warning signals are used to posture airbases for attacks, warn of attacks in progress, initiate post-attack recovery actions, and return the airbases to a wartime state of readiness. Although warning signals are primarily designed to provide air, missile, artillery, and ground attack warning, they may also be used to warn you if a covert attack with a chemical, biological, or radiological weapon is discovered. Alarm warning signal variations might be used in some geographic regions. If they are, you'll be notified what those variations are before you depart your home station or when you arrive in that region. For example, Alarm Blue is used instead of Alarm Red in South Korea. Alarm Blue will be announced and blue flags will be displayed.

USAF STANDARDIZED ATTACK WARNING SIGNALS FOR NBCC MEDIUM AND HIGH THREAT AREAS

ALARM CONDITION	IF YOU	THIS INDICATES	GENERAL ACTIONS
GREEN	HEAR: ALARM GREEN SEE: GREEN FLAG	ATTACK IS NOT PROBABLE	■ MOPP 0 or directed [1,3] ■ Normal wartime condition ■ Resume operations ■ Continue recovery action
YELLOW	HEAR: ALARM YELLOW SEE: YELLOW FLAG	ATTACK IS PROBABLE IN LESS THAN 30 MINUTES	■ MOPP 2 or directed [1] ■ Protect and cover assets ■ Go to protective shelter or seek best protection with overhead cover [2]
RED	HEAR: ALARM RED, SIREN (WAVERING TONE) SEE: RED FLAG	ATTACK BY AIR OR MISSILE IS IMMINENT OR IN PROGRESS	■ Seek immediate protection with overhead cover ■ MOPP 4 or as directed [1] ■ Report observed attacks
RED	HEAR: GROUND ATTACK, BUGLE (CALL-TO-ARMS) SEE: RED FLAG	ATTACK BY GROUND FORCES IS IMMINENT OR IN PROGRESS	■ Take immediate cover [2,3] ■ MOPP 4 or as directed ■ Defend self and position ■ Report activity
BLACK	HEAR: ALARM BLACK, SIREN (STEADY TONE) SEE: BLACK FLAG	ATTACK IS OVER AND NBC CONTAMINIATION AND/OR UXO HAZARDS ARE SUSPECTED OR PRESENT	■ MOPP 4 or as directed [1,3] ■ Perform self-aid/buddy care ■ Remain under overhead cover or within shelter until otherwise directed

NOTES: 1. Wear field gear and personal body armor (if issued) when outdoors or when directed. 2. Commanders may direct mission-essential tasks or functions to continue at increased risk. 3. This alarm condition may be applied to an entire installation or assigned to one or more defense sectors or zones.

Prescribed by AFI 10-2501, Supercedes AFVA 32-4011, 1 December 1997. Distribution: F

Individual Protective Equipment (IPE)

IPE is the minimum personal clothing and equipment needed to protect wearers from most CBRNE hazards. Use buddy assistance for donning and doffing when available.

Overgarment (OG)
- Chemical protective overgarment (CPO)
- Joint Firefighter Integrated Response Ensemble (JFIRE)

- IPE for ground operations (overgarment, field gear)

- Field gear (web belt, canteen, M1 canteen cap, helmet, load bearing equipment), body armor (if issued)

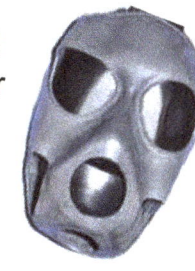
- Second skin (for MCU-2 Series or M45 mask)

- C2 series canister

- M8 and M9 Paper

- Gloves and glove inserts

- Overboots

- Decontamination kits

Chemical Protective Overgarment (CPO)

Ref: TO 14P3-1-141

*SEE Page 214, Quick Reference, **CPO Checklist***

- Two-piece permeable material garment (coat and trousers) with an integral hood that is compatible with MCU-2 Series and M45 protective masks.
- Coat and trousers packaging includes resealable bags
- Store resealable bags in trouser pocket and retain for reuse
- Wash/wear life for **training purposes**, unlimited for CPO
- Do not attempt to wash contaminated suits
- Do not starch, bleach, dry clean, or steam press any items
- Do not attempt stain removal on mission-ready items as it may result in damage to clothing

Use buddy checks when possible

CPO Labels

Coats and trousers have labels to record when they're removed from the factory bags and the number of times they're washed.

Preparation for a new garment

- Remove coat and trousers from factory vacuum-sealed bags
- Perform preventive maintenance checks
- Mark label with date that garment was removed from package

CPO Wash/Wear Life

| X | 2 | 3 | 4 | 5 | 6 | | | |

CPO has 120-day service life once removed from factory sealed bag. The wash/wear life for an uncontaminated CPO is six launderings or 45 days (whichever occurs first.) With a permanent marker, mark the "laundry label" after each wash.

Preparation for a used garment

- Remove CPO from resealable bags
- Check wear date marked on label
- Perform preventive maintenance checks

Replace CPO

Change the CPO within 24 hours after contact with chemical agents.

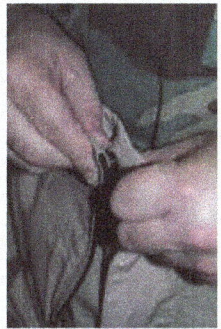
Secure closures.

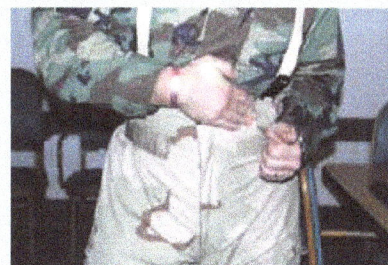
Adjust waistband.

Don trousers.

CPO Donning Procedures

To provide maximum protection, all closures should be as tight fitting as practical. The following donning order is provided as a guide.

CPO Trousers

Adjust suspenders.

Don the trousers by placing the legs into the trousers and pulling them up. Then:
- Close the slide fastener (front zipper) and fasten the two fly opening snaps
- Pull the suspenders over the shoulders and fasten the snap couplers (plastic clips)
- Adjust the suspenders for the proper inseam and leg length
- Adjust the waistband hook-and-pile fastener tapes for a snug fit

Multipurpose Lightweight Overboot (MULO)

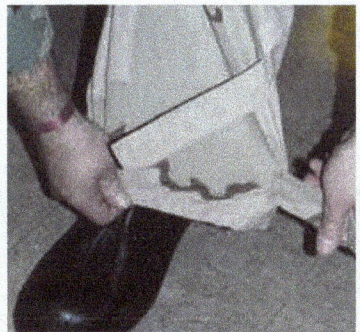
Secure legs.

Don MULOs over the combat boots and adjust and secure the strap-and-buckle fasteners. Pull the trouser legs over the MULOs and secure the two hook-and-pile fastener tapes on each ankle so that they fit snugly around the boot. If the MULO is not available, use the black vinyl overboot or the green vinyl overboot.

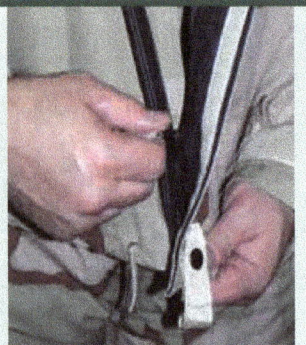
Secure closures.

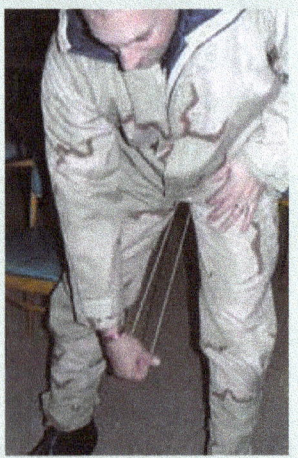
Retention cord.

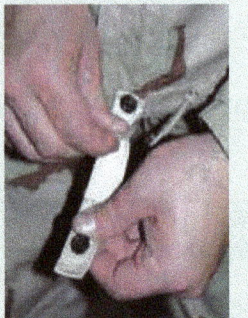
Webbing strip.

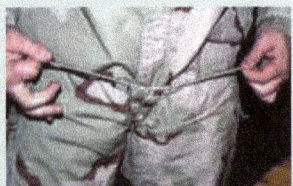
Waist drawcord.

CPO Coat

Don the coat by placing the arms into the sleeves and pulling on the coat. Then:
- Close the slide fastener (zipper) and the front closure flap up as far as the chest
- Pull the bottom of the coat down over the trousers and adjust the waist for a snug fit using the waist drawcord
- Secure the coat-retention loop. Bend over, reach between your legs and grasp the loop on the back of the garment coat. Pull on the loop so that the bottom of the garment coat fits snugly over garment trousers. Bring the loop forward between your legs. Place the loop over the webbing strip at the bottom of the coat

NOTE: Secure the coat's retention-cord loop in the manner previously described when directed to immediately assume MOPP Level 4. When directed to perform MOPP Level 1 or 2, pull the coat's waist cord through the front of the coat and tie it in a bow

- Fasten the snap on the webbing strip to keep the coat's retention-cord loop in place. Re-tie the coat's retention-cord, if needed. This may result in some discomfort in the crotch area

Additional items for completing CPO donning:
- Field gear
- M9 Paper (tape)
- Identification marking

CPO Doffing Procedures

Doffing CPO in an uncontaminated environment is the reverse order of the donning procedures. After contamination, doff CPO in a CCA.

Mission Oriented Protective Posture (MOPP)

Ref: AFI 10-2501; AFMAN 10-2602; AFTTP(I) 3-2.46; AFVA 10-2512; TO 14P3-1-141; TO 14P3-1-181

MOPP, like standardized attack warning signals, quickly increases or decreases personal protection against CBRNE threats. The senior commander controls MOPP levels for the airbase. Subordinate commanders may, however, be granted authority to reduce MOPP levels or employ MOPP options for people under their control. Field gear (A-Bag) includes helmet, web belt, canteen, and body armor (if issued). IPE includes chemical defense ensemble (C-Bag and D-bag) and field gear.

MOPP Level 0

Available for immediate donning
- Individual protective equipment (IPE)

Carried
- Protective mask with C2 series canister or filter elements and hood installed
- Field gear worn when directed
- Aircrew–protective mask/hood with C2 series canister

Primary use
- Pre-Attack
- During periods of increased alert when the enemy has a chemical, biological, radiological, or nuclear (CBRN) offensive capability
- There is no indication of CBRN use in the immediate future

Marking

Print **USAF**, **rank**, **first** and **last name** in **all capital letters** with a **black** permanent marker on **OD green** duct tape. Attach tape to:
- **helmet** (front and rear)
- **protective hood** (horizontally above the eyelens in the front and in the approximate middle of the back of the hood)
- **jacket** (over wearer's right breast)

NOTE: An additional MOPP level commanders can use is called MOPP Ready. In MOPP Ready, personnel are in a MOPP 0 configuration but instead of carrying IPE, personnel store it in a location where they can access their IPE within 30 minutes.

Groundcrew　　**Aircrew**

MOPP Level 1

Worn
- Overgarment and field gear
- Aircrew-overgarment and field gear

Carried
- Overboots, protective mask and gloves
- Aircrew–overboots, protective mask/hood, gloves, and overcape

Primary use
- Pre-Attack
- During periods of increased alert when a CBRN attack could occur with little or no warning
- When CBRN contamination is present or suspected and higher levels of protection are not required

Aircrew

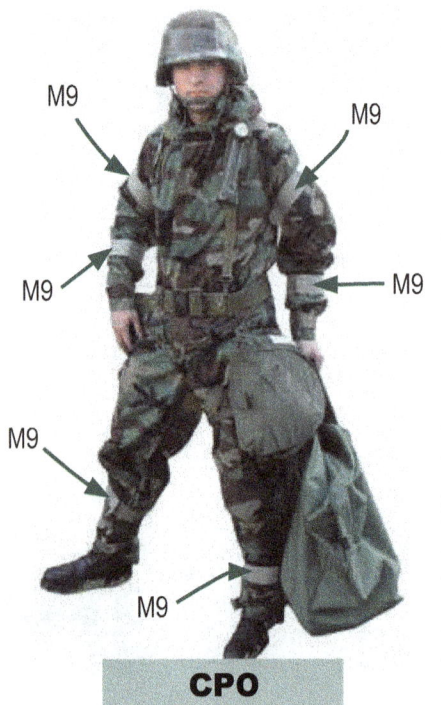

CPO

JFIRE

JFIRE: MOPP Level 1 Plus.

MOPP 1 Plus is worn when doffing from MOPP Level 4.

MOPP Level 2

Worn
- Overgarment, overboots and field gear
- Aircrew—overgarment and field gear

Carried
- Protective mask and gloves
- Aircrew—overboots, protective mask/hood, gloves, and overcape

Primary use
- Pre-Attack or Post-Attack
- During periods of increased alert when a CBRN attack could occur with little or no warning
- When CBRN contamination is present or suspected and higher levels of protection are not required

JFIRE: no MOPP Level 2.
Fire protection personnel follow UCC instructions on MOPP Level.

Aircrew

CPO

MOPP Level 3

Worn
- Overgarment, protective mask, overboots, and field gear
- Aircrew—overgarment, protective mask/hood

Carried
- Gloves
- Aircrew—overboots, gloves, field gear, and overcape

Primary use
- Pre-Attack or Post-Attack
- During periods of increased alert when a CBRN attack could occur with little or no warning
- When CBRN contamination is present or suspected and higher levels of protection are not required

> **JFIRE: no MOPP Level 3.**
> Fire protection personnel follow UCC instructions on MOPP Level.

Aircrew

CPO

MOPP Level 4

Worn
- Overgarment, protective mask, gloves, overboots, and field gear
- Aircrew–overgarment, mask/hood, gloves, overboots, and overcape (see notes this page)

Carried
- Aircrew–field gear (new; as required)

Primary use
- Post-Attack
- When a CBRN attack is imminent or in progress
- When CBRN contamination is present or suspected or the highest level of protection is required

CPO

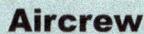

Aircrew

MOPP 4 Firefighting Mode

JFIRE

NOTE 1: Overboots and overcape only worn outside or in transit when overhead cover is not available.

NOTE 2: Overcape only worn outside during the hazard deposition phase of an attack. 10 foot rule requires wear of overboots but not the overcape.

NOTE 3: Use extreme caution when wearing the aircrew overcape. Potential hazards include; Carbon dioxide/extreme heat build-up, and material interference with breathing inlet locations.

Additional Information For All MOPP Levels

- Carry M8 and M9 Paper, the M291 and M295 decontamination kits, and nerve agent antidotes in MOPPs 1-4. Refer to AFI 10-2501, *Air Force Emergency Management (EM) Program Planning and Operations* for IPE components and basis of issue
- Depending on the threat and mission, MOPP levels may vary within different areas of the airbase and operating location
- Refer to AFTTP(I) 3-2.46, *Multiservice Tactics, Techniques, and Procedures for Nuclear, Biological, and Chemical (NBC) Protection*, for options to the MOPP levels and tactics, techniques and procedures to optimize the use of MOPP levels and alarm conditions
- Wear field gear and personal body armor (if issued) when outdoors or when directed
- Specialized clothing, such as rain and cold weather gear, is worn as the outside layer of clothing over groundcrew chemical ensemble

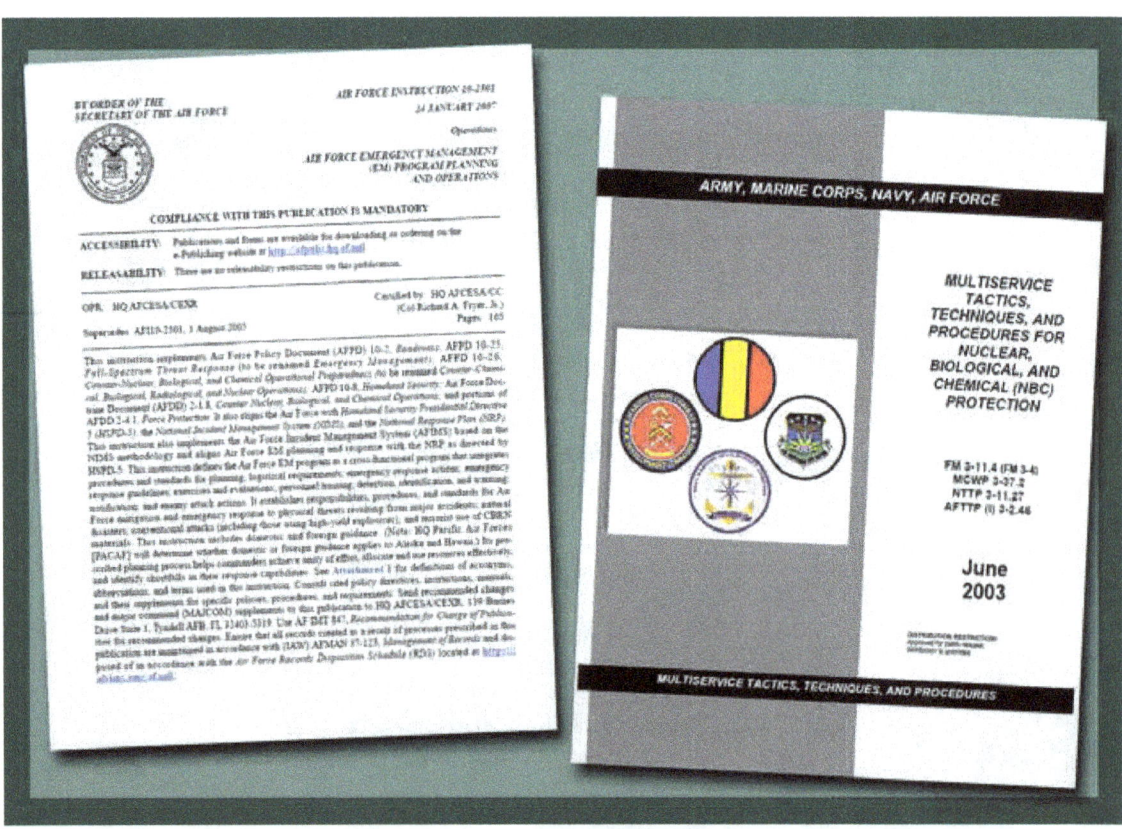

Mask only option.

MOPP Options

Ref: AFMAN 10-2602

To accomplish some missions, the senior commander may need to authorize certain MOPP options to reduce the heat burden on those affected people. MOPP options might similarly be authorized when threats do not require full body protection. The commander has three MOPP options:

Mask-Only Option—wear your protective mask only without the hood. Wear your battle dress uniform or flight suit with sleeves rolled down. Use the mask-only option after post-attack reconnaissance is complete. If an attack warning is announced and you're wearing the mask-only option, assume the directed MOPP level.

No Battle Dress Uniform or Flight Suit Option—do not wear your BDU or flight suit under your overgarment. However, do not use this option if you're reusing previously contaminated IPE.

Ventilation Option—open your overgarment jacket to increase ventilation and reduce thermal build-up. This option is automatically revoked with each MOPP level increase, unless specifically reauthorized by the commander.

Ventilation option.

Split-MOPP Concept

Ref: AFMAN 10-2602

This tactic divides the airbase into multiple sectors or control zones and assigns threat-based protective actions and MOPP for each area that's independent from one another. This provides commanders with the flexibility to respond to threats in specific areas and continue operations within areas unaffected by the incident or at lower risk from the threat. Your Unit Control Center (UCC) controls your movement between one sector and another. Ensure you understand what alarm condition and MOPP level applies before entering a sector or zone.

Split-MOPP

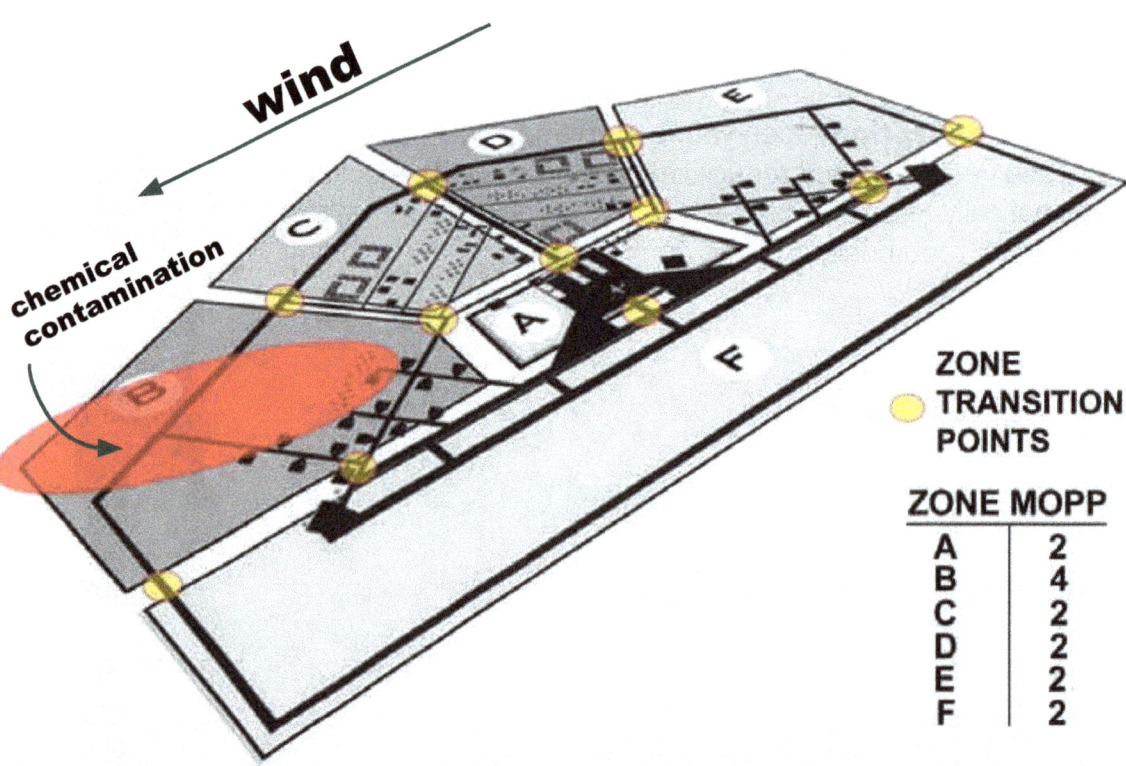

**Follow UCC instructions for movement between zones.
Call UCC before leaving or entering zones.**

Zone transition point signs include:
- Zone designator
- Zone MOPP Level
- Time/date posted
- Individual actions

Zone transition point supplies often include:
- M8 and M9 Paper
- Potable water
- Decon kits
- Glove and boot decon troughs

Before entering a dirty zone:
- Assume required MOPP
- Have full canteen
- Have M8 Paper
- Have decon kits

Before returning into a clean zone:
- Get UCC authorization
- Check self/assets for contamination
- Operationally decon self/assets
- Mark contaminated assets

10-Foot Rule

Provides guidelines for residual chemical hazards "probable duration times", but are not absolute guarantees of safety.

- Remain alert for evidence of chemically-induced symptoms
- Take appropriate first aid steps should these symptoms occur

Initial Phase: Lasts approximately 24 hours

- Remain in MOPP 4 when within 10 feet of contaminated equipment

Follow-on Phase: Greater than 24 hours

- Relatively small amounts of agent may still be present
- Use any sort of gloves when handling contaminated equipment
- Avoid bare skin contact with agent residue

Lifting and Carrying Safety

Ref: AFOSHSTD 91-46

Before you begin, remove all jewelry, wear work gloves, steel-toed boots, and use proper lifting and handling techniques. Use two or more people to lift heavy and bulky objects and use a forklift to position very heavy items.

Team Lifting
- Check the object for slivers, sharp edges, and rough or slippery surfaces
- Keep fingers away from pinch and shear points
- Don't carry a load that obstructs the view of where you're going
- Clear your travel path
- Make whole body turns and crouch down to lower the object–don't turn at the waist to change direction or to put an object down
- When you carry objects up or down stairways:
  - Use a helper as a guide
  - Move a couple small safe loads over one large unsafe load
  - Adjust loads for maximum visibility

Team lifting increases safety.

Lifting

Position your feet.

Crouch close to the load.

Lift materials with a full palm grip.

Keep back as straight as possible... start movement.

Section 3
Employment

Arrival at Deployment Location

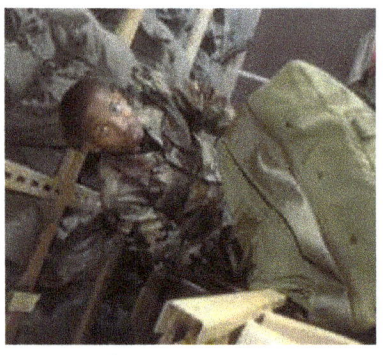

Arrival actions include in-processing, status briefings, and palletized mobility bag retrieval. If you're first to arrive at a bare base, status briefings may be delayed until initial beddown actions are complete. Review functional checklists that pertain to your particular specialty.

Briefings–generally include local alarm signals and warning systems, FPCON, MOPP, sector or zone operations, Contamination Control Area locations, shelters and bunkers, local phone numbers, billeting and feeding, EOD, EOR, fire safety, intelligence, rules of engagement, health threats/medical support, and unique local information.

Base Operating Support–varies with deployment strength and mission. A Main Operating Base will have a full range of services. A Bare Base will be limited–especially during the early days after arrival.

Personnel Support–will be available at most deployed locations.

Finance–service is sometimes limited to cashing checks and answering pay inquiries–may not be able to process military pay changes. Complete financial affairs actions before you deploy!

Chaplain Service–responsible for religious activities, worship services, pastoral counseling, work area visitation, and pastoral and religious rites. Chaplains and chaplain assistants form Religious Support Teams (RSTs) and they normally deploy with you.

Chaplains provide a wide range of services.

Medical and Dental Support–Varies with deployment strength and mission. Support ranges from self-aid/buddy care and preventive medicine to treatment of minor medical and surgical problems (colds, diarrhea, and injuries) to fully-equipped expeditionary hospitals.

Legal Services–if available, contact the judge advocate (JA) representative for claims. If claims cannot be processed, keep receipts, photos, statements, etc., to substantiate loss. File all claims upon return to home station. You have two years from date of loss to file military claims.

Legal Defense–Defense services are available if you become the subject of a criminal investigation or other disciplinary action. Contact the ADC directly or, if not available, through the judge advocate, first sergeant, or commander.

Laundry support.

Services–provides food service support, lodging, recreation and fitness, laundry support, mortuary affairs, protocol, and nonappropriated fund (NAF) resale operations.

Supply–provides IPE bulk storage and replaces exhausted supplies to individuals, teams, and contamination control area operators through the Consolidated Mobility Bag Control Center.

Communications–services will vary. Expect minimal services during early weeks of deployment (especially at bare base) and improved services and evolving communications support throughout build-up.

Food service.

Communication services will vary.

Arrival Actions

Use this list as a reminder of what to do upon arrival–your arrival briefing may satisfy many of these items.

- Confirm FPCON, Attack Warning Signals, Alarm Condition, MOPP, sector/zone layout
- Recover pallet loaded mobility bags (if not hand-carried) and inspect contents
- Be alert for and report suspicious individuals/ activities to AFOSI or Security Forces
- When Directed
  - Retrieve operational overgarment from vapor bag
  - Place identification tape on IPE
  - Mark tape on IPE with personal information
  - Place M9 Paper (Tape) on overgarment (see page 28)
  - Place operational filter on mask
  - Place second skin (as applicable) on mask
  - Wear field gear and personal body armor (if issued)
  - Remove contact lenses (if worn) wear protective mask spectacles
  - Keep nerve agent antidotes at hand (when issued)
- Hydration
  - Sanitize your canteen and mask drinking tube with 0.5% chlorine solution. (1 part 5% chlorine solution to 9 parts water).
  - Fill canteen with approved drinking water and keep it full
  - Ensure M1 canteen cap is functional with protective tab attached
  - Store personal bottled water at work area and billeting quarters
- Review local threats (including criminal) and attack reporting procedures
- Review unexploded ordnance (UXO) hazard charts, marking procedures, location(s) of mined areas
- Review fire safety, alarms, alarm locations, reporting, evacuation routes and procedures

Annotate canister information.

Prepare IPE for use.

SEE Page 216, Quick Reference, Fluid Replacement Guidelines

Keep canteen full.

- Review smoking area rules
- Review tent heater operation
- Review medical warnings, advisories, sick call and casualty collection procedures
- Annotate local contact information and locations:
  - Personal weapon(s) and ammunition
  - Shelter, bunker, nearest evacuation area(s)
  - Unit Control Center (UCC)
  - Base Defense Operations Center (BDOC)
  - Unit firefighting equipment, first aid equipment
  - Casualty collection point(s)
  - Unit and base resupply point
  - Emergency Operations Center (EOC)
  - Emergency Communications Center (ECC)
  - Fire reporting alarm/phone number
  - Medical treatment facility
  - Contamination Control Area(s) (CCA)
  - Contaminated waste disposal point
  - AFOSI
  - Security Forces
  - Sector/zone transition points
- US services and coalition forces (familiarize yourself with their uniforms)
- Attend spin-up or CBRNE defense familiarization training as directed.
  - Post-attack reconnaissance
  - UCC, EOC, CCA operations
  - Shelter or collective protection
  - Contamination control
  - Contamination avoidance and control measures
  - Nerve agent antidotes
  - Hardening and dispersal
  - SABC
  - Driver training (flightline, blackout)
  - Combat skills
- Inspect and conduct preventive maintenance checks and services on protective mask—carry a copy of mask fit and mask assessment and fill out DD Form 1574 documentation in mask carrier

Know where bunkers are located.

Follow MOPP Levels.

Conduct preventive maintenance checks.

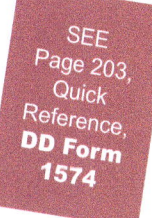
SEE Page 203, Quick Reference, DD Form 1574

The Improvised Explosive Device (IED) Threat

Ref: TO 60A-1-1-22; 60A-1-1-4; AFMAN 91-201

Terrorist attacks are a threat at home just as they are abroad and the terrorist weapon of choice is the homemade bomb or IED. During contingencies the threat is normally greater. In recent operations, IEDs have been used against US Forces with deadly effect. As the name implies, these are homemade explosive items—and the design and complexity are limited only by the ingenuity of the builder. Safety is paramount with any IED. IEDs are made from whatever materials are easily obtainable and can take almost any form. IEDs might be hidden or not easily recognized.

The IED–in various forms–is the weapon of choice by terrorists.

IED using gas and propane.

You May Be A Target
Never lower your guard. Constantly maintain situational awareness—know where you are and remain alert for all types of entrapment situations. IEDs can be planted to stir your curiosity and lure you within their lethal explosive range. There have been instances of bombers causing an explosion just to draw in the curious, the would-be rescuers and first responders—and then detonating a second device. If there is one IED, there may be more in the area.

SEE Page 202, Quick Reference, **IED Reporting and Evacuation**

A battery and car alarm system used as a remote control detonator.

How They Work
Time Delay or Command Detonated. An IED can function at a preset time or be detonated remotely using a hand held transmitter/receiver. Remote control devices of every sort can be used (e.g., car alarms, door bells, garage door openers, or cell phones).

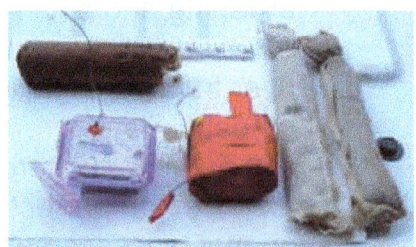
Clock, batteries, and explosives from a time-delay IED.

Booby-Traps. An IED can also be triggered mechanically if you disturb it. This is commonly known as a "booby trap." IEDs can be built so that any force or movement such as tugging, lifting, turning a doorknob (any normal day-to-day function) will detonate it.

How They're Used

In the workplace, IEDs can be contained in or made to look like ordinary items—a common item such as a backpack, a discarded box, or a soda can.

In outside areas, in addition to smaller items, IEDs have been camouflaged as trashcans, cement blocks, flower containers, pieces of curbing, and crates.

Small IEDs found in a cardboard box and a soda can.

Pipe bomb.

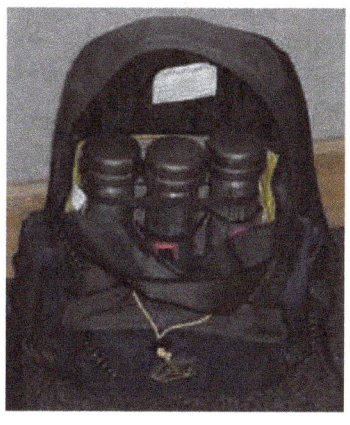

IED disguised as a backpack.

Remote control receiver hidden in plaster.

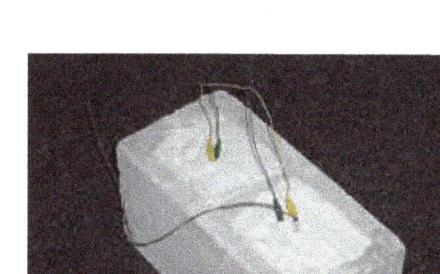

IED camouflaged as a cement block.

In a convoy ambush, IEDs can be used to disable a vehicle, followed-up with a secondary attack. If you're the target of an IED attack (in a convoy or otherwise), DO NOT drop your guard–stay on high alert, maintain 360° security, and be ready to defend yourself against a follow-up ambush and be observant for other IEDs designed to attack dismounted Airmen or responding forces. Know your rules of engagement–work as a team.

Hidden 155 mm projectile.

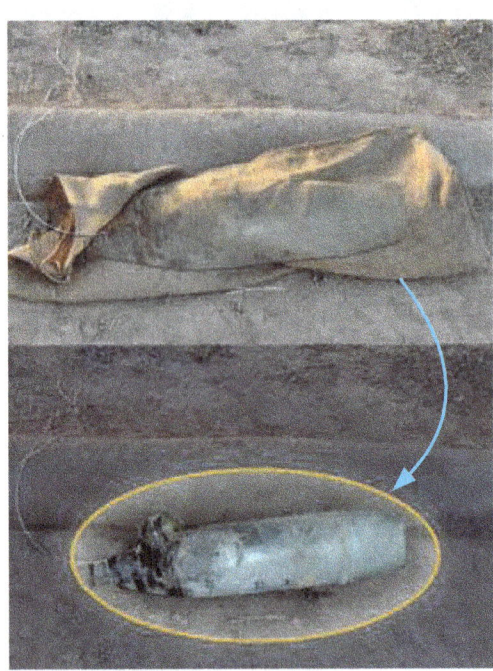

Explosive hidden beneath burlap.

Roadside IEDs can be concealed in very innovative ways. Watch for:
- Potholes covered with dirt or freshly paved areas
- Camouflaging devices such as bags along side or in the roadway
- Dead animal carcasses, or bits of a car wreck that's strewn across a highway
- An obvious IED in the open–a decoy–to slow or stop convoys

Vehicle Borne Improvised Explosive Device (VBIED) come in all shapes and sizes from donkey carts to simple passenger cars and ambulances, to delivery trucks. An attack may even involve multiple vehicles. Possible indicators of a VBIED are:
- An auto rides low on the springs or resting low in the rear

Explosive charge in a compact car.

- Large boxes, crates, bags, or containers in plain view
- A control box, switch, or "circuitry" on the front seat/floor near the driver
- An acrid smelling smoke coming from the trunk or passenger compartment
- Curious fuel-like (diesel or kerosene) odors from the trunk or passenger compartment

The Suicide/Homicide Bomber is another form of IED threat. There is no stereotypical suicide bomber. Bulky clothing, and nervous appearance may be clues, but the best defense is vigilance in performing your duties.

Use Common Sense. When you recognize something is suspicious - get yourself and others away from the threat and report the situation immediately. If you find a suspected IED, use the 5-C's (Confirm, Clear, Cordon, Check and Control) to manage your response. While the 5-C's are conducted in no specific order, the response must be instinctive, effective and based on situation. See the 5-C's on page 202a/202b. When you suspect an IED threat, DO NOT second-guess yourself, and do not be embarrassed to ask the experts for help.

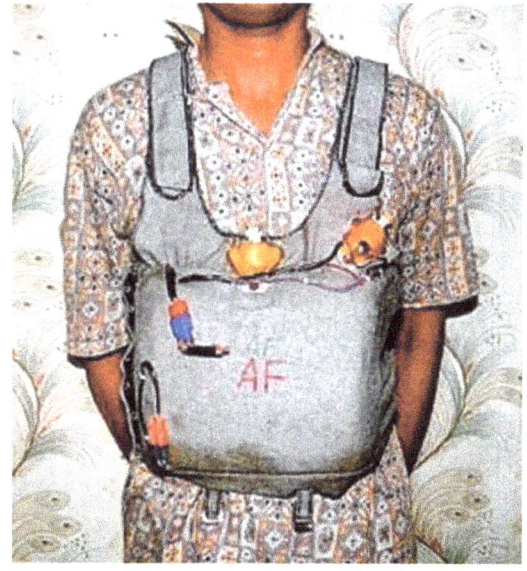

Suicide vest.

Tropical

Desert

Arctic

Health Concerns During Deployment

Many foreign countries have environments that you have to experience to fully understand. Medical threats from heat, cold, water, food, disease, poor sanitation, and pollutants are real. Remember, in the history of warfare, more people are lost to disease than to combat.

Drink before you get thirsty.

Heat
- Heat can be incapacitating or deadly
- Drink water before you get thirsty. Consume 1/2 quart per hour during moderate work in temperatures over 82°F
- Avoid caffeine (cola, coffee) as it increases water loss and promotes dehydration
- Follow appropriate work/rest cycles
- Your IPE increases your need to hydrate
- If urinating, that's a good sign you're hydrated

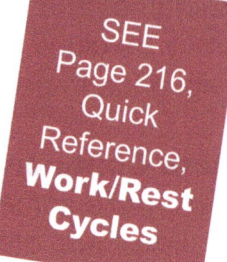
SEE Page 216, Quick Reference, **Work/Rest Cycles**

Cold can cause injury or death.

Cold
- Cold can cause serious injury or death
- Wear the proper cold weather gear and layer your clothing for added warmth
- Limit the amount of time you must spend outdoors
- Watch for signs of frostnip, frostbite, and hypothermia
- Eat all meals to maintain energy

Drink only approved water.

Food and Water
- Local food and water can cause serious illness and may contain parasites
- DO NOT eat local foods or drink any water, including bottled water and ice, until approved by US military medical authorities

Personal Hygiene
Diseases are a major concern. Good personal hygiene helps prevent illnesses, fights off infections, helps maintain good morale, and supports good general health. Proper field hygiene requires constant attention. To help prevent disease...
- Wash your hands frequently
- Practice good oral hygiene
- Maintain clean, dry clothing
- Change your socks daily
- Use foot powder to prevent fungal infections
- Bathe only in approved water and as often as practical
- Wash where you perspire if a shower is unavailable
- If you think you have a sexually transmitted disease, seek medical attention

Change socks daily.

Practice good oral hygiene.

Insects
- Insects may transmit life-threatening diseases
- Use insect repellent, such as DEET on exposed skin
- Pretreat uniform with permethrin. Spray application offers protection for 6 months or 10 washes. The "kit" application offers protection for the life of the uniform unless it's drycleaned. Read all directions before use
- Sleep under a bed net treated with permethrin–tuck bed netting under the mattress all the way around
- DEET and permethrin re-supply can be obtained through your deployment supply channels
- Obtain anti-malarials, if required, from medical personnel and take as instructed

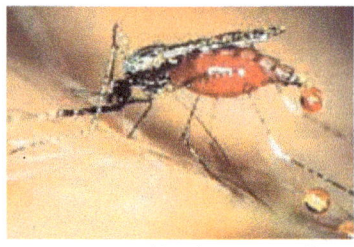
Use insect repellant.

Watch out for ticks and fleas.

Other Concerns
Be sure to shake out your bedroll and boots, you never know what you might find.

Scorpion   Camel spider

Animals
- Avoid contact with ALL animals–many species can transmit rabies and other diseases
- DO NOT keep local animals as pets or mascots
- If bitten or scratched by any animal, wash the wound with soap and water and seek medical attention immediately

Avoid contact with all animals.

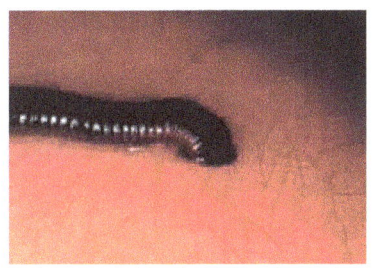
leech

Rivers, Lakes, Swamps, Canals
- Waterways may contain obstacles or parasites that can penetrate unprotected skin and cause serious illness
- Avoid stagnant water and open sewers–they attract mosquitoes and other disease vectors
- DO NOT swim or bathe in rivers, lakes, swamps, or canals
- If you must wade, avoid direct contact between your skin and the water if possible

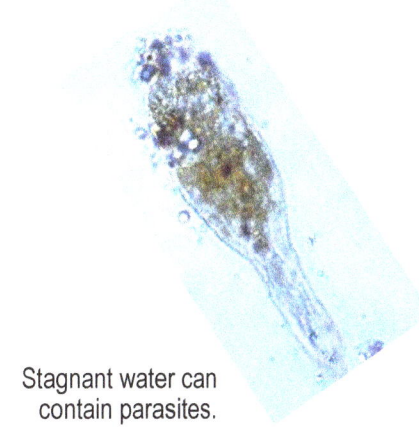
Stagnant water can contain parasites.

Asp.

Cobra.

Cottonmouth (water moccasin).

Rattlesnake.

Mental Health

Talk with a chaplain.

Self-Maintenance
Taking care of yourself is the most effective way to manage stress. The key components to self-maintenance are basic: get sufficient sleep, eat a healthy and balanced diet, and participate in a regular exercise program. Take advantage of leisure activities during non-duty hours. It's good for you and your unit's morale—you may enjoy the experience and contribute to everyone else's well-being.

Communicate
Keep in touch with your family and friends. Reassure them that you're well and you have a good attitude about what you're doing. This will make you feel better and minimize the worry and concern that your family and friends back home have for you.

Stay in touch.

Avoid Unnecessary Stress
How you live when you're deployed directly affects your physical and mental well-being. Stress left unchecked can degrade your health and performance. If you feel stress building, seek relief by talking to your buddies, your supervisor, a chaplain, or a medical counselor.

Participate and stay active.

Enjoy your time off.

Fire Safety

Ref: AFPAM 10-219, Vol 3; AFI 32-2001; AFOSH Std 91 - 501

Unfamiliar environments, crowded accommodations, a high operational tempo (OPTEMPO) and carelessness can adversely affect fire safety. The key to fire-safe mission execution is fire prevention– make it part of your daily routine.

General Fire Prevention
- Smoke only in designated smoking areas
- Use proper receptacles for discarding smoking materials
- Practice good housekeeping in personal and storage areas
- Set up a fire alerting system
- Use carbon monoxide detectors, if available, when heating equipment may produce carbon monoxide vapors
- Test smoke detectors often
- Know fire escape plans and participate in unit fire drills
- Keep pathways to emergency exits clear
- Know your assembly location
- Know the location and operation of fire extinguishers
- Ensure fire extinguishers are operational and installed near exits and hazardous operations areas
- Only use approved undamaged electrical cords and appliances
- Clear self-help projects through Civil Engineering

Practice good housekeeping.

Fire Precautions Within Tent City

- No smoking inside any tents
- Preposition emergency water supplies and firefighting equipment
- Use only approved tent lighting and electrical kits
- Check with fire prevention specialists before you use any type of heat generating sources
- Keep combustible materials away from heat sources
- Flammable items used as tent partitions increase fire loads and fire intensity
- Ensure all tent exits are not blocked or tied shut
- Keep access roads to tents clear for fire vehicles

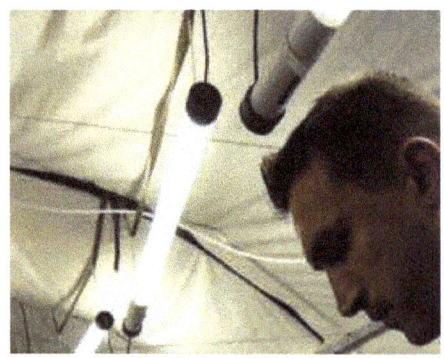
Only use approved lighting.

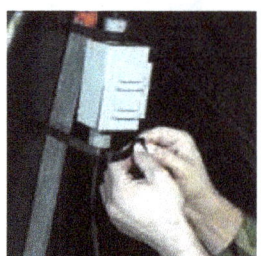
Don't overload receptacles.

Expedient Firefighting

Ref: AFPAM 10-219, Vol 3; AFI 32-2001

If you're faced with a fire, efficient reporting, evacuation, and quick extinguishing will significantly reduce the loss of critical resources. Become familiar with fire reporting procedures and be ready to perform expedient firefighting tasks as an auxiliary firefighter.

Know where extinguishers are stored.

- **P** Pull the pin
- **A** Aim nozzle at base of fire
- **S** Squeeze handle
- **S** Sweep side-to-side

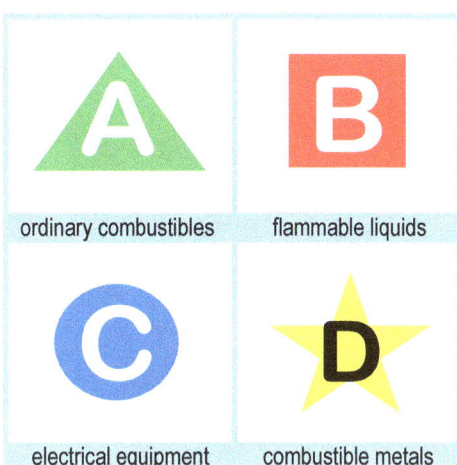

Firefighting Agent Resources
- Dry Chemical Extinguisher: ABC rating (all fires except metals)
- Dry Powder Extinguisher: D rating (metal and metal-alloy fires)
- Halon Flightline Extinguisher: BC rating (petroleum fuels and electrical)–used for aircraft and related equipment only
- Water
- Sand

Fire Reporting
- Sound the alarm
  - Yell "FIRE, FIRE, FIRE" or as directed locally
  - Use fire alarm, triangle, air horn
  - Report all emergencies even if the fire goes out
- Notify the fire department and report
  - Name and rank
  - Location of fire
  - Nature and status of emergency
  - Status of personnel
- Evacuate the area and account for personnel, try to evacuate upwind from any fire
- Extinguish small fires (trash can size), if possible
- Direct firefighters to the fire

Direct firefighters to fire.

General Firefighting
- Fight small fires with available firefighting resources
- Always maintain an escape route
- Separate fuel sources from ignition sources
  - Shut off fuel and gas valves
  - Shut off electrical equipment
- Munitions involved in a fire are unpredictable
- Wildland fires can generate intense heat and move rapidly

Your CBRN protective mask won't protect you in smoke filled environments.

Tent City Firefighting—depending on the camp layout and environmental conditions, fires can rapidly spread if your initial attempts to extinguish them fail. Timely reporting and evacuation are critical. Life, safety, and tent evacuation is a prime concern.

- Focus on preventing the spread of fire
    - Get well ahead of the fire to make a stand
    - Wet tents down
    - Cut supports and let tents collapse
- Cut the power to tent city
- Never enter a burning tent

Never enter a burning tent.

A tent can completely burn in just 2-3 minutes

Waste Control

Ref: AFI 32-7080

Large amounts of solid waste can be generated during a deployment. Proper sanitation practices help to inhibit the spread of disease and it controls disease carrying vectors such as insects and rodents. Because accumulated waste provides a breeding ground for these vectors, aggressively strive to maintain a healthy living and work environment. If you're authorized to burn waste, do it in a CE approved area. Diesel fuel is preferred over gasoline to start fires because its higher flash point increases your safety when igniting.

Proper sanitation inhibits disease.

Human Waste
During a deployment, you may use bathrooms ranging from a straddle-trench to highly engineered systems. Always wash your hands after using the bathroom.

Sanitation
Depending on your deployed site population, you could see different methods of trash and garbage control that range from burning and burying techniques to full-service host

nation trash collection contracts. Don't allow trash to accumulate, and place trash in sturdy containers—preferably those with a secure cover.

Trash

Dry combustible waste may be burned on-site when landfills are nonexistent or if they're too far away for timely disposal. If you must burn, make sure the smoke won't interfere with base operations. Burn only in a fire service approved open pit or metal containers such as 55-gallon drums.

- Food leftovers and trash in your work areas and defensive fighting positions invite rodents and insects
- Use waste collection points—minimize the chance of disease and bacteria in your areas of operation

Open pit burning may be authorized.

Contaminated Waste Control and Disposal

Properly dispose of contaminated waste.

Ref: AFH 10-222V4; AFMAN 10-2602; AFTTP(I) 3-2.60
Chemical and biological attacks can generate significant quantities of contaminated waste. Contaminated items will include IPE and field gear, contaminated M8 and M9 Paper, M291 and M295 decon kit components, contamination avoidance covers and bulk plastics, and personal equipment. The waste that accumulates at waste disposal points, contamination control areas, and at cargo transload sites must be collected and properly disposed to limit hazards.

Depending on the type and quantity of contaminated material, waste accumulation areas themselves could increase local hazards and require increased protective measures within the areas. In addition, the airbase is responsible for limiting, to the greatest extent possible, post-conflict cleanup and restoration actions. Effective actions to identify, control, and mark waste will reduce problems with waste accumulation and disposal.

Mark contaminated waste receptacles.

Unit Contaminated Waste Collection Points—establish work center, facility, and base-wide contaminated waste collection points during the pre-attack phase. Collect and dispose of non-reusable contaminated items. Use plastic bags, trash cans, barrels, or empty munitions cans for contaminated waste storage. Trash barrels with multiple layers of plastic bags are easy to obtain and simplify waste removal. Appropriately mark contaminated waste using NBC Marking set markers or their equivalents.

Collection points should be at least 10 feet away and downwind from facilities, bunkers, fighting positions, or Contamination Control Areas. Clearly identify the collection point and prepare contaminated marking signs in advance to mark containers after use. Be prepared to relocate the collection point when the wind direction changes. Units must periodically move their contaminated waste to installation contaminated waste disposal area.

Site collection points downwind from facilities.

Installation Contaminated Waste Disposal Area—the airbase consolidates contaminated waste from unit waste collection points and stores it at one or more waste disposal areas. There are three primary ways of handling large amounts of contaminated waste: open storage, burying, or burning. Open storage is the method of choice followed by burning. Bury contaminated material only as a last resort.

The airbase consolidates contaminated waste.

Food Consumption

Ref: AFI 48-116

Meals Ready to Eat will be your primary food source until arrangements can be made to provide hot meals. Services will provide hot meals as soon as possible using the Single Pallet Expeditionary Kitchen and Unitized Group Ration (UGR).

UGRs include utensils and paper products. However, there may be times when you may still need to use your mess kit to eat. A clean mess kit helps prevent food borne illnesses. If you use the mess kit, follow the posted mess kit cleaning process. Always wash your hands before you consume food.

Services will provide hot meals ASAP.

Scrape leftover food into trash can.

Prewash in first can of soapy water. Thoroughly wash in second can of soapy water.

Rinse in third can of clear water.

Sanitize in fourth can of sanitizing solution–submerge at least 30 seconds. Air dry before packing up.

Resources Protection and Crime Prevention

Don't display large amounts of cash.

Ref: AFI 31-101

Although Air Force installations overall enjoy a lower crime rate than that of other communities, crime still occurs at deployed locations. A situational awareness of what's going on and knowing how to protect resources and one's self goes a long way in preventing crime and maintaining mission readiness. General concerns include:

- Secure all equipment and property when unattended—particularly sensitive items such as small arms, ammunition, computers, and bulk explosives
- Avoid showing large sums of money
- Permanently mark all government property, especially highly pilferable items, and provide adequate storage for them
- Have accurate and up-to-date inventory controls and sign out highly pilferable items on an AF Form 1297/Temporary Issue Receipt
- Establish accountability procedures to control lock combinations, keys, locks, and containers
- Secure all personal property the best way possible
- Stay in groups, even on base, and don't lower your guard with people you don't know
- Promptly report confirmed incidents to Security Forces or AFOSI

Secure high value items.

Keep lockers locked.

Passive Defense

Ref: AFMAN 10-2602

Passive defense are measures you take to lessen damage from enemy attack. Most measures are typically quickly executed, inexpensive, and require minimum manpower and material.

Expedient berms protect assets.

Hardened Structure (rarely available)
- Allows occupants, systems, and support infrastructure to operate during and after attacks
- May include a collective protection system
- Typically constructed below ground level and under rock or concrete cover
- Provides substantial protection against direct attacks with chemical, biological, and conventional weapon threats
- Protects against small arms fire
- Protects against most collateral effects of nuclear weapons (blast, heat, fallout, radiation, electromagnetic pulse)

Hardened structures may include collective protection systems.

Semi-Hardened Structure

- Allows occupants, systems, and supporting infrastructure to survive attacks and continue to operate immediately following attacks
- May include a collective protection system
- Typically constructed at or below ground level
- Provides protection against the collateral effects (blast, heat, fragmentation, shock, and contamination) of attacks with chemical, biological, and conventional weapon threats
- Protects against small arms fire
- Protects against some collateral effects of nuclear weapons (blast, heat, fallout, radiation, electromagnetic pulse)

Semi-hardened bunker, without collective protection.

Splinter Protected

- Allows occupants to survive attacks and limits damage to systems, supporting infrastructure, and resources
- May include collective protection system
- Limits collateral effects (blast, heat, fragmentation, and shock) of conventional weapon attacks
- Provides limited protection against small arms fire
- Provides limited protection against collateral effects (blast, heat, fallout, radiation, electromagnetic pulse) of nuclear weapons

HESCO concertainer revetment for splinter protection.

Expedient Hardening

Ref: AFPAM 10-219, Vol 2; AFMAN 10-2602

Sandbagging provides expedient hardening to protect resources from conventional weapons effects. Sandbags can be built into freestanding barriers. To reduce the chemical contact hazard duration, use burlap bags in lieu of plastic bags (when available) as chemical agents will sorb more rapidly into burlap bags than plastic materials. Check with the base civil engineer before commencing any sandbag effort. Earth berms may be your only protection until a sandbagging plan is approved.

Sandbag Wall Construction

- Fill bags three-fourths full with earth or a dry soil-cement mixture
- Tuck in bottom corners after they're filled
- Place tied-off ends and side seams away from the threat
- Lay the first course as a header
- Build the wall with alternating stretchers courses
- Position sandbags so the layers have the same pitch as the base
- Stack sandbag at a slope ratio of 1:4 or 1:5
- Create L-shaped ingress/egress points
- The top row should be placed as a header

elevation

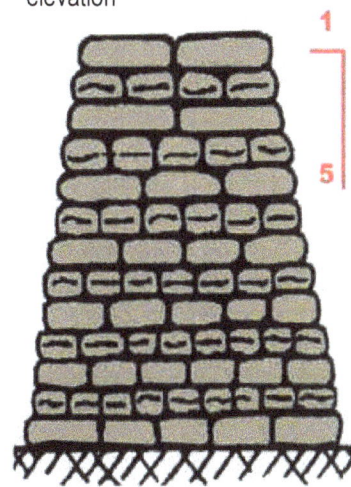

Build a side slope of 1:4 or 1:5 to prevent collapse

Camouflage, Concealment, and Blackout

Ref: AFPAM 10-219, Vol 2; AFMAN 10-2602
Camouflage, concealment, and blackout primarily applies to conventional aircraft and ground force enemy attack.

Camouflage Nets—breaks up outline of covered assets. In Chem/Bio threat areas, resist using camouflage nets as much as possible. Chemical agents rapidly sorb into net surfaces and cause an extended chemical hazard. Be extremely careful around contaminated camouflage nets and wear the appropriate MOPP gear.

Don't bunch up assets.

Dispersal—spread critical assets out to maximize their survival. Take advantage of natural cover. Distribute and hide critical resources outside of the effective range of shoulder-fired weapons that enemy ground forces may possess and not along the perimeter. When possible, disperse assets in or near the work area they'll support.

Ideally, each dispersal site should have at least two entry/exit routes on concrete or asphalt (if possible, due to rapid chemical agent sorption rates on these surfaces.) Don't bunch vehicles up into one area. Disperse more than just vehicles. Also disperse equipment, tires, and other critical supplies. In medium and high CBRNE threat areas, disperse with overhead cover and use reinforced facilities when available. Effective dispersal lessens the odds of contamination and damage.

Cat's eye headlights.

Blackout—a method to limit nighttime illumination of areas, facilities, and vehicles. Turning off interior and exterior lights, covering doors and windows, and creating "cat's eyes" on vehicle running lights are forms of blackout.

Limitations—except for an enemy's real-time satellite surveillance capability, camouflage, concealment, and blackout countermeasures are ineffective against low tech Tactical Ballistic Missiles and Unmanned Aerial Vehicles, and high tech threat missile systems and global positioning system guided weapons. Camouflage, concealment, and blackout efforts, however, are valuable strategies against penetrating ground force attacks and many intelligence gathering efforts.

Airfield blackout may be necessary.

Noise—the enemy is listening—keep it down
- Practice noise discipline continuously
- Talking, coughing, sneezing, and sniffing can reveal your position—especially at night
- Bumping walls, tapping fingers, rattling paper, or shuffling your feet can also give your position away
- Noise can help identify an enemy—the noise an enemy makes can give them away

Litter– eliminate it. You may attract more than the enemy as it can reveal your presence... and it's a nuisance.

Keep light to a minimum.

Light Discipline—Given a chance, an enemy will watch you day and night. At night, there might be times when you'll need flashlights or chemical light sticks to do your job. That's ok, but don't unnecessarily draw attention to yourself by leaving a flashlight on or exposing chemical light sticks when they're not needed. Learn how to safely move around at night using natural light. At entry control points, don't silhouette sentries with lights or cause them to lose their "night vision" by shining a light directly in their eyes. It could take several minutes or longer for their eyes to readjust back to low light.

During a post-attack phase when M8 Paper is pre-positioned, only use a white light to read the paper at night. Using a flashlight with a colored lens or using chemical light sticks could cause you to miss color changes on the detector paper and make you think that chemical contamination is not present when the opposite might be true!

Read M8 Paper only with white light.

Defensive Fighting Position (DFP)

Ref: AFMAN 10-2602; AFH 10-222V14

Use overhead cover to inhibit contamination.

The DFPs provide all-around cover from enemy fire and allow defenders to observe and repel enemy forces, however, beware that in CBRNE threat areas, DFPs may present dangerous environments due to the interaction between chemical agents and many materials used in DFP construction. Reduced airflow, the inability for defenders to leave a contaminated area, and the close proximity of the occupant's respiratory tract to the contaminated surface (inches instead of feet) all provide survival challenges.

DFP Construction—to inhibit falling chemical droplets from entering, build DFPs with two-foot overhangs above the observation ports unless it interferes with weapon firing. Also, build small L-shaped entrances to inhibit contamination intrusion. If you're given the option, use unpainted concrete for DFP construction as that allows chemical agents to absorb faster than any other likely construction material. Floor construction similarly makes a difference to DFP occupants during the post attack environment, so consider chemical agent interaction with floor surfaces.

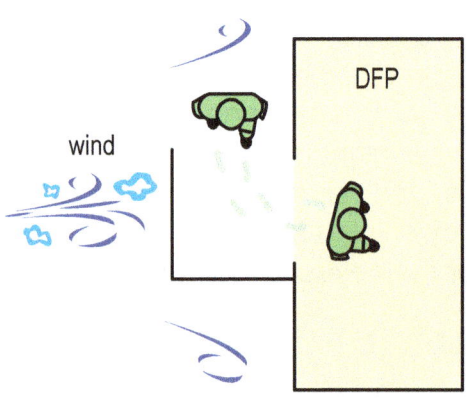
L-shaped entrances inhibit contamination.

DFP Camouflage–use exterior latex paint to create camouflage patterns. Latex lets liquid agents rapidly sorb below the surface and minimizes the contact hazard period. Unless required for tactical operations, don't use camouflage nets near DFPs since chemical hazards will exist for an extended period.

Hasty DFP.

Hasty DFPs
- Temporary–provides partial protection from enemy fire
- Select position that provides ample frontal coverage
- Should be a small depression or hole that is at least 18 inches deep

Fighting DFPs
- Construction–build for two people with unrestricted observation and enemy engagement ports
- Position to provide frontal cover to engage the enemy without exposing yourself
- Construct 6 feet long (1.8 m), 3 feet wide (0.9 m), and arm-pit deep
- Build grenade sumps one entrenching tool wide and deep at both ends
- Provide at least 18 inches (0.5 m) of dirt overhead. Use adequate amount of stringers to support the weight
- Camouflage with natural and artificial foliage to conceal occupants
- Check camouflage daily–view it from 40 yards (36 m) in front–it's good if you can't easily spot it
- Foliage that you might have utilized to camouflage your position must be changed as soon as it starts to standout from foliage of the surrounding area

Build DFPs for two people.

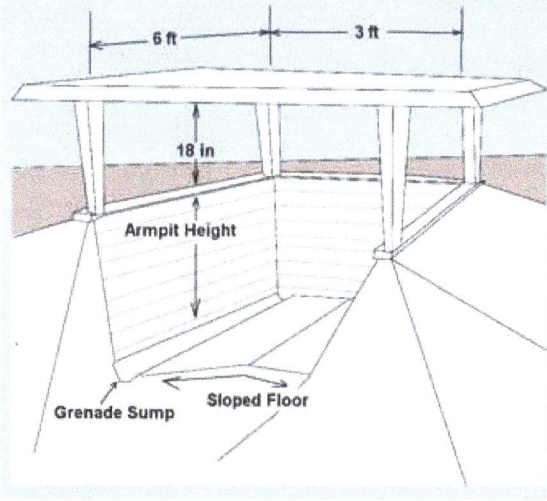
Cut-away DFP.

61 / Section 3 / Employment   AFPAM 10-100 / 1 March 2009

Contamination Avoidance and CBRN Pre-Attack Preparation

Ref: AFMAN 10-2602

In CBRNE Threat Areas, contamination avoidance is the key to prevent assets from becoming contaminated. Place assets beneath an overhead cover when they're not in use. If overhead cover is unavailable, wrap or cover assets with at least one layer of barrier material such as repellent plastic sheets, canvas, tarpaulins, or specialized CBRN protective covers (if available.) Wind can cause havoc on contamination avoidance covers. Ensure all barrier material is tightly secured around assets stored outdoors and roll excess material beneath the asset.

Move vehicles beneath overhead cover.

Protect palletized cargo.

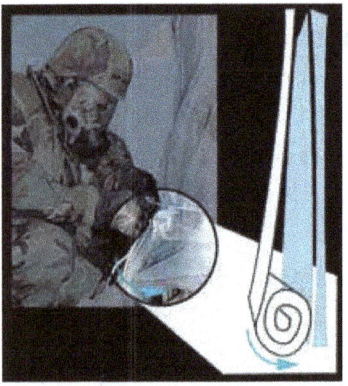

Secure barrier material. Roll excess material beneath asset, away from contaminants.

Two Cover Layers—use two cover layers when possible so the exposed cover, along with any contamination, can be easily removed, safely discarded, and replaced. Discard contaminated barrier material and M8 paper in your unit contaminated waste collection point. Periodically take accumulated trash to the installation contaminated waste disposal area. Place M8 Paper on the exposed horizontal layer of barrier material and don't forget to mark and date its time of placement.

Cover outside assets beneath two barrier layers.

Protect Facilities—close all facility windows, turn off ventilation systems (or close outside air intake—Heating, Ventilation and Air Conditioning (HVAC), respirators, air compressors, etc.) at the time of attack, and implement single-entry procedures. Pre-plan specific actions when attack threats increase. Add these actions to your work center operational checklists.

Keep doors closed.

Boot and glove decon.

Limit Contamination Spread–create, place, and use boot and glove decontamination troughs at entries to shelters, work centers, large frame aircraft doors, hatches, loading ramps, and around work areas. Fill the troughs with a 5% chlorine solution (household bleach), and replace the solution every 48 hours or after 400 people have used it (whichever comes first), or as directed.

Chemical Agent Detection-pre-position M8 Paper throughout your work area on flat horizontal surfaces that are likely to become contaminated during a chemical attack. Avoid surfaces that could reach temperatures above 125° F as the dye will deteriorate quickly. Place M8 Paper so it can be easily seen during post-attack surveys. Mark time and date on tape affixing M8 Paper to object.

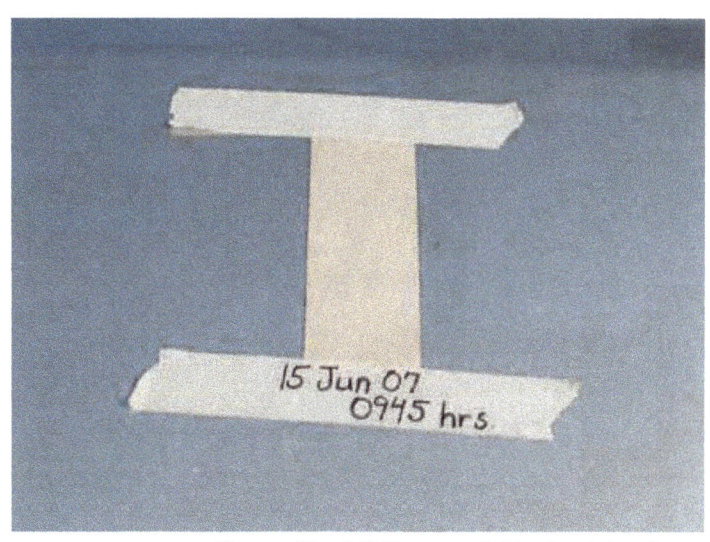

Pre-position M8 Paper on flat horizontal surfaces.

Contingency Operations–Air Mobility Command will move strategic airlift cargo regardless of the chemical or biological environment at the deployment site. Contamination avoidance is the key to air mobility movement. If you're deploying to a CBRNE threat area, triple-wrap each pallet and affix M8 Paper on the outside and on each internal layer of the barrier material. The technique is to place one barrier layer below the cargo net and two over the top. If a pallet should become contaminated, discard and replace the outer layer. Contaminated pallet netting presents a residual vapor hazard, it can't be decontaminated, and must be treated as contaminated waste. When you've completed pallet build-up and protection, it should look much like this example:

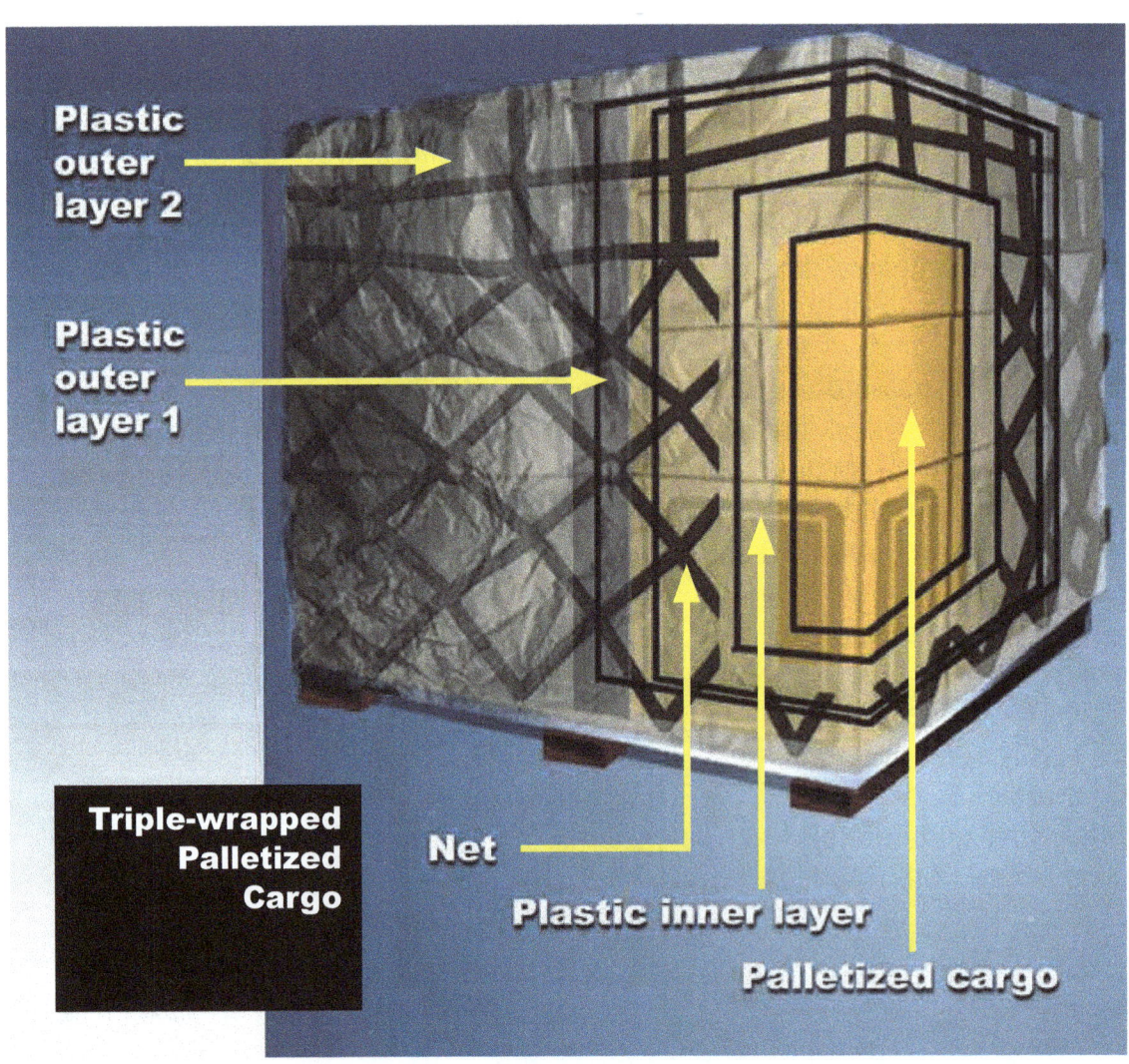

Command and Control

Ref: AFMAN 10-2602; AFI 10-2501

Effective command and control is essential to mission accomplishment and base survivability. You may notice some command and control differences at your deployed location compared to your home station, especially in joint operations.

Installation Control Center (ICC)–the top echelon of airbase operations led by the senior Air Force Commander.
- Primary focus is flight operations, airbase security, and airbase support
- Focal point for resource allocation, mission tasking, status reporting, and decision making
- The Commander's Senior Staff includes senior officers from the medical, mission support, operations, and maintenance groups
- Senior officers representing major tenants or host-nation forces may be present
- Directs FPCON, MOPP, and alarm signal changes

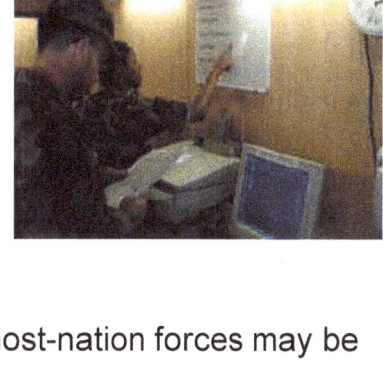

Emergency Operations Center (EOC)– is the C2 support elements that direct, monitor, and support the installation's actions before, during, and after and incident. The EOC is activated and recalled as necessary by the Installation Commander.

Unit Control Centers (UCC)–focal points for unit command and control functions
- Directs and monitors unit contamination control and dispersal actions
- Rapidly provides alarm condition and MOPP Level changes to unit personnel
- Directs and monitors unit pre-, trans-, and post-attack actions
- Directs unit personnel movement through base Split-MOPP sectors or zones
- Monitors unit shelter operations and works closely with shelter managers
- Collects vehicles and equipment contamination status reports, logs and upchannels information
- Remains in contact with alternate control center (if assigned)
- Tracks locations of all known contamination and unexploded ordnance that may affect unit's mission
- Warns unit personnel of hazards and directs their movements accordingly

Emergency Support Functions (ESFs) are groupings of capabilities that provide the support, resources, program implementation, and services that are most likely to be needed during emergency response. The 15 ESFs serve as the primary operational-level mechanism that provides support during an incident.

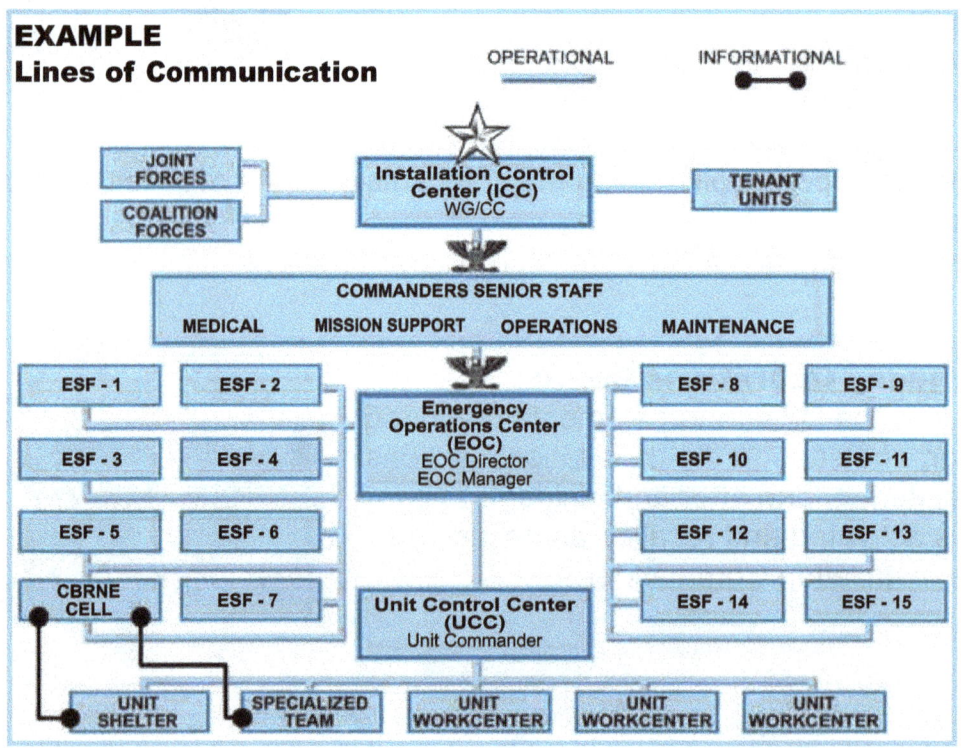

Field Communications

Ref: AFH 31-302

Communication is essential to mission accomplishment. If you encounter unfamiliar equipment, your communications function will instruct you on its use. Local area networks and email may also be available—follow the established guidelines when using these capabilities.

Communications Security (COMSEC)
- Non-secure phone, radio, and computer network systems are subject to monitoring
- Never discuss sensitive or classified information over non-secure systems
- Never talk around, paraphrase, or use code words to disguise sensitive or classified information
- Always use secure systems to discuss sensitive or classified information

Observe COMSEC.

Telephone Bomb Threats
If you receive a bomb threat over the telephone, obtain and retain as much information about the call and caller as possible. Use the AF Form 440, Bomb Threat Aid, if available or take notes during the call. Try to keep the caller on the phone as long as possible. Do not hang up the phone after the caller ends the phone call. Immediately report the incident to Security Forces and follow their instructions.

Personal Anti-Terrorism Force Protection Actions

Ref: DOD 0-2000.12H; JS Guide 5260; AFI 10-245

Terrorists don't discriminate! If you're an American, you're a potential terrorist target. Follow these key steps to lessen your threat.

Keep a Low Profile
- Your dress, conduct, and mannerisms should not attract attention
- Make an effort to blend in
- Avoid publicity, large crowds, demonstrations, and civil disturbances

Vary your routes.

Stay Unpredictable
- Vary your route, time, and mode of travel
- Vary where and when you go
- Vary your appearance
- Let others know where you're going and when you plan to return

Be Alert
- Watch for anything suspicious
- Do not release personal information
- If you believe you're being followed, go to a predetermined safe area
- Immediately report any suspicious incidents to Security Forces and AFOSI
- Carry important phone numbers, i.e. US embassy, security forces, UCC, EOD, etc.

If You Are Taken Hostage
The chances of you being taken hostage are very remote. But should it happen, remember your personal conduct can influence your treatment. If you're taken hostage there are three important rules to follow:
- Analyze the problem so as to not aggravate the situation
- Make educated decisions to keep the situation from worsening
- Maintain discipline to remain on the best terms with your captors

Be Suspicious

Ref: AFVA 32-4022

Hate is a profound feeling that makes some people do terrible and irrational things. Because you're a US military member, there are some very dangerous people in this world who hate you and hate what you stand for. So, be suspicious, but not reckless!

Improvised explosive device.

Hostile governments and terrorists often use improvised explosive devices (IED) to destroy their targets or to generate mass hysteria. Only the imagination and the talent of the builder limit IED construction techniques– there is no standard identification chart that will tell you what the next IED will look like.

- Become familiar with workcenter surroundings
- Keep your workcenter neat and organized so it's easy to spot anything that may seem out of place or unknown
- Get to know your coworkers so you can more easily spot people who don't belong in your area
- Rely upon your training and sometimes your "gut" feeling if you discover an item you suspect might be an IED
- React by following the 5-C's - Confirm, Clear, Cordon, Check and Control. (see page 202)
- Never risk your life by moving or opening an IED to get a better description

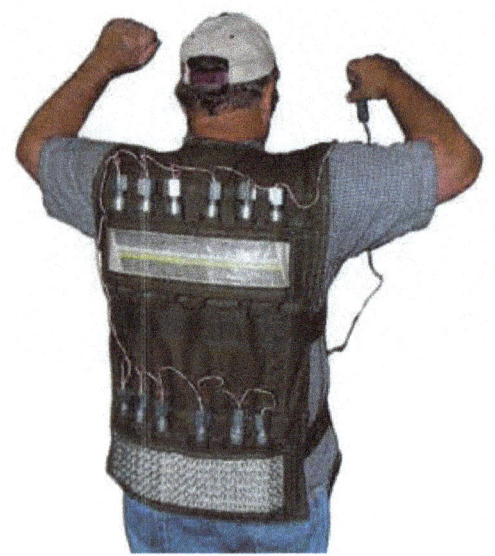

Suicide bombers are a real threat as well! As with IEDs, there is no standard identification or description that will tell you who the next suicide bomber will be, what they'll look like, or how they'll act. Suicide bombers have already targeted public areas overseas where Americans and other foreigners congregate.

- Be security conscious and know the off-limits and areas of concern
- Challenge or report unknown people around your work area
- If you get a "bad feeling" about something, many times there's a reason–tell your coworkers when you think something doesn't feel right
- Follow your training and your "instinct" when uncomfortable situations arise

New surroundings can feel uneasy.

It's normal to have feelings of uneasiness after you arrive at your deployment location. But, don't become consumed by fear. Slowly adjust to your new surroundings, learn all you can from more experienced people, and follow your training.

Terrorist Threats and Vehicles

There are no typical vehicles associated with vehicle bombs. Terrorists are imaginative and cunning and will go to great lengths to kill you and further their cause. With vehicles, they easily blend into their surroundings and don't need to rely on the cover of darkness to strike. Watch for unusual and creative approaches a terrorist might use to slip through a cordon or past a checkpoint–perhaps using an emergency response vehicle (i.e. ambulance) following an incident, to deliver a bomb. To engage this effort, a terrorist may even create the incident to lure first-responders to the scene then entrap and attack them with explosive devices. Watch for suspicious behavior or refusal to obey orders. Know your rules of engagement. If you're one who responds to emergencies, stay on high-alert while you're performing your duties.

Terrorists use all types of vehicles.

Vehicle Search Procedures—If you're tasked to do a vehicle search, you're not only looking for the "big bomb" but for any type of weapon, improvised explosive device, or explosives. Ask the vehicle driver to open all compartments, doors, the hood, and trunk (if applicable.) Look for things that don't belong there or things that appear out of place. For example, in a dirty engine compartment, be suspicious of shiny new wires or a box or carton you find stored behind the vehicle's grille. If you find anything suspicious, follow your local reporting procedures. Even if everything appears to be in order, you can still consider a vehicle as suspicious if the driver refuses to open any compartment (e.g. hood, trunk, passenger doors, glove box, or even a package.) If this happens, heighten your vigilance and immediately notify your supervisor or Security Forces and request help. If a previously searched vehicle has been left unattended in an unsecure environment, another vehicle search should be conducted. This also applies when receiving a rental car.

INSPECT:
under seats, glove box, and all compartments

- Dash board
- Engine compartment
- Behind/under front and rear bumper
- Behind grill
- Wheel well and tires
- Door panels and interior
- Undercarriage
- Spare tire
- Fuel tank
- Cargo area

Pre-Attack Actions

Ref: AFMAN 10-2602

Alarm Green–normal condition of readiness in wartime. Attack is not probable and there is no active threat of attack at present. However, local procedures may vary.

No active attack threat.

As Directed
- Perform pre-attack preparations
- Remove contact lenses and wear protective mask eyeglasses
- Wear field gear and personal body armor
- Inspect IPE and assume MOPP 0
- Implement contamination avoidance actions
- Implement contamination detection actions
- Protect facilities, equipment, aircraft, vehicles
   - Close windows, doors, hatches, and access panels
   - Pre-position M8 Paper throughout work areas and on exposed assets–mark time and date of placement
   - Store assets beneath overhead cover, inside shelters, within revetments, or similar structure
   - Cover exposed assets with contamination avoidance material–double wrap where practical
- Implement hardening and dispersal actions

Prepare equipment for use.

- Know immediate and operational decon actions
- Know post-attack reconnaissance (PAR) procedures
- Know Split-MOPP zone or sector operation procedures
- Know local alarm signals and actions
- Keep supervisor and UCC informed of progress
- Remain vigilant for possible threats

Prepare equipment.

Reverting Back to Pre-Attack... Alarm Green following Alarm Red or Black–CBRNE hazards (damage, UXO, and CBRN contamination) may be present. However, they're not an operational risk for people in MOPP 0 outside of marked hazard areas.
- Perform pre-attack preparations, recovery actions, and stay alert for hazards
- Verify NBCC and other hazard markers remain visible day and night
- Verify UCC receipt of hazard, UXO, damage, and casualty reports

- Replace exhausted supplies and contamination avoidance material (CCA, decon, firefighting, self-aid and buddy care (SABC), water, shelter supplies)
- Replace contaminated M8 and M9 Paper (Tape)–mark time and date of placement
- Discard used decon kits and detection paper as contaminated waste
- Inform UCC of contaminated waste accumulation
- Casualty care
  - Decontaminate casualty as necessary
  - Verify zone or sector hazards along travel route
  - Return casualty's weapon and ammunition to armory
  - Keep IPE with casualty

Watch for hazards.

Continue pre-attack actions.

 **Alarm Yellow**–attack probable in less than 30 minutes. Focus upon final protection and contamination avoidance measures to mitigate attack effects. Commanders may direct mission-essential tasks or functions to continue.

Listen for warnings.

- Notify others within the immediate area and over communications systems
- Remain in shelter, go to shelter, or seek protection with overhead cover
- Do buddy checks to verify correct IPE wear
- Quickly and safely terminate routine or non-critical operations
- Protect and cover assets
- Park vehicles indoors or under cover
- Close doors, windows, vents, hatches, openings
- Shut off HVAC systems
- MOPP Implementation:
  - If you are currently in MOPP 0 or MOPP 1, implement MOPP 2 or as directed
  - If you are currently in MOPP 3, MOPP 4, or the MASK ONLY option, remain in that MOPP and stay masked unless otherwise directed

Shut off HVAC.

Assume MOPP as directed.

Additional Attack Preparations Under Alarm Yellow

Ref: AFMAN 10-2602

A hardened aircraft shelter (HAS) provides optimum protection for aircraft, vehicles, and equipment. Use extreme caution when you drive a vehicle into a HAS that contains aircraft or equipment. Once inside, close the HAS doors. If there's no room for your vehicle inside a HAS, park near the side of the shelter, cover your vehicle with contamination avoidance material, and run inside.

Aircrews should be transported in covered vehicles. Passengers should don the appropriate MOPP while the driver heads toward the squad-operations facility for shelter. Running aircraft may be ordered to launch-to-survive or told to return to a HAS, shut down, and seal the HAS doors.

DO NOT cover refueling vehicles or liquid oxygen and liquid nitrogen equipment with plastic barrier materials. Plastic sheets can accumulate static electricity and discharge sparks at any time–particularly during removal.

With munitions handling equipment, if you must choose between protecting a bomb trailer's cargo surface or the tongue, protect the cargo surface. Also, if space exists, drive forklifts into igloos, shut them off, and close the igloo doors.

Military working dog (MWD) patrols should go to the nearest collective protection shelter or nearest protection with overhead cover. For missile attacks, put the MWD inside a vehicle, cargo aircraft, or other area that avoids agent fallout. Handlers and dogs should remain sheltered until you hear MOPP 0, 1, 2, or directed otherwise.

Services personnel should disperse food assets into fixed or hardened shelters, or refrigeration units. Cover the units with plastic and seal their openings with tape.

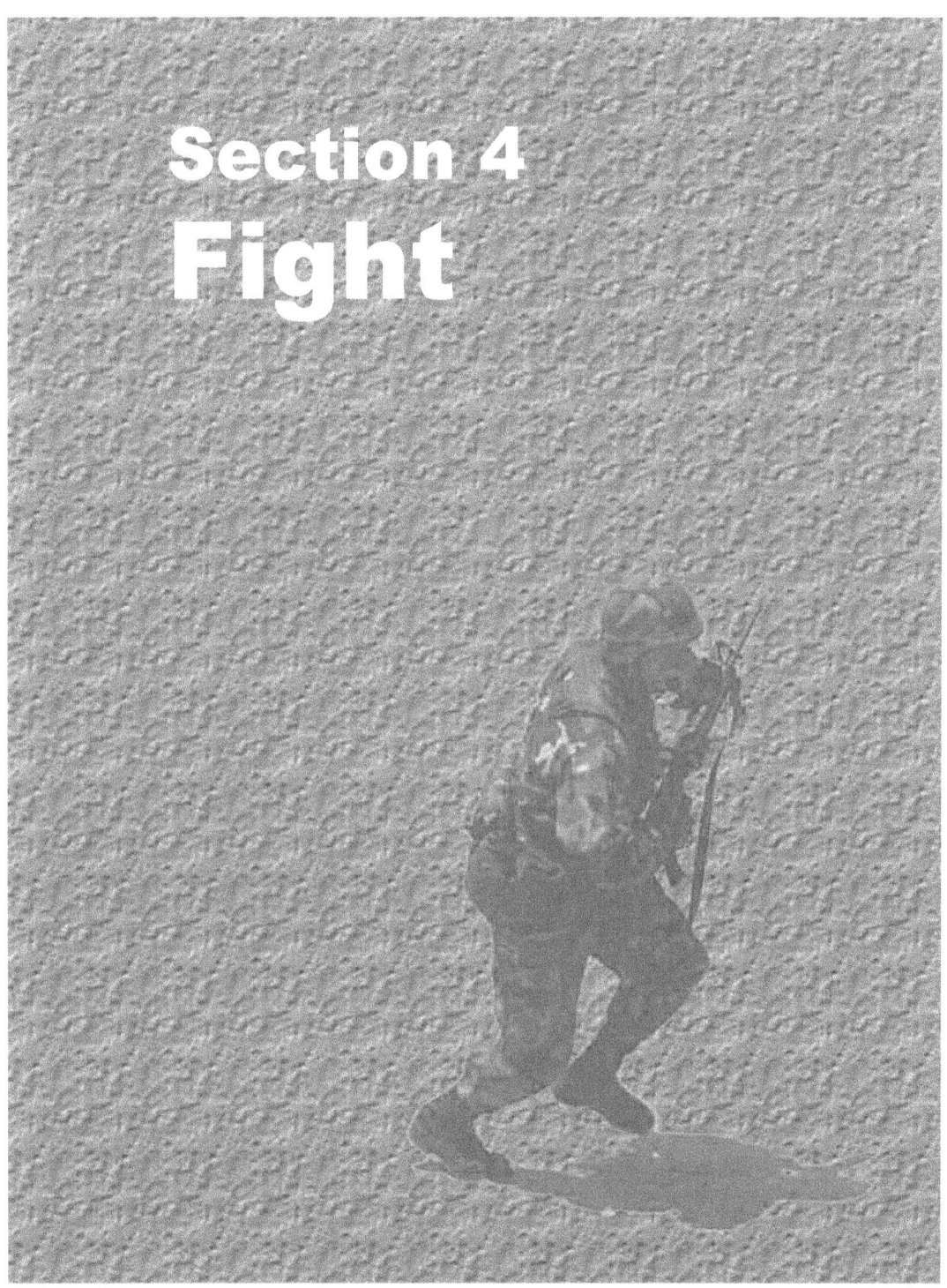

Section 4
Fight

Integrated Base Defense (IBD)

Ref: AFTTP 3-10.1

IBD provides full dimensional protection for people and assets. It provides the framework for a fully integrated base defense that ensures our forces can pursue the defeat of any adversary or control of any situation across the threat and conflict spectrum. Most importantly, you and every Airman play an extremely vital role as a sensor and potential defender in the Force Protection (FP) and IBD battlespace.

FP battlespace covers airbases, detached sites, transient forces and convoys. IBD battlespace begins with the flightline, Protection Level (PL) resources (i.e. critical USAF resources that are designated a separate level of protection), and cantonment areas. It expands out to, and beyond, the base perimeter. IBD battlespace dominance can be achieved through interacting capabilities channeled through an integrated command and control network.

Capabilities essential to IBD

- **Mitigate** – Minimize enemy success
- **Deceive** – Distort adversary's view, mislead
- **Deter** – Discourage adversaries. Make consequences clear
- **Deploy** – Rapidly respond. Gain positional advantage
- **Anticipate** – See adversary's options. Prepare accordingly
- **Neutralize** – Render adversary ineffective
- **Detect** – See all potential threats
- **Assess** – Analyze defense effect, leverage
- **Deny** – Deny adversary the time, space and means to attack
- **Delay** – Increase adversary's risk

These interacting measures aid in the Air Forces' ability to See First, Understand First, and ultimately, Act First.

See First
- Relentless Intelligence and Information Capture–Gather, collate and disseminate effectively, information on defense related activity within and beyond the IBD battlespace

Gather information.

- Detect and Identify Threats—Analyze collated information and deduce likely threats. Maintain a reconnaissance, intelligence, surveillance and target acquisition capability
- Predict Threat Courses of Action (COA)—Use planning tools to process information and deductions and arrive at likely threat COAs

Understand First
- Identify Vulnerabilities—Critically assess the effectiveness of the defense that is in place. Aggressively examine the integrity of the defense, know the weaknesses that exist and plan accordingly
- Know and Manage Risks—Where the burden of a shortfall exists in the defense, ensure that it is carried unobtrusively and in a manner that minimizes the risk to assets in priority order. To minimize risk, manage any shortfall commensurate with the emerging situation and changes in defense resources

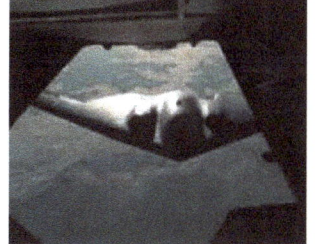

Analyze information.

Act First
- Determine Options—Identify broad COAs open to IBD defenders to meet the perceived threat. Consider each COA against the defense mission
- Decide First—Taking into account the advantages and disadvantages of each COA, the decision must be a logical result of the analysis process. The absence of ideal conditions, such as when defense forces are undermanned, does not preclude the selection of the best COA in the prevailing circumstances

Remove threat.

- Act to Remove Threat—Action to remove a threat could be the initiating of a lethal or non-lethal engagement at a time and place of the Air Force's choosing. Equally, amending the defense posture and thereby rendering ineffective an adversary's preferred line of attack, constitutes acting to remove a threat

Security Procedures

Cordons
Ref: AFI 10-403; AFMAN 91-201; AFMAN 10-2602

A cordon protects people.

Block cordon entrances.

A cordon protects people, equipment, and classified material during major incidents, and it's normally marked off with rope, tape, and appropriate signs. Where no toxic or explosive materials are involved, its size is dictated by the affected area and the area disaster response force teams need to conduct unhindered operations. Security Forces personnel may direct non-security force personnel to act as cordon sentries. If you're needed to work as a cordon sentry, strictly follow your instructions. Some situations that may warrant a cordon are:
- Discovery of unexploded ordnance
- Bomb threat/suspicious package
- Damage caused by a natural disaster
- Major accidents
- Contaminated areas following an enemy attack

Cordon Sentries
- Secure their assigned posts on the cordon perimeter–prevent access to incident site
- Direct arriving people to report to the entry control point
- Report the names of anyone who evacuates the cordon at your post
- Do not enter the cordon area or leave your post until properly relieved

Report evacuees.

Passing Through Entry Control Points
- Control entry into installations, controlled and restricted areas, Chemical, Biological, Radiological, Nuclear, and high yield Explosives (CBRNE) incidents, and major incidents

- Entry Authority Lists are checked to gain access to controlled and restricted areas
- Be prepared to show your identification card
- You and your belongings may be searched
- Your vehicle may be searched
- Know the local MOPP entry control procedures, sign/countersign, or chem code

Entry control point.

Be continually vigilant.

Challenging Intruders

Ref: AFMAN 31-222

Intruders can be aggressive or passive, male or female, adult or child, and can show up at any location, at any time. Be continually vigilant. Challenge all intruders. Treat all individuals or groups as hostile whether weapons are present or not. Challenge an individual, but always maintain proper cover and concealment while doing so. NOTE: Cover and concealment means to place yourself out of harms way by concealing your location and being in a protective position in case you are fired upon. Challenges are divided into two areas: individuals or groups.

Challenge Steps
- Upon hearing or seeing a group or lone person approach, command the group or person to "**Halt**" just loud enough to be heard. Shouting the command can give away your position. Note: Learn the word "halt" in the language of the country you are currently in.

Halt!

If challenging a vehicle, DO NOT stand directly in the path of the vehicle to get it to stop—if the vehicle flees, note the direction of travel, and immediately report the incident to your UCC or Security Forces

- When the group or person stops, command, "**Who goes there?**"
- The challenged person should respond with their **Rank**, **Name**, and **Unit**
- After the person identifies him or herself, command "**Advance To Be Recognized!**" Note: If in a group, command only one person forward
- When the person comes within 10 feet, command "**Halt**" and issue the **Challenge Word** or **Sign**, just loud enough to be heard without being heard by others
- If the person responds with the correct **Password** or **Countersign**, let the person pass. Note: If in a group, that person you called forward must then identify the members of that group as they pass
- If the person fails to stop or answer at anytime during the challenge, immediately notify your UCC and Security Forces
- Command the unidentified person or group to "**Halt!**" again
- Once they've stopped, command the person or group to "**Turn Away From The Sound of My Voice!**" Note: If they fail to heed your commands, follow the Rules of Engagement established for your Area of Responsibility.

Who goes there?

Advance to be recognized.

Turn away from the sound of my voice and drop slowly to your knees.

- Notify your UCC and SF control center of your situation by using the S-A-L-U-T-E report (see page 91) and your location.
- Follow UCC instructions. Note: If a weapon(s) is visible, instruct the person or group to place their weapon(s) on the ground and move six to eight steps forward (away from you)
- Command the person or group to "**Drop Slowly To Your Knees and Lie Down on Your Stomach!**" Note: Separate each person from a group before you place them on the ground. Remember to keep them in a position where you can observe them until help arrives

Lie down on stomach.

- Command the person or group to "**Move Your Arms Away From Your Body and Spread Your Feet Apart!**"

Move arms away from body and spread your feet.

- Remain vigilant over the person or group until responding forces arrive
- Continually scan the entire area for other intruders

Codewords

Sign/Countersign—words or numbers can be used as the sign and countersign. For example, if the words of the day are Blue Cards and the challenge word is Blue, the correct response is Cards. The number of the day must be between two and 10, so if the number of the day is 7 and you say 3, the correct corresponding number would be 4 making the sum of 7. These numbers or words, also known as chem. codes, can be used to identify people who are in MOPP 4.

Sign/countersign.

SEE Page 217, Quick Reference, **Square Grid Matrix**

Authentication Codes—These codes are a constant changing list of numbers and letters developed into a square grid matrix to necessitate a different response to the possible combinations of challenge codes. This is a very secure method, but the most difficult to operate. Normally used in radio or telephone communications to authenticate the identity of the person you are talking to.

Duress Words—can be any unusual word that is not normally used in the course of routine conversation, like giraffe or scarecrow. It can be inserted into the conversation in order to communicate inconspicuously that a person is under some form of duress. For example "How are you today, SSgt Smith?", "Did you see the giraffe at the zoo?" Security Forces publish duress words on a periodic basis.

How are you today, SSgt Smith? Did you see the giraffe at the zoo?

Search all EPWs.

Handling Prisoners and Defectors

Ref: Geneva Convention; AFI 31-304 (I)

Taking enemy prisoners of war (EPW) and defectors can happen at any time. When it does, immediately notify your Unit Control Center and request Security Forces to take custody. In the meantime, search, segregate, silence, speed to the rear, safeguard, and tag your detainees.

Search
- Immediately search the EPW with an armed colleague monitoring
- Look for anything that could be used as a weapon or an escape aid
- Thoroughly search for items of potential intelligence value
- Allow prisoners to keep uniforms and any protective clothing, (e.g., bad weather and IPE gear) insignia, medals, ID and all personal property

Segregate
- Separate defectors, deserters, and EPWs (male and female)
- Separate military and civilians
- Separate military into subgroups
   - Officers
   - Enlisted

Separate EPWs.

Allow EPWs to keep uniforms.

Do not allow EPW's to gain operational intelligence.

Silence
- Limit communication between EPWs as much as possible
- If you don't understand the language, don't allow it
- Record anything the EPW says and send it up the chain of command

Speed to the Rear
- Contact your UCC as soon as possible
- Much of the intelligence received from the EPW is time-sensitive
- Do not allow EPW's to gain operational intelligence.

Safeguard
- Protect EPWs from local nationals
- Protect EPWs from friendly and allied forces
- Protect EPWs from CBRNE attacks
- Protect yourself and others from EPWs
- Sick and wounded prisoners will be evacuated separately, but in the same manner as US and allied forces

Tagging
- Complete a DD Form 2745, Enemy Prisoner of War Capture Tag, if available for each detainee, weapon, and piece of equipment
- If not, use any source available
- At a minimum you should include:
  - Date/time of capture
  - Capturing unit/branch
  - Place of capture
  - Circumstances surrounding capture

Complete an EPW tag.

Audible and Visual Warnings

Ref: AFMAN 10-2602

Commanders continually assess existing and potential threats, vulnerabilities, and the OPSTEMPO when balancing how to protect people and accomplish mission objectives. They use:
- Alarm warning signals
- FPCONs
- MOPP levels
- MOPP variations
- Split-MOPP
- Shelter strategies

All of these will be ineffective unless you understand what they are, what they mean, and how to react. Installation warning systems vary based upon:
- Size of the base
- Number of assigned personnel
- Base layout
- How long the base has been in operation

Well established bases may have:
- A public address system
- Electronic signs
- Flags
- Cable television and computer network systems
- Tactical radios and/or land/mobile radios
- Cell phones, pagers, and an AM/FM radio broadcast system

Most deployment bases and sites, however, will be limited to a primary and secondary public address/siren system and a land mobile radio system for audible communication, and simple flags and signs for visual communication.

The command post normally operates the primary base warning/siren system while assigned and attached units maintain visual warning indicators throughout the base and at geographically separated units. Places you may see these warning flags include:
- Entry control points
- Flag poles
- Vehicles
- Shelters and workcenters
- Split-MOPP transition points
- Geographically separated units
- Maintenance areas and facilities

Note: Security Forces and Fire Protection often provide back-up audible alarms when primary systems fail and will often display alarm condition flags on their vehicles throughout operations.

A public address alarm signal announcement generally identifies the:
- Announcer
- Alarm signal
- MOPP Level
- FPCON
- Appropriate warning siren/bugle/sounds

As an example, a missile attack warning may sound something like:
"This is the base command post, Alarm Red (Alarm Blue in Korea) Missile Attack, FPCON Charlie, MOPP Level 4, Take Cover, (they may repeat this warning) then sound a wavering tone siren."

Unit control centers will also make radio announcements throughout their radio networks.

Learn what to listen for and where to observe visual indicators at your base!

Attack Warning

Ref: AFMAN 10-2602; AFVA 10-2511

If an attack warning is given, and you don't know what type of attack will or has occurred, quickly follow the protective actions for a missile attack. Always wear your helmet and body armor (if issued.) Also, always try to cover your face and ears during an attack.

Listen for announcements.

Alarm Red/Alarm Blue–Attack by air or missile is imminent or in progress
- Audible wavering tone siren
- Visual red flags (Blue in Korea)

Your location is under missile attack, aircraft attack, or an attack will begin within minutes. Assume MOPP 4 or as directed by the commander.

Alarm Red/Alarm Blue, Ground Attack–Attack by ground force is imminent or in-progress
- Audible bugle Call-to-Arms
- Visual red flags (blue in Korea)

Bugle call means ground attack.

Your location is under attack by a ground force, or an attack will begin within minutes–assume MOPP Level 4 or as directed by the commander. For a small arms attack, take a defensive position behind cover. Prepare to defend yourself, your area, and watch out for Security Forces or other friendly forces to prevent fratricide. For a mortar or rocket attack, immediately shout "Incoming" and lay down in the prone position–ideally in a low lying area. If better cover is available nearby, move to that safer position between incoming rounds and avoid gathering in large groups. If you witness where mortars or rockets are fired/launched, notify Security Forces as soon as possible. Use the S-A-L-U-T-E format (see page 91) to report enemy activity and support Security Forces where possible.

Trans-Attack Procedures in NBC Threat Areas
- Immediately report observed attacks or enemy force sightings to your UCC or work center
- Defend yourself under ROE–coordinate actions with others in your area

- Use buddy checks to verify proper IPE wear–assist other personnel with donning
- Assist the injured if possible, otherwise, remain in position and under cover until alarm change
- For missile attack warning, seek the best available protection (building, bunker). If unavailable, find overhead cover
  - Remain inside vehicles/equipment (windows up, doors closed, and engine off), and don IPE
- If you're attacked without warning, don mask, move to closest protection, and don remaining IPE. Seek overhead cover (rain gear, poncho, tarps, or plastic)
- When attack warning sounds or notification is received, vehicle and equipment operators should drive to the best available protection (building, aircraft shelter, bunker, or hangar) while passengers don IPE
- Drive vehicles and equipment into or under shelter if possible
- Keep shelters closed. Shelter teams or senior personnel in each shelter should ensure shelter doors remain closed as much as possible to limit infiltration of contamination, and control personnel entering and exiting the shelter
  - Keep shelterees away from exterior walls
  - Desks and interior rooms provide additional protection inside unhardened facilities

Use buddy checks.

Assume directed MOPP.

Seek overhead cover.

Keep away from exterior walls.

Reporting an Attack

Ref: AFH 31-302

Use the **S-A-L-U-T-E** report as a quick and effective way to communicate ground enemy attack information up the chain of command.

Report Area	Information to Report
Size	The number of persons and vehicles seen or the size of an object
Activity	Description of enemy activity (assaulting, fleeing, observing)
Location	Where the enemy was sighted (grid coordinate or reference point)
Unit	Distinctive signs, symbols, or identification on people, vehicles, aircraft, or weapons (numbers, patches, or clothing type)
Time	Time the activity is observed
Equipment	Equipment and vehicles associated with the activity

Example of a S-A-L-U-T-E Report: "Six enemy soldiers, running away from the command post, heading towards the flightline. Uniforms solid green fatigues–possibly Republic Guards. Time was 0230 hours. Equipment– AK-47 rifles, backpacks and gas mask being carried."

Use the most expedient means necessary/possible for the urgency you place on the information you have to up channel. If your report needs to get to the commander **NOW**, use **any means** available!

- **Messenger**–most secure-most time consuming
- **Wire/telephone**–more secure than radio-not mobile and may be monitored
- **Radio**–fast and mobile-least secure. However, a secure radio lessens the possibility of being monitored

Radio Discipline

- Think before you push-to-talk
- Be brief. The radio is not a phone
- Speak clearly into the microphone and use proper call signs
- Protect your radio
- Conduct radio checks
- Comply with OPSEC standards for radios, phones, PDA's, and computers
- Periodically check physical condition and battery connections
- Know your unit radio manager
- DO NOT hang anything from antenna

Practice radio discipline.

OPSEC is Everyone's Job... DO NOT:

- Use ranks and names of supervisors or commanders
- Broadcast social security account numbers, phone, or credit card numbers
- Discuss classified information
- Disclose specific locations
- Use profanity

SEE Page 195, Quick Reference, **Procedure Words (Prowords)**

Speak clearly.

Don't discuss classified information.

OPSEC is everyone's job.

Reactions to Flares

Don't watch flares.

Both friendly and opposition forces rely on nighttime illumination to conduct military operations. US forces often use high-tech night vision devices to see without using illumination flares, but strategically placed ground flares with triggering devices are sometimes used in areas where it's difficult to monitor certain terrain even with the use of night vision devices. Unsophisticated opposing forces usually are not as well equipped as US forces–they don't have night vision devices and may rely heavily on low-tech aerial flares to harass friendly forces, illuminate targets, or for signaling purposes. If you spot an aerial or ground flare at night, follow these common procedures to maximize your protection and safety:

- Remain stationary and assume the prone position–don't move.

- Report flare activity to your unit control center

- Don't look toward a burning flare– protect your night vision by closing or covering one eye (preferably your "shooting" eye) while observing with the other. Close both eyes if you can

- Wait until the flare(s) is completely burned out before moving

- Your eyes may take up to 30 minutes to readjust to darkness after exposure to light

Notify control center.

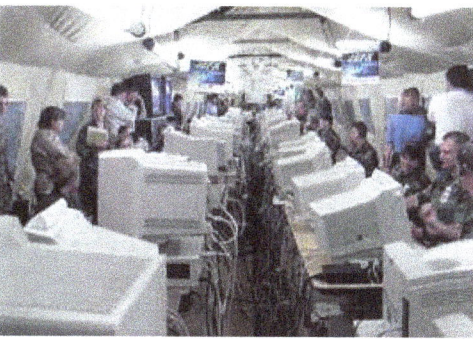

AFPAM 10-100 / 1 March 2009   93 / Section 4 / Fight

Vehicle and Equipment Protection, Marking, and Decontamination

Ref: AFMAN 10-2602

Seek overhead cover and close facility doors.

When attack warning occurs, drive your vehicle to your designated shelter or seek cover beneath the best available overhead protection. Turn-off the engine, close hatches and doors, install protective covers, and pre-position M8 Paper on horizontal surfaces. Equipment operators should likewise shut-down equipment, close access doors and panels, install protective covers, and pre-position M8 Paper. Take cover!

After the attack (when you're released) check the pre-positioned M8 Paper for contamination. If contaminated, remove the barrier material and dispose as contaminated waste. Notify your UCC of the contamination status. Check the asset again with M8 Paper. If contaminated with a liquid chemical agent, operationally decontaminate the asset within 1 hour from the time of contamination. Nonporous surfaces (i.e. glass, unpainted metal) won't let liquid chemical agents quickly penetrate the surface—that represents the most dangerous area on a contaminated surface. Use M295 decon kits and decon surfaces that must be continuously touched. A 5% chlorine bleach solution can augment the decontamination process (if available).

Remove contaminated barriers.

Can't decon textiles.

There's no operational method of decontaminating textiles (canvas storage covers, seatbelts, webbing, carpet) once they've become contaminated with a liquid chemical agent. Place barrier material over these items or replace them if possible.

Contaminated vehicles and equipment are not unserviceable—don't abandon or stop protecting them if they were previously contaminated. If you wear the right IPE and follow appropriate measures, you can continue to use contaminated vehicles and equipment.

Follow procedures when using contaminated vehicle.

Mark vehicles and equipment with the appropriate NBC hazard marker (or equivalent) to show they were contaminated. For vehicles, place the marker in the lower center portion of the windshield. Annotate the AF Form 1800-series operator's form when the marker is placed. Equipment operators should use the appropriate inspection form outlined in the equipment technical data. Include the date and time of contamination, the agent type, and the location of the contamination on the vehicle. If the inspection form is not available or itself becomes contaminated, provide the same information, along with the vehicle registration or equipment identification numbers to your UCC.

Mark vehicles.

SEE Page 200, Quick Reference, NBC Hazard Markers

Vehicle operators and passengers should place barrier materials on seats if they or seat areas are (or were previously) contaminated. Body heat and pressure (from sitting) increases the potential for liquid chemical agents to penetrate the overgarment. Also, consider covering steering wheels with barrier material—this is especially important for vehicles with open cabs or driver compartments.

Convoy Procedures

Ref: AFTTP(I) 3-2.58

If you must travel in a vehicle convoy, pay close attention to the predeparture convoy briefing that's applicable to both drivers and riders.

Drivers:
- Be qualified to operate the vehicle
- Inspect your vehicle every 24 hours
- Annotate AF Form 1800, Operator's Inspection Guide and Trouble Report
- Ensure your vehicle is properly equipped
  - Check for spare tires, tire changing equipment, first aid kit, flashlight, fire extinguisher, etc.
- Guard vehicle anytime convoy has stopped

Drivers and Riders Must Know:
- Primary and alternate travel routes, checkpoints, and timelines
- Everyone must be alert to possible threats or hazards during the entire convoy and be prepared to defend against them
- Order of movement
- What to do during road blocks and breakdowns
- Speed limits
- Distance and intervals

Vehicles are force multipliers.

Convoy Attack Procedures

Air Attack
- Sound a series of short blasts on the vehicle horn
- Pull vehicle off the road, maintain intervals
- Seek cover away from the vehicles
- Notify UCC–give time, location, and activity using S-A-L-U-T-E
- Remain under cover until "All Clear"

Watch vehicle interval spacing.

Watch for ambush.

Ambush (IED, Rockets, Mortars, Small Arms)
- Take an alternate route
- Notify UCC–give time, location, and activity using S-A-L-U-T-E
- Speed up and drive out of the kill zone or halt convoy
- Dismount and return fire as a last resort
- Assemble and move out of the area
- Assemble at a safe distance

NOTE: See page 38 for IED threats.

Vehicle Break Down
- Repair the vehicle, if possible
- If irreparable, tow it if possible
- If towing isn't possible, call for a wrecker
- Ensure personnel left behind have equipment, food, water, communications, and currency
- If vehicle may fall into enemy hands, destroy or disable it

Roadblock
- Lead vehicle notifies convoy
- All vehicles stop
- Disperse in a defensive posture
- Assess the roadblock
- Watch for booby-traps or ambush
- Look for IEDs made to look like roadside garbage or debris
- Report the location and nature of the roadblock to UCC
- If roadblock can be moved or breached, do so immediately
- If the roadblock can't be moved or breached, switch to an alternate route

Go around roadblocks.

Weapons Skills–Rifle

Ref: TO 11W3-5-5-41, Operator's Manual; AFMAN 31-229, USAF Weapons Handling Manual

You must be able to competently handle your assigned weapon. Prior training, along with this information, will keep you ready if you must fulfill your force protection role.

Weapon Safety
- Never point your weapon at anyone or anything you're not willing to shoot
- Consider all weapons as loaded
- Clear all weapons during issue and turn-in at a designated safe place or as instructed by superiors
- Keep your finger off the trigger until you're prepared to engage your target
- Don't shoot anything you can't positively identify
- Know what's behind your target
- Keep weapon on safe until ready to shoot

Don't shoot at anything you can't identify.

Keep weapon on safe until ready to shoot.

M16A2 Characteristics

- Maximum rates of fire:
  - Semiautomatic, 45 rpm
  - Automatic (3-round burst), 90 rpm
  - Sustained, 12 to 15 rpm
- Maximum range, 3938 yds (3600 m)
- Maximum effective ranges:
  - Point target, 602 yds (550 m)
  - Area target, 875 yds (800 m)

M4 Carbine Characteristics

- Maximum rates of fire:
  - Semiautomatic, 45 rpm
  - Automatic (3-round burst), 90 rpm
  - Sustained, 12 to 15 rpm
- Maximum range, 3938 yds (3600 m)
- Maximum effective ranges:
  - Point target, 547 yds (500 m)
  - Area target, 656 yds (600 m)

Clearing Procedures

1 Attempt to place weapon on Safe

2 Remove magazine from weapon by pressing magazine release button

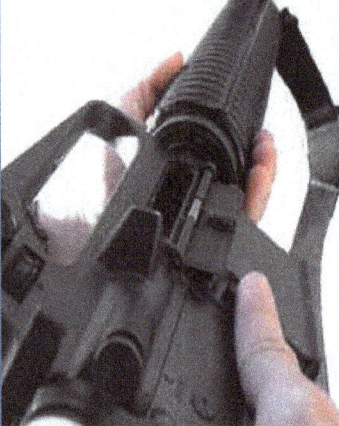

3a If bolt locked to rear. Visually inspect chamber and receiver area for live rounds or obstructions

3b If bolt is in forward position, push in on BOTTOM of bolt catch, then pull charging handle all the way to rear. After bolt has been locked back, ensure charging handle is placed fully forward

4 Check to make sure weapon is on safe

Disassembly (Fieldstrip)

1. Clear weapon
2. Send bolt forward
3. Remove sling
4. Remove handguards (may use buddy system)
5. Separate upper and lower receivers
6. Remove bolt carrier group and disassemble
   a. Pull back charging handle and bolt carrier
   b. Remove bolt carrier, then charging handle
   NOTE: Use charging handle to hold small parts
   c. Remove firing pin retaining pin
   d. Remove firing pin from the rear of the bolt carrier
   e. Push bolt into bolt carrier, rotate cam pin 1/4 turn, then lift out of the bolt carrier
   f. Remove bolt assembly from carrier
   g. Press the rear of the extractor relieving spring pressure and press out extractor pin
   h. Remove extractor and spring (do not separate spring from extractor)
7. Remove buffer and action spring

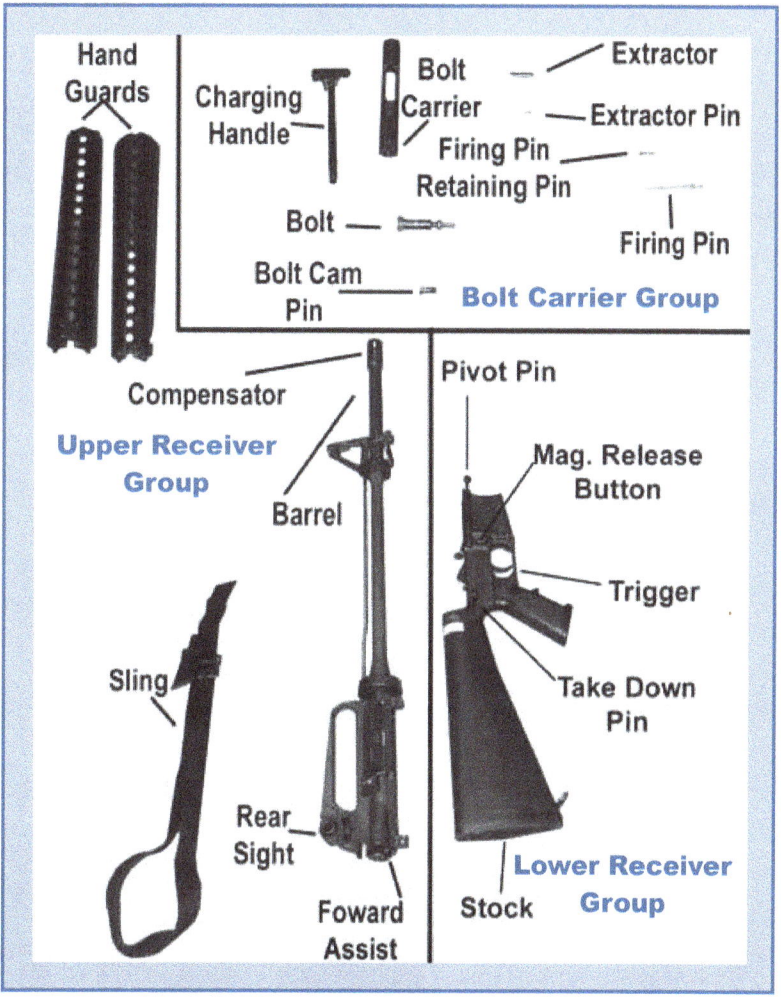

Magazine Disassembly
1. Remove base catch with end of cleaning rod
2. Remove spring and follower

Function Check
- Start with a CLEARED WEAPON, bolt forward, on SAFE
- Pull the trigger
- Weapon should not dry fire (hammer should not fall)
- Place on SEMI and pull the trigger
- Weapon should dry fire (hammer falls)
- Hold the trigger to the rear and charge the weapon
- Release trigger slowly and smoothly (you should hear an audible click)
- Place the weapon on BURST and pull the trigger
- Weapon should dry fire (hammer falls)
- Hold the trigger to the rear and release the weapon charging handle three times
- Release the trigger. Pull the trigger and hammer should fall

Magazine Disassembly.

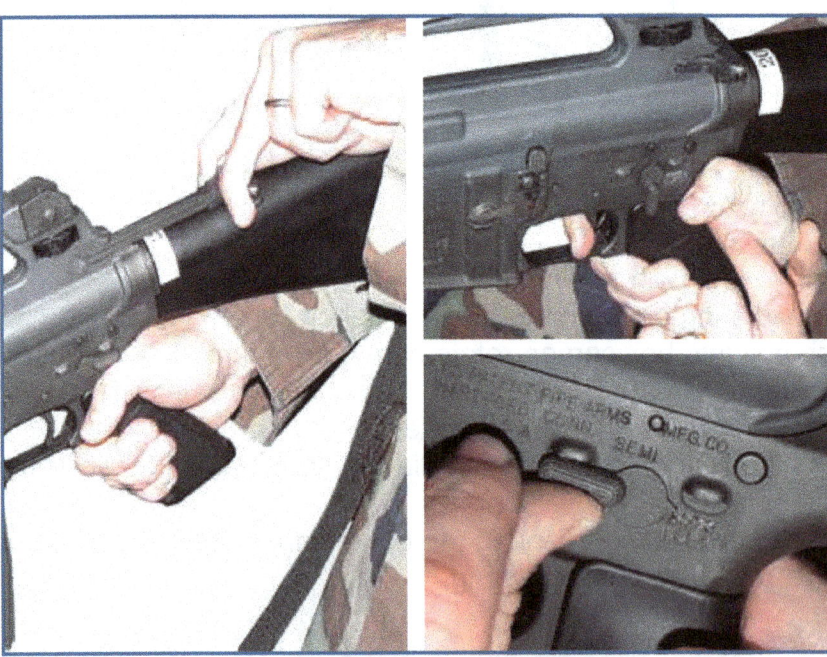

M16A2 and M4 Carbine Ammunition
- M855 Ball with green tip
- M856 Tracer with orange tip

These are the standard rounds for the M16A2 and M4 Carbine.

Care of Ammunition
- Store six inches off ground (pallet)
- Keep closed until ready for use
- Protect from moisture, high temperatures, and direct sun
- Do not disassemble
- Do not lubricate or clean with solvents
- Clean with dry cloth

M855 Ball

M856 Tracer

Insert magazine.

Loading Procedures
- Visually inspect rifle to ensure weapon is on safe and no ammunition is present in chamber or receiver
- Send bolt forward by slapping bolt release on left side of weapon
- Insert magazine, pull down to ensure magazine is locked in position

Firing the Weapon
- Pull charging handle fully to the rear and release (allow bolt to slam forward)
- Hit forward assist
- Place weapon to Semi
- Aim and shoot

Know what's behind your target.

Insert new magazine.

Reloading Procedures
- Remove empty magazine
- Insert new magazine, pull down to ensure the magazine is seated
- Slap bolt release to allow bolt to go forward
- Continue to fire

Clearing Procedures
- Place selector lever on Safe if possible
- Remove magazine
- Lock bolt to rear
- Ensure selector lever is on Safe
- Visually inspect chamber and receiver area
- Press Bolt Catch and release bolt forward (unless handing weapon over to another individual)

Remove empty magazine.

Immediate Action Procedures (SPORTS)
If the weapon fails to fire:
- **S** Slap upward on bottom of magazine to ensure magazine is fully seated
- **P** Pull charging handle to rear
- **O** Observe to see if a round or cartridge casing was ejected and chamber and receiver area are clear (if chamber or receiver is not clear, proceed to remedial action)
- **R** Release charging handle (allow bolt to slam forward)
- **T** Tap forward assist button to ensure bolt is fully forward
- **S** Shoot

Remedial Action Procedures
If immediate action does not correct problem, or an obstruction is found during immediate action:
- Clear weapon
- Check again for jammed cartridge case
  Note: inspect closely, a ruptured cartridge case can be difficult to see
- If cartridge case is detected, use a cleaning rod to remove
- Reload weapon
- Select Semi
- Fire

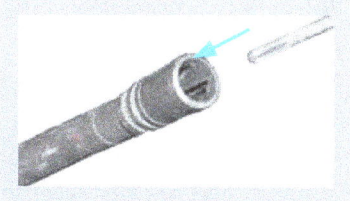

Shove rod into barrel to clear jammed cartridge.

Hot Weapon Procedures
If your weapons stops firing with a live round in the chamber of a hot barrel:
- Remove round fast (within 10 seconds) WARNING: KEEP YOUR FACE AWAY FROM THE EJECTION PORT!
- If you could not remove the round, wait 15 minutes
- Clear weapon

Note: Firing 140 rounds rapidly and continuously will raise the temperature of the barrel to the COOKOFF POINT.

Light Recoil Procedures
If an audible "POP" or reduced recoil is experienced during firing, IMMEDIATELY CEASE FIRE! DO NOT APPLY IMMEDIATE ACTION!
- A projectile may be lodged in barrel
- DO NOT apply immediate action, weapon could explode if fired!
- Clear weapon
- Inspect bore for obstruction

Fundamentals of Shooting and Firing

- Establish steady firing position
- Establish GOOD stock weld (face should be in firm contact with stock of weapon.) Ensure tip of nose is no further than two fingers width behind charging handle to establish proper eye relief
- Align sights (sight alignment)
- Align sights on target (sight picture)
- FOCUS on FRONT SIGHT
- Place no more than first pad of finger on trigger
- Hold your breath
- With steady, increasing pressure, press trigger to rear
- After weapon recoils, realign sights and start fundamentals process again (do not break stock weld)
- Remember to be consistent with face placement, sight alignment, sight picture, and breath control. Be as motionless as possible while pressing trigger to rear

M68 Sight

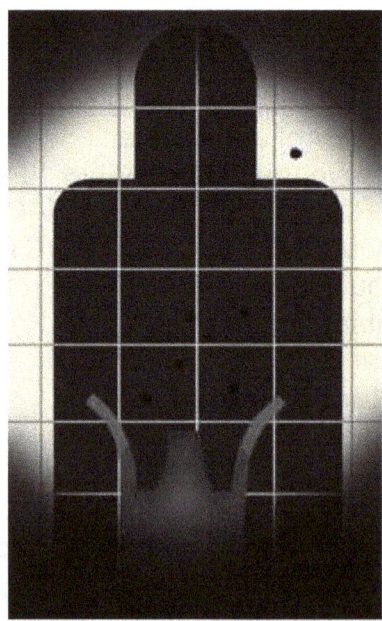

Iron Sight

MOPP Equipment Fire Training

Immediate Action
Under increased MOPP levels, this may take as long as 10 seconds to successfully complete.

Marksmanship Fundamentals
1 *Steady Position*
- Adjust firing positions for stability and comfort as needed due to added bulk of the over garment
- Adjust the positioning of your head to place your eye directly behind the sight. This may be an awkward position due to the shape of the protective mask, but is necessary to maintain a consistent spot or stock weld

2 *Aiming*
- While wearing a protective mask, rotate (cant) the rifle the least amount possible to see through the rear aperture and line up the sights. Center the tip of the front sight post on the ideal aiming point

1. Ideal Sight Picture.

2. Right-handed cant.

3. Left-handed cant.

MOPP Equipment Fire Training

2 Aiming continued...
- Use center-of-mass aiming until you know what aiming adjustment is needed. Right-handed shooters usually adjust the point of aim to the right and high; left-handed shooters usually adjust to the left and high

M16A1   **M16A2**

(Aiming high and right to compensate for cant)  **RIGHT-HANDED FIRER'S CANT**  (Aiming center mass)

Engagement of 175 Meter Target

NORMAL AIMING   (Rotating around aiming point)  (Aiming high and right to compensate for cant)

Engagement of 300 Meter Target

3 Breath Control
- Emphasize rapid target engagement...there is a limited amount of time you can control your breathing while encumbered by the bulkiness and breathing restrictions of IPE

4 Trigger Manipulation
- Be aware that wearing protective gloves alters your ability to grasp the pistol grip and press the trigger with your index finger
- Release the swing-down trigger guard if the fit of the glove restricts the trigger finger

M16A2 Sight Adjustment

front sight

Front Sight Adjustments
- Make elevation changes during weapons zeroing only
- Use the tip of an ammunition round to depress the front sight detent, and then rotate the sight clockwise to raise the bullet strike or counter clockwise to lower the bullet strike
- One click = 3/8 inch (0.9 cm) at 82 ft (25 m) or 1 3/8 inch (3.5 cm) at 328 ft (100 m)

rear sight, elevation

rear sight, windage

Rear Sight Adjustments
- Make changes in the right and left movement (windage) of the bullet and elevation or range distance corrections
- Windage correction is one click = 1/8 inch (0.3 cm) at 82 ft (25 m) or 1/2 inch (1.25 cm) at 328 ft (100 m)
- Rear sight elevation adjusts for proper target distance as long as the weapon was properly zeroed
- Elevation correction is one click = 1/4 inch (0.7 cm) at 82 ft (25 m) or 1 inch (2.8 cm) at 328 ft (100 m)

Backup Iron Sight

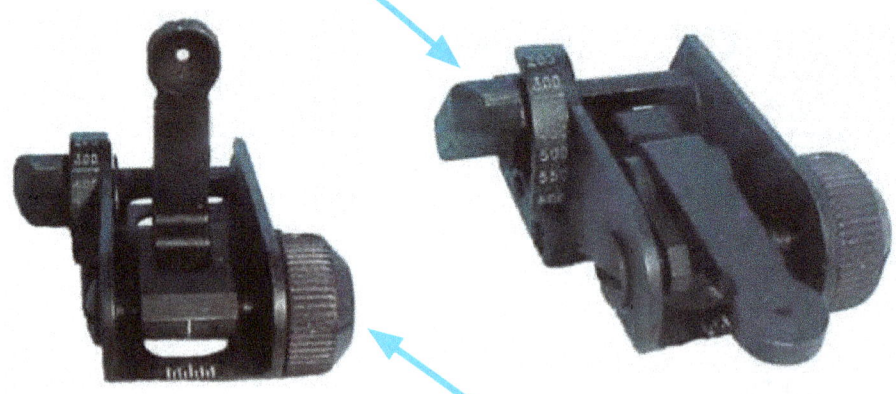

Elevation Scale

Windage Knob

Rear Sight Adjustments
- Make changes in the right and left movement (windage) of the bullet and elevation or range distance corrections
- Windage correction is one click = 3/16 inch (0.5 cm) at 82 ft (25 m) or 3/4 inch (1.9 cm) at 328 ft (100 m)
- Rear sight elevation adjusts for proper target distance as long as the weapon was properly zeroed
- Elevation correction is one click = 1/2 inch (1.2 cm) at 82 ft (25 m) or 1 7/8 inch (4.8 cm) at 328 ft (100 m)

Care and Cleaning of Small Arms M4, M9, M16

Cleaning Equipment

The ideal cleaning kit consists of:
- Handle section, three-rod sections, swab holder, and swabs
- Chamber, small arms cleaning brush (nylon bristle toothbrush), and pipe cleaners; and the bore is required for the M16 and M4 rifles
- Cleaner, Lubricant, and Preservative (CLP), ½-oz bottle
- Other authorized cleaning equipment:
  - Lubricating oil weapons (semi-fluid LSA)
  - Lubricating oil, arctic weapons (LAW)
  - Under all but the coldest arctic conditions, LSA and CLP are the lubricants to use in temperatures above -10°F (-23°C)
  - LAW is used when temperatures range below -10°F (-23°C)

Always wear eye protection when cleaning your weapon.

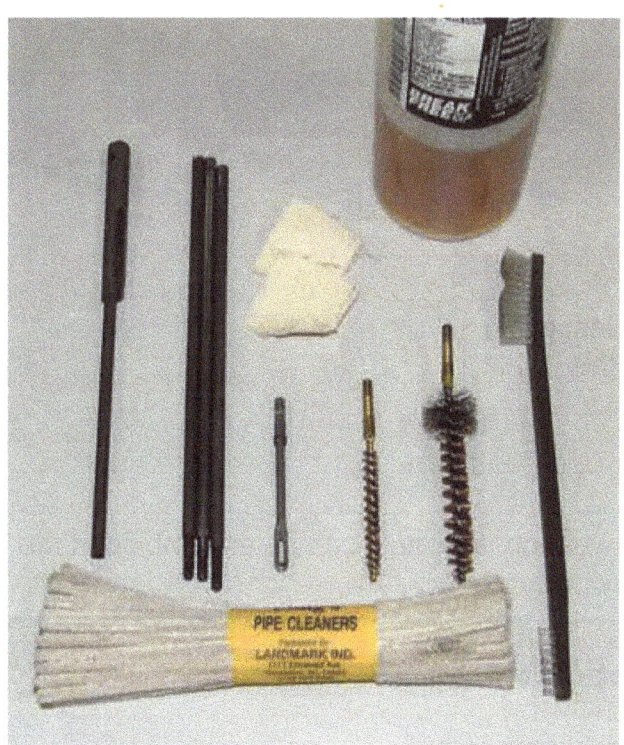

Cleaning the Weapon

1 First clean, inspect, and lubricate the upper receiver and barrel assembly

2 Next clean, inspect, and lubricate the charging handle and bolt carrier group

3 Clean, inspect, and lubricate the lower receiver and extension assembly

4 Finally clean, inspect, and lubricate the magazine

5 Now that the weapon is clean it can be assembled in the reverse order of disassembly

Field Expedient Cleaning
- Clear weapon
- Clean bolt carrier assembly
- Clean barrel

Note: Required daily when in a field environment.

Weapons Decontamination

Ref: AFMAN 10-2602

Operational and Thorough Decontamination
- Operationally decontaminate Chem/Bio contaminated weapons within minutes after exposure (if possible)
- Use M291 or M295 decon kits
- Use water-soaked rags to remove decon powder residue
- To thoroughly decontaminate, disassemble and soak or submerge in 5% chlorine solution for the duration identified by CBRNE Control Center
- Always wear gloves when cleaning or handling previously contaminated weapons
- Decontaminate cleaning tools (cleaning rods and brushes) with a 5% chlorine solution
- Dispose of used weapons cleaning materials as contaminated waste

Operational decon.

Contaminated Weapons Handling in Armories or Closed Spaces
If not thoroughly decontaminated, previously contaminated weapons may become vapor hazards to unmasked people within closed or unventilated areas. When a previously contaminated weapon is not needed for immediate use, double-wrap in a plastic bag and mark the bag. The bag will reduce the residual hazard and prevent exposure to low-level Chem vapors.

Use vapor barriers.

NOTES

#2 pencil works best

Weapons Skills–Pistol/M9

Ref: TO 11W3-3-5-1, Operator's Manual; AFMAN 31-229
USAF Weapons Handling Manual

You must be able to competently handle your assigned weapon. Prior training, along with this information, will keep you ready if you must use your weapon.

Weapon Safety
- Never point your weapon at anyone or anything you're not willing to shoot
- Consider all weapons as loaded
- Clear all weapons each time you handle them
- Keep your finger off the trigger until your sights are on the target
- Don't shoot anything you can't positively identify
- Know what's behind your target

Characteristics
- Weapon will fire both single and double action. Safety feature includes a manual decocking lever and firing pin block, hammer half cock notch
- Maximum effective range is 55 yd (50 m) with a maximum range of 1.1 miles (1800 m)

firing pin block

Nomenclature
- Slide assembly consists of the decocking lever, firing pin, extractor, barrel, firing pin block, locking block, and sights

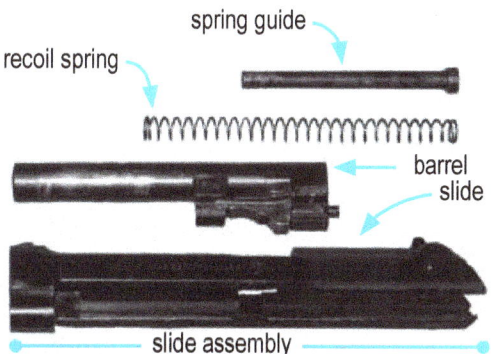

spring guide
recoil spring
barrel
slide
slide assembly

- Receiver assembly consists of disassembly button and lever, slide stop, trigger, magazine catch assembly/release button, grips, hammer, and lanyard loop
- Magazine assembly consists of the floor plate, magazine spring, follower, and magazine tube

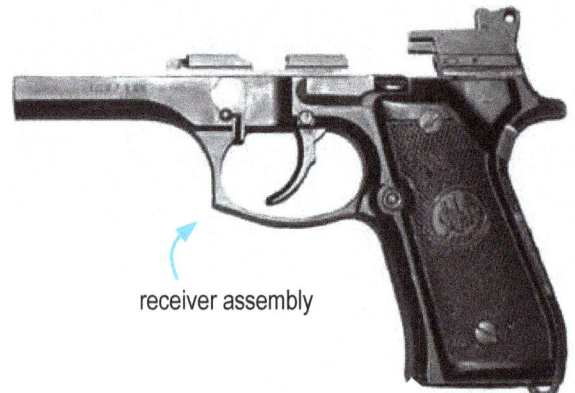
receiver assembly

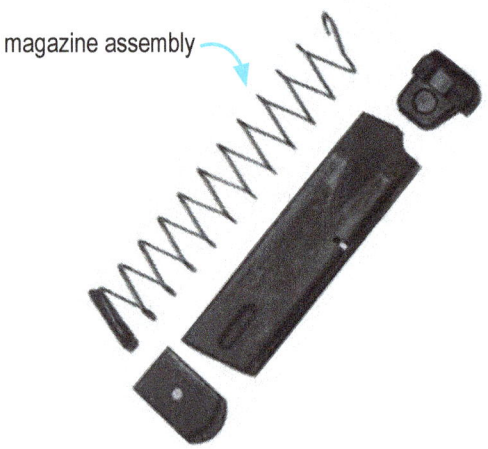
magazine assembly

Types of Ammunition
- M882 Ball– 124-grain jacketed bullet, basic cartridge for field use
- No tracer round is authorized for use in the M9

Care of Ammunition
- Store six inches off ground (pallet)
- Keep closed until ready for use
- Protect from moisture, high temperatures, and direct sun
- Do not disassemble
- Do not lubricate or clean with solvents
- Clean with dry cloth

M882 Ball

Clearing Procedures

1 Holding the pistol in the right hand, move the **decocking lever** DOWN to the SAFE position

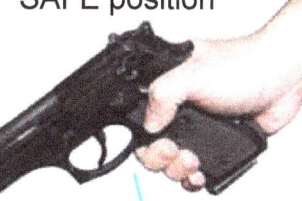

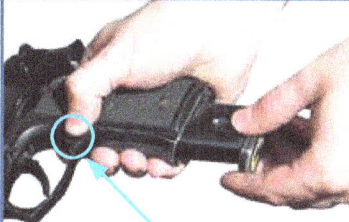

2 Press the **magazine release button** and remove the magazine

3 Grasp the slide with the left hand, cupping the **left hand over the ejection port**

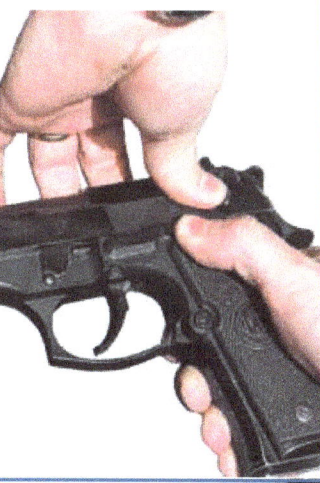

4 Next, rotate the weapon slightly to the right while **pushing the slide to the rear**

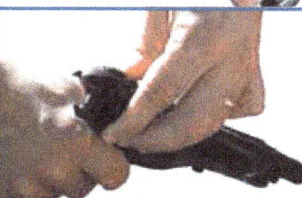

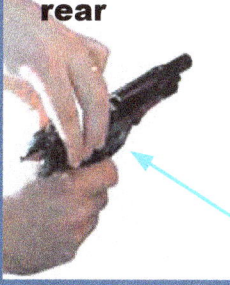

5 Catch the ejected round in the left palm and lock the slide to the rear

6 Visually inspect the chamber and receiver area to ensure there is no ammunition present

Disassembly (Fieldstrip)
- Clear the weapon and then allow the slide to go forward
- Hold pistol in right hand with muzzle slightly elevated
- Press in on the disassembly button and hold
- Rotate the disassembly lever down until it stops
- Pull slide and barrel assembly forward and remove from the receiver– use caution when separating recoil spring and guide as they're under spring tension and can cause injury
- Lift and remove the barrel and locking block assembly from the slide

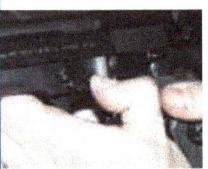   

Magazine Disassembly
- Unload magazine
- Remove floorplate (use barrel locking block plunger)
- Remove magazine spring
- Remove follower

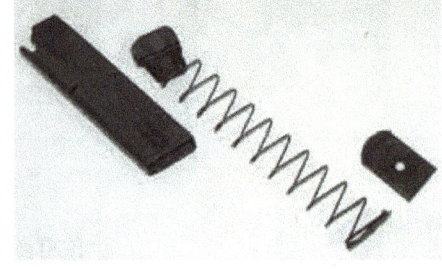

Function Check
- Clear the weapon
- Release the slide and insert an empty magazine
- Retract the slide, once the slide moves all the way to the rear, the magazine follower should hold the slide to the rear
- Remove the magazine
- Ensure the decocking lever is down, release the slide forward (hammer should fall fully forward)
- Press/release the trigger (firing pin block should move up and down and hammer should not move)
- Move decocking lever UP to FIRE position
- Press the trigger (weapon should dry fire double action)

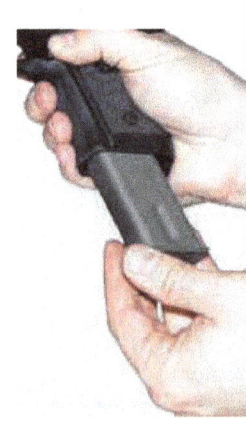

- Press the trigger and hold to rear
- Retract and release slide
- Release the trigger (you should hear a click and hammer should not fall forward)
- Press trigger to check single action (hammer should fall)

Loading Procedures
- Starting with cleared pistol
- Visually inspect pistol to ensure decocking/safety lever is in safe position (down)
- Insert magazine
- Send slide forward by depressing slide stop
- Place weapon on fire

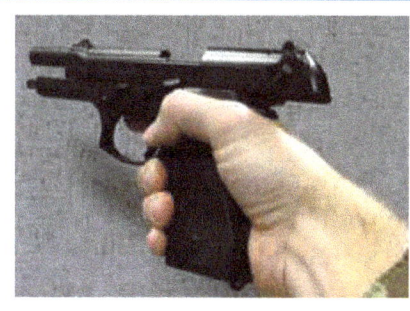
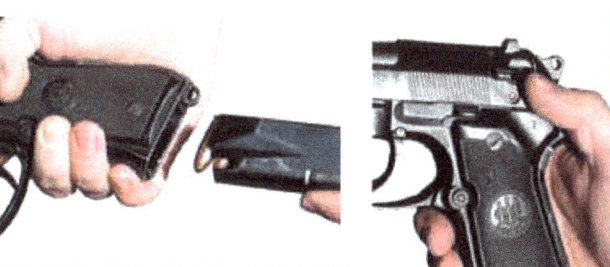

Reloading Procedures
- Remove empty magazine
- Insert new magazine
- Release slide
- Fire

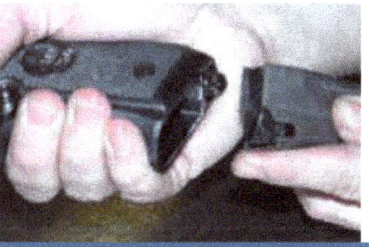

Weapon is on fire during a reload.

Immediate Action Procedures

If the weapon fails to fire:
- Ensure decocking /safety lever is in the fire position (up)
- Smack upward on bottom of magazine to ensure it is fully seated
- Rack the slide to the rear and release
- Fire

If Pistol Still Does Not Fire
- Remove magazine
- Eject chambered round
- Insert new magazine
- Rack slide to rear and release to chamber new round
- Attempt to fire
- If pistol still does not fire, clear pistol and perform detailed inspection to determine cause of stoppage

  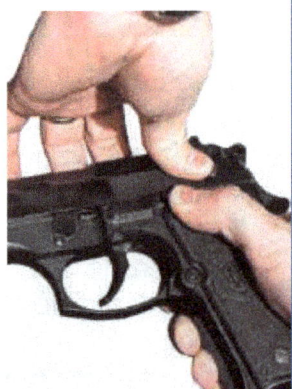

Fundamentals of Pistol Shooting

- Establish firm handshake grip (ensure no part of hand is above tang of weapon)
- Push shooting hand towards target, non-shooting hand pulls back towards shooter
- Raise sights to eye level and align
- Place aligned sights on target
- FOCUS on FRONT SIGHT
- Place first pad of finger on trigger
- Hold breath
- With steady, increasing pressure, press trigger to rear
- After weapon recoils realign sights and apply fundamentals for subsequent shots
- Remember to be consistent with sight alignment, sight picture, and breath control. Be as motionless as possible while pressing trigger to rear

tang of weapon

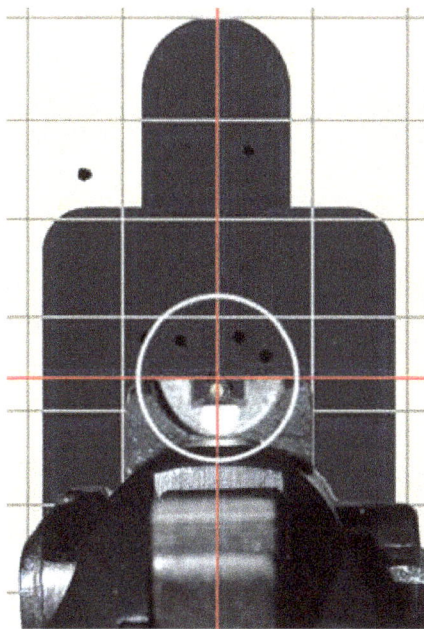
Good sight picture.

M9 Cleaning Procedures
(Also see p. 111)

1. First clean, inspect, and lubricate the upper receiver and barrel assembly
2. Next clean, inspect, and lightly lubricate the slide assembly
3. Finally clean, inspect, and lightly lubricate the magazine
4. Now that the weapon is clean it can be assembled in the reverse order of disassembly

Field Expedient Cleaning
- Clear weapon
- Clean receiver
- Clean slide

Note: Required daily when in a field environment.

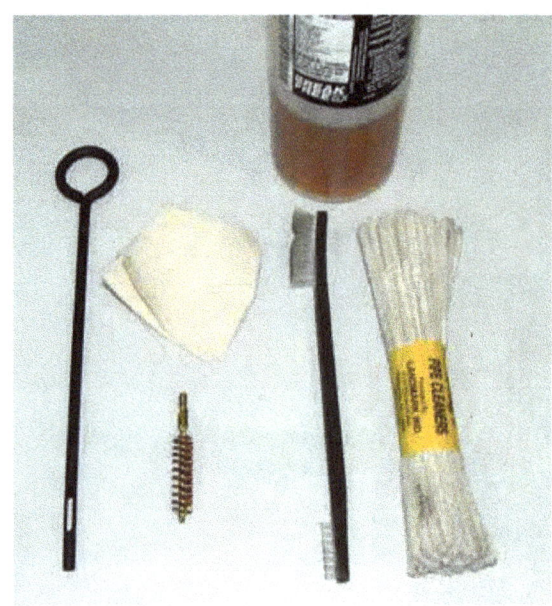

Section 5
Survive

Alarm Black–Attack Is Over, Initiate Base Recovery

Ref: AFMAN 10-2602; AFVA 10-2511
- Audible steady tone siren
- Visual Black Flags
- Assume MOPP 4 or as directed by the commander
- CBRNE hazards (facility damage, UXO, CBRN contamination) are likely to be present but may not yet be marked or reported
- Perform self-aid and buddy care (SABC), and perform immediate decontamination (if contaminated)
- Base specialized and unit Post-Attack Reconnaissance (PAR) teams begin surveys when directed by the commander
- Commanders will release mission critical personnel in phases

Perform SABC.

Post-Attack Reconnaissance

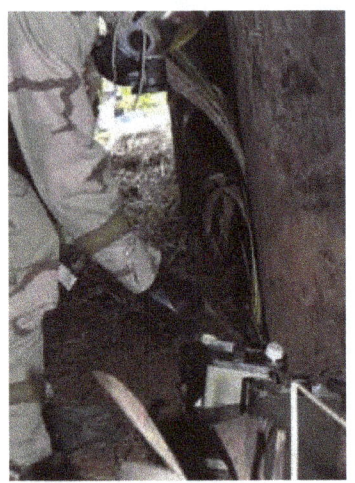
Check for contamination.

Ref AFMAN 10-2602
- Remain in a shelter or under cover unless otherwise directed–mission essential personnel outside only. Keep exposure to a minimum and remember contamination avoidance
- When contamination is present and movement is required, don't move between sectors or zones without prior approval–follow appropriate contamination control procedures
- Check the prepositioned M8 Paper throughout the immediate area for signs of contamination
- Check all detectors in your area–listen for audible alarms
- Check for UXOs
- Report positive and negative findings to your UCC
- Negative detector readings don't necessarily equate to hazard-free assets; liquids may have absorbed but low level vapors may still be present

- Replace prepositioned contaminated M8 Paper with new paper–mark date and time on tape affixing paper to object
- Treat contaminated M8 Paper as contaminated waste
- Avoid contact with objects and areas that may be contaminated
- Use M291/M295 kits to operationally decontaminate areas you must touch to perform your mission (within the first hour of contamination if possible)
- If double or triple layer sheets of barrier material covered contaminated assets, carefully remove the outer layer, and replace it as time permits
- Treat contaminated barrier material as contaminated waste
- If contamination is found in the area, identify assets as contaminated
- Mark contaminated assets according to Air Force installation procedures
- Place NBC marking kit signs or their approved equivalents on all sides of contaminated assets
- Mark and update signs at Chem/Bio zone transition points once established
- At night, use portable lights or chemical light sticks to call attention to markings, however, use only white light to read M8 and M9 Paper

SEE Page 218, Quick Reference, **Grid Maps**

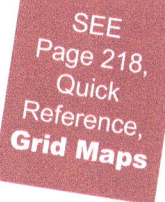
Mark contaminated buildings.

Post-Attack Damage and Casualty Checklist Items

1. Call your UCC or EOC representative and report:
   a. Name/rank
   b. Unit
   c. Phone/radio net
   d. Date/time/type of contamination
2. Report the location of the incident:
   a. Facility/**grid coordinates**/other relevant information
   b. Report any known damage:
   c. Condition of area/facility/equipment/vehicles/assets
3. Report the number of casualties:
   a. Dead = D
   b. Injured = I
   c. Missing = M
4. Report casualty disposition:
   a. Evacuated to Casualty Collection Point
   b. Applied first aid
   c. Awaiting transport

Unexploded Ordnance (UXO)

Ref: Counter IED Field Manual FM 3-90.119/MCIP 3-17.01 5-5

If a suspected IED is found, the following basic confirm, clear, cordon, check, and control (5-Cs). to ensure that the situation is dealt with quickly and safely.

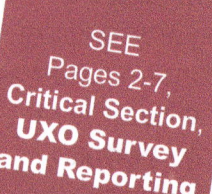

CONFIRM
- The presence of a UXO from a safe distance
- Behind cover use spotting equipment (binoculars and scopes)
- Indentify the features: size, shape, color and condition
- Report the UXO to your UCC (if using a radio transmit from a safe distance of 25 ft or 100 ft for vehicles

SEE Pages 2-7, Critical Section, UXO Survey and Reporting

Mark UXO.

CLEAR
- Clear personnel to a safe position and distance (see page 127 for distances)
- If evacuation is impossible, isolate or barricade the area to restrict access
- Leave the area the same way you came in

CORDON
- Cordon off area (see page 127 for evacuation distances)
- Prevent unauthorized personnel from entering the site
- Use standard UXO or mine markers or other available materials to mark the UXO
- Ensure markers are visible in all directions and at night

CHECK
- Check your immediate area for other UXOs

CONTROL
- Control the area
- Only emergency services (medical, firefighting, or EOD) should be allowed to enter the cordon

Warn others.

- Divert all traffic
- Direct EOD responders to UXOs

Follow UXO checklist.

WARNING:
Modern ordnance is complex and sensitive and can incorporate anti-disturbance or anti-removal devices. Clearing any UXO without proper training, tools, and information could be LETHAL. DO NOT attempt to move or disturb these items.

Protective Measures–three methods are used to protect people and equipment: evacuate, isolate, and barricade

Evacuation–upon identification of a UXO:
- Retire to a safe distance and enforce evacuation measures when evacuation is possible
- Evacuate and use available cover to an initial distance of:
    - 300 feet for munitions smaller than 5 inches in diameter
    - 500 feet for munitions 5 to 10 inches in diameter
    - 1,000 feet for munitions 10 to 20 inches in diameter
    - 1,500 feet for munitions greater than 20 inches
- Do not remain in the immediate danger area any longer than necessary
- Seek EOC guidance via your UCC to determine the appropriate evacuation distances for UXO present

Stay out of craters.

SEE Pages 2-7, Critical Section, UXO Survey and Reporting

Isolate—sometimes, for mission-related, operational, or other reasons, evacuation of people or equipment isn't possible or it's impossible to leave a particular area. In these situations, isolate the assets (people, equipment, and operations) from UXO by establishing a safe area and limiting exposure. Contact EOD if you must work in an area you suspect UXO or landmines may be present.

Barricade—limits blast and fragmentation from an explosion
- Suppressive barricades are constructed around a UXO to suppress an explosion, shock wave, and fragments
- Protective barricades are constructed around exposed resources to shelter from overpressure and fragments
- Use natural protective barriers whenever possible
- If natural barricades are inadequate, construct artificial barriers
- While building barricades, DO NOT disturb the UXO and wear all appropriate protective equipment (to include Kevlar helmets and personal body armor)

Small.

Small UXO—generally **less than 3 inches in diameter**, carefully construct a double-wall thickness of sandbags within 3 to 4 ft around the UXO. Stack the sandbags to at least 3 ft high and thick enough (minimum two sandbags deep) to protect personnel and equipment from the blast and fragmentation.

Medium UXO—generally from **3 inches to 10 inches in diameter**, a wall thickness of four or five sandbags within 5 to 7 ft should surround the UXO. Stack the sandbags to a height of at least 5 ft to protect assets.

Medium.

Large UXO—over 10 inches in diameter are generally too large to build effective barricades around them. In these cases, barricade the equipment and personnel activity areas.

Large.

Reporting Unexploded Ordnance

UXO Spot Report—clearly identifies the location of the UXO, briefly describes the item, and provides the opportunity to include other significant information.

- The first-echelon report that is sent when an observer detects UXO
- Forward the UXO Spot Report to the Unit Control Center or chain of command
- Once the information is recorded, the report is sent or called in to the EOC EOD representative by the fastest means available

Warning–do not transmit or key radios within 8 meters (25 feet) of a UXO when using a handheld radio or within 30 meters (100 feet) of a UXO when using a vehicle radio. It may cause a detonation.

Don't transmit within 25 ft.

Unexploded Ordnance Checklist Items

1. Call your UCC or EOC to report
   a. Unit
   b. Date/time
2. Report the location and cordon size of the UXO
   a. Bldg number, grid coordinate, distance from landmark or building, etc.
   b. Explain how the UXO is marked and the distance between the UXO and the marker
3. Report the "Class" or shape (i.e., "Bravo 1" UXO)
   a. See Critical section, page 3, for UXO identification
4. Report any identifying features
   a. For example, the color, size, length, and markings
5. Report the condition of the UXO
   a. Is it leaking?
   b. Is it intact?
   c. Is it broken?
6. Report any other significant information

NOTES

#2 pencil works best

Contamination Control

Ref: AFMAN 32-4005

In a chemical and/or biological environment, contamination control is essential to sustained operations. You must remove contaminated IPE within 24 hours by processing through a Contamination Control Area (CCA).

Contamination control area.

Collective Protection

CBRN collective protection enhances survival. Collective protection systems provide overpressure, filtration, controlled entry/exit, and a contamination-free environment for relief from continuous wear of IPE. Collective protection supports two mission sustainment areas that quickly erode in an CBRN environment; personnel rest and relief (breaks and sleeping), and work relief (command and control, medical treatment, MOPP recovery time after maximum work effort). Transportable and expedient collective protection measures are also used to augment existing capabilities. Your unit Shelter Management Teams are trained to operate and maintain collective protection systems (where assigned).

Temporary structure with collective protection.

Contamination Control Area (CCA)

A form of thorough decontamination incorporates these features:

- Transportation drop off point
- Entrance and holding area
- Contact hazard area (CHA)
- Vapor hazard area (VHA)
- Mask decon and refurbishment area
- Toxic free area (TFA) where you can operate without chemical protective equipment

A CCA is a form of thorough decon.

Trained CCA assistants will usually help you process safely through the CCA. You can expedite your CCA processing experience by closely listening to the CCA assistants and doing exactly what they tell you to do, and by reading and understanding each processing step before you perform that task.

SEE Pages 198 and 199 Quick Reference, **CCA Layouts**

Follow CCA procedures.

Use the buddy system.

Watch out for problems that might arise in the CCA processing area during high wind conditions.

M8 Chemical Agent Detection Paper
Ref: TO 11H2-14-5-1

Detection

- Detects G and V nerve agents and H and L blister agents
- Provides a manual liquid detection capability
- Supplied in booklets of 25 perforated pages of paper containing chemical agent sensitive dyes
- Inspect prior to use. Discard M8 Paper that shows signs of wetness, wrinkling, dirt, damage, or discoloration
- If M8 Paper is not pre-positioned, blot (do not rub or scrub) over nonporous surface like glass or bare metal surfaces suspected to be contaminated
- Mark date and time of placement on tape used to secure paper

Operational Limitations

- Use only white light to read
- M8 Paper will function in snow, rain, and sleet, but not if saturated with water
- If M8 Paper is saturated with water, it should be replaced
- M8 Paper reaction is immediate at temperatures above 32°F and slow to several minutes below 32°F
- Dye will rapidly deteriorate at temperatures above 125°F
- Some items such as wasp spray and cleaning supplies may produce false positives
- M8 Paper shelf life is 10 years

Positive M8 Paper Results

When liquid nerve or blister agents contact M8 Paper, a color change takes place. **Report color changes to your UCC.**

Color	Agent
Gold or Yellow	G-series nerve
Pink or Red	H- or L- series blister
Blue or Dark Green	V-series nerve
Red-brown*	GF nerve agent

*This positive indication is not presented on the color comparison chart inside the cover of the M8 packet.

The average size of a VX-Nerve liquid droplet that reaches the ground is expected to be 200-250 microns in size—at the beginning detectable threshold for the average eye to see, under optimum light levels. Now, imagine reading M8 Paper results through your protective mask, during darkness, with a flashlight, and under a high OPSTEMPO! Knowing what to look for will help you prepare for this difficult challenge.

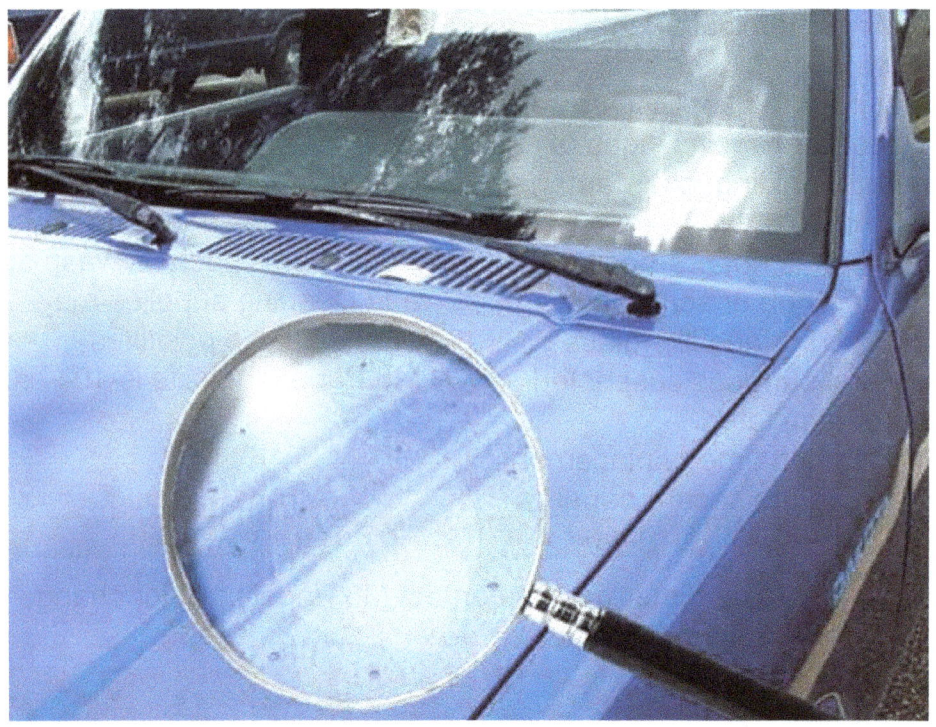

200-250 micron drops will be difficult to see with the naked eye.

M8 Paper showing VX nerve contamination at approximately 250 microns, with three examples of various deposition patterns.

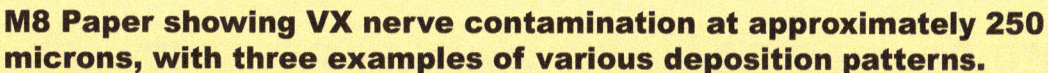

Deposition pattern #1.

Deposition pattern #2.

Can you see these green spots?

Deposition pattern #3.

Now, can you see these?

NOTE: The M8 detector paper may cause Dermatitis when exposed to bare skin. If susceptible to skin Dermatitis, individuals should wear protective gloves or limit contact to bare skin.

M9 Chemical Agent Detection Paper (Tape)

Ref: TO 11H2-2-21

Intended Use

M9 Paper is worn on clothing or attached to vehicles or equipment. Preferred operating range is 32°F to 125°F, with relative humidity up to 100%.

Sensitive Dyes

M9 Paper contains sensitive dyes that change color in the presence of liquid G- and V- series nerve agents and H and L blister agents.

Color Changes

Color changes identify agent presence, (**Not Agent Type**.) Liquid agent positive indicators include: pink, any shade of red, red-brown, and red-purple. Blue, yellow, green, gray, or black spots on M9 paper (Tape) are not from a liquid chemical agent.

Warning– Always wear protective gloves when touching the detector paper. Do not place the detector paper in or near your mouth or skin.

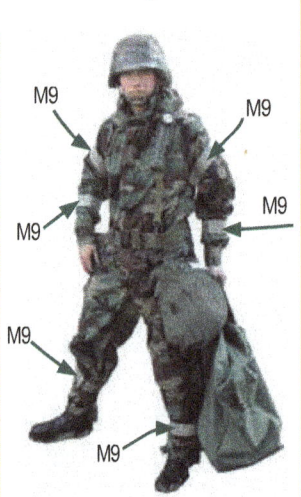

Inspection

Inspection is a user responsibility. Inspect shipping bag and dispenser. If shipping bag is torn or open, discard roll. Check dispenser for shelf life date stamp and discard if shelf life has expired. If dispenser is crushed, wet, or cutting edge is missing, discard. Check paper for discoloration, tears, creases, or dirt. If paper comes apart from backing, discard.

Operational Life

One year in temperate, tropic, and desert regions. Two years, in frigid zones after removal from the shipping bag. After M9 dispenser is removed from shipping bag, immediately write or stamp current date on the dispenser. Determined useful life by adding one or two years to the current date based upon region. The useful life can **never** extend beyond the discard date printed on the dispenser.

Operational Limitations

- Temperatures above 125°F cause false responses
- Brake fluid, hydraulic fluid, gasoline, aircraft, and automotive grease, and insect repellents cause false responses
- M9 Paper does not provide rapid results at temperatures below 32°F, but will function

Nuclear Attack/Radioactive Individual Protective Actions

Ref: AFMAN 10-2602

Initial Actions

- Store or remove flammable materials from the populated shelter areas and work centers
- If advanced warning of a detonation is received, find shelter that provides the greatest protection
- Use window barriers and shielding to improve protection for buildings or shelters
- Upon seeing the nuclear flash, seek protection from the blast wave, heat, and flying debris
- If a detonation occurs without warning, immediately drop to the ground in a prone position. Tightly cover your face with both hands. Do not move until the initial blast wave and any reflected blast waves have passed

Follow-on Actions

- Remain within protected areas or shelters until directed otherwise
- Perform damage assessment, self-aid and buddy care, and reporting actions
- Decon yourself by brushing dust/fallout off of your clothing or by blotting away with adhesive tape—Rinse exposed skin
- Limit radiation exposure by minimizing time spent outside in contact with fallout, and maximizing time in shelter and distance from radiation

Nuclear and Biological Protection

Ref: AFTTP(I) 3-2.46; AFMAN 10-2602

Nuclear Concerns
The primary products of a nuclear detonation are:
- Blast and shock
- Thermal radiation (heat)
- Nuclear radiation
- Ballistic debris for surface and shallow sub-surface bursts

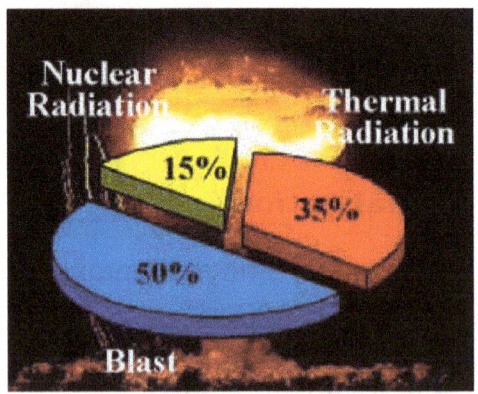

Nuclear blast energy distribution.

Electromagnetic Pulse (EMP)
May cause widespread communications and/or electrical problems after a nuclear detonation.

Types of Nuclear Radiation
Can affect you initially at the time of the burst, or delayed as fallout.
- Alpha–harmful if internalized
- Beta–may cause skin burns; harmful if ingested
- Gamma–destroys living cells; harmful when exposed
- Neutron–emitted only during detonation, but 20 times more harmful than Gamma

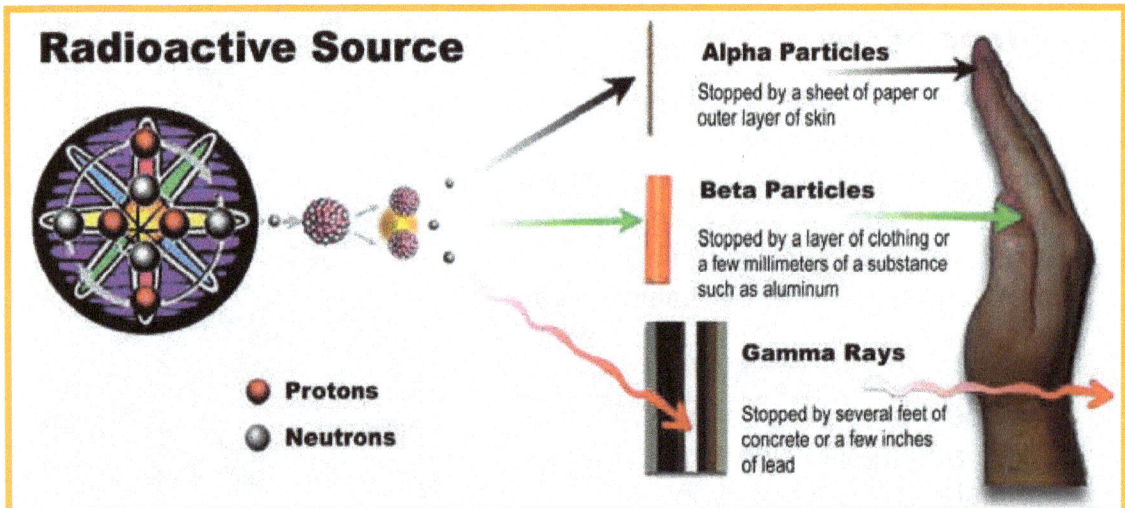

Radiation hazards.

Radiological Dispersal Device (RDD)–is any device that causes the purposeful dissemination of radioactive material across an area without a nuclear detonation. An RDD could function as a terror weapon or terrain-denial mechanism. One type of RDD could function by using conventional explosives to blow-up and scatter radioactive source debris across a relatively small area-also known as a dirty bomb.

Radiation Sickness
- Caused by radiation destroying cells within the body at a rate the body cannot overcome
- Radiation sickness is not contagious
- Early symptoms are nausea, vomiting, loss of appetite, and illness
- Subsequent symptoms, severe body fluid loss, internal hemorrhaging, and diarrhea

Individual Decontamination
- Radioactive material can't be neutralized–it must be removed from affected surfaces
- Brush dust from uniform and footwear
- Thoroughly wash dust from skin and body
- Avoid breathing dust by covering nose/mouth with dust mask, handkerchief, or equivalent
- Limit time spent in fallout environment

Biological Agent Individual Protective Actions

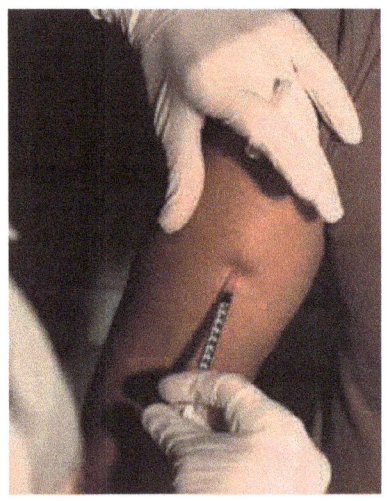

Immunizations and Preventative Medications

Keep your immunizations current.

Physical Health

Poor physical health reduces your body's ability to resist and fight infections. Regular exercise and balanced meals build and maintain your body's natural resistance to diseases.

Personal Hygiene

Frequently washing with soap and water prevents and eliminates most areas where biological agents multiply. Protecting skin cuts and abrasions also denies biological agents additional pathways of entry into your body.

Food and Water Sanitation

Wash all fruits and vegetables before eating and ensure that all foods are thoroughly cooked. Additionally, drink only from approved water sources, and only use ice that's approved for consumption.

Self-Monitoring

Individuals noting and reporting the onset of unusual symptoms and providing precise information as to the time symptoms began. This is key to detection and enhances medical surveillance and assists medical personnel in administering appropriate treatment. Supervisors should assist in identification of potentially affected individuals.

Biological Warfare and Biological Terrorism

Ref: AFI 10-2604

Biological agents include viruses, bacteria, fungi, and toxins cultured from living organisms that are developed to produce death or disease in humans, animals, or plants. Biological agents may be found as liquid droplets, aerosols, or dry powders and can be adapted for use as a terrorist weapon.

Advantages of Biological Agents as Weapons:
- Easy to obtain, inexpensive to produce
- Potential for high number of casualties from a small amount of agent
- Can overwhelm medical services and resources
- Threat of use may be enough to create widespread panic

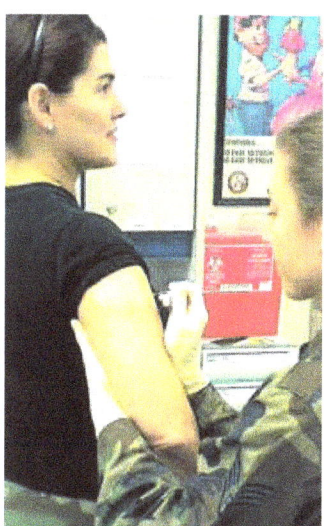

Keep immunizations up-to-date.

Routes of Infection:
- Skin
  - Cuts
  - Abrasions
  - Mucous membranes (eye, nose, mouth)
- Gastrointestinal
  - Food–Potentially significant route of delivery
  - Water–Capacity to affect large numbers of people
- Respiratory
  - Inhalation of spores, droplets, and aerosols
  - Aerosols are an effective delivery method

What can be done?
- Awareness
- Individual and collective protection
- Detection and characterization
- Vaccination, prophylaxis, and medical treatment
- Safe practices

Immunizations and Treatment—keeping immunizations current is paramount. In some cases, you may be issued a pretreatment based upon the deployed region and the specific threat. If you're given a prevention or treatment, like certain powerful antibiotics for inhaled anthrax, you MUST NOT deviate from taking your prescribed dose at the required interval until directed otherwise.

Disease	Incubation	Symptoms	Transmission	Protection
Inhaled Anthrax	2-6 days Range: 2 days-8 weeks	Flu-like symptoms Respiratory distress (Anthrax infection of skin sequence: Initial itching bump on skin, 1-3 cm painless ulcer, dead skin tissue center; fever)	Aerosol inhalation No person-to-person transmission	3 of the 6 anthrax shots could protect; powerful antibiotics after infected
Botulism	12-72 hours Range: 2 hrs-8 days	Difficulty swallowing or speaking Weakness Respiratory dysfunction No sensory dysfunction No fever	Aerosol inhalation Food or water ingestion No person-to-person transmission	Personal hygiene to protect; Antitoxins after infected
Plague (pneumonic and bubonic)	1-3 days by inhalation	Sudden onset of fever, chills, headache Pneumonic: cough, chest pain Bubonic: painful lymph nodes	Inhalation of the organism Person-to-person transmission in pneumonic forms	Hygiene and gloves, mask; Antibiotics after exposed
Tularemia "pneumonic"	2-5 days Range: 1-21 days	Fever, cough, chest tightness, painful and difficult respiration	Inhalation of agents No person-to-person transmission but laboratory personnel at risk	Respiratory protection; Antibiotics longer than 7 days after infected
Smallpox	12-14 days Range: 7-17 days	High fever and muscle pain; itching; abdominal pain; delirium Rash on face, extremities, hands, feet; confused with chickenpox which has less uniform rash	Person-to-person transmission	Hand wash, immunization to protect Respiratory protection– Treat symptoms after infected Airborne precautions– Negative pressure Clothing and surface decontamination

Operational Differences Between Chemical Warfare and Biological Warfare Agents

Ref: AFMAN 10-2602

Chemical and biological agents can be employed with equally deadly effects. However, there are some distinct differences in their employment and detection. One difference is the quantity of agent needed to generate a widespread effect and the methods needed to carry-out their effective use. It takes considerable effort to deliver a chemical weapon that holds a militarily significant amount of agent needed to produce widespread coverage. Bacteria, viruses, and biological toxins, on the other hand, can be delivered with relative ease when compared to chemical agent delivery. This table shows some of the differences:

	Chemical Warfare Agent	vs.	Biological Warfare Agent
Release Site of Weapon	Quickly discovered, possible to cordon off contaminated/attack areas		Difficult to identify, probably not possible or useful to cordon off area of attack
Manifestation of Symptoms	Rapid, usually minutes to hours after an attack		Delayed, usually days to weeks after an attack (except toxins)
Distribution of Affected Patients	Downwind area near point of release		Widely and rapidly spread, difficult to track or predict
Signatures	Easily observed (colored residue, dead foliage, pungent odor, dead insect and animal life)		Typically no characteristic signatures immediately after attack
Medical Countermeasures	Chemical antidotes		Limited vaccines, antibodies, and/or antitoxins and antivirals for some agents
Casualty Management and Contamination	After decontamination and/or weathering, no further need for protective measures or risk of further contamination		Patient isolation/quarantine crucial if communicable disease is involved

During increased threats and in high threat areas, trained teams continuously monitor bases with specialized detectors that can warn you of the presence of chemical and biological warfare agents. Listen closely for public address announcements and radio updates, and listen for alarms from detectors that are spread throughout the base to provide you with an early warning of attack.

Chemical Agent Individual Protective Actions

Nerve Agents

Characteristics
- Some may have a fruity smell or camphor odor, others may be odorless
- Most lethal of all agents
- Symptoms can be immediate; lethal within minutes.
- Affects nervous system
- May be inhaled, ingested, or absorbed through the skin
- In vapor, solid, or liquid form
- Antidotes may be effective even if given to a victim having advanced symptoms, as long as the victim continues to breathe

Symptoms
- Pinpointing of pupils and muscular twitching
- Dimness of vision and runny nose
- Tightness of chest and difficulty in breathing
- Excessive sweating, drooling, nausea and vomiting, and involuntary urination and defecation
- Convulsions, coma, death
- Intermittent cumulative exposures to very low amounts can lead to the same ultimate effect as a single exposure to a higher amount

Protection
- Take Pyridostigmine Bromide tablets (P-Tabs) as directed **NOTE: These are effective against Soman (GD) only**
- Wear IPE (MOPP 4), or as directed
- Practice contamination avoidance and expedient decontamination
- Use nerve agent auto-injectors when experiencing symptoms
- Flush eyes and open wounds with water and protect from further contamination
- Use decon kits to absorb agents on skin
- Seek medical attention as soon as possible after any exposure or as soon as symptoms appear

Nerve Agent Antidote Injectors

Ref: AFH 36-2218, Vol 2
**Use Auto-Injectors for Nerve Agents ONLY!
Wear protective mask.**

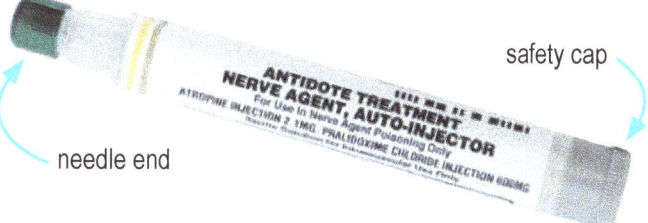
ATNAA Antidote Injector.

Prior to deployment, you will be issued three Antidote Treatment, Nerve Agent, Autoinjector (ATNAAs) and one Convulsant Antidote for Nerve Agent (CANA). The ATNAA is a single autoinjector that contains both atropine and 2-PAM chloride nerve agent antidotes.
Self-Aid: If you receive notification of a chemical attack and experience any or all of the nerve agent mild symptoms, you must immediately put on your protective mask and self-administer one ATNAA.

- Remove one ATNAA and remove safety cap
- Position injector against injection site and administer one ATNAA by applying firm, even pressure until needle is triggered
- Hold injector firmly in place for 10 seconds
- Carefully remove injector and bend needle; attach the used injector to the front or sleeve pocket of your outermost upperbody piece of IPE

WARNING: If within 5-10 minutes after administration of the first ATNAA, your heart beats very quickly and your mouth becomes very dry, do not inject a second ATNAA.

- If mild symptoms persist after 10 to 15 minutes, administer a second ATNAA
- Seek medical help

Remove cap

Inject antidote

Pin to IPE

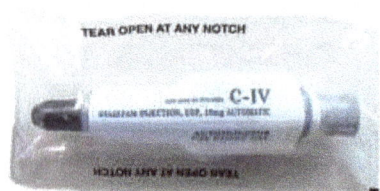

Diazepam injector.

With Severe Symptoms
Buddy Care: Before initiating Buddy Care, determine if any ATNAAs have already been used so that no more than three kits of the antidote are administered. Buddy Care also includes administering the CANA with the third ATNAA to prevent convulsions.

Use buddy care.

Administer all three ATNAAs followed by the CANA injector to prevent convulsions. Do not wait between administering ATNAA kits. In cold weather, store kits in an inside clothing pocket to protect the antidote from freezing.

Warning: Do NOT use more than three ATNAAs. The white injector, CANA, is to be used when there is a presence of severe nerve agent poisoning symptoms and all three ATNAAs have been administered. Never use your injectors on somebody else!

Mark 1 kit
Some Air Force personnel may deploy with the Army and be issued Mark 1 kits rather than ATNAA once they are in theater. The Mark 1 kit contains individual autoinjectors for the atropine and 2-PAM chloride nerve agent antidotes. When using the Mark 1 kit, follow all of the ATNAA steps above, but inject one atropine autoinjector followed by one 2-PAM chloride autoinjector (large injector) instead of the single ATNAA.

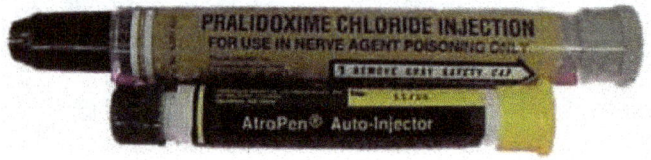
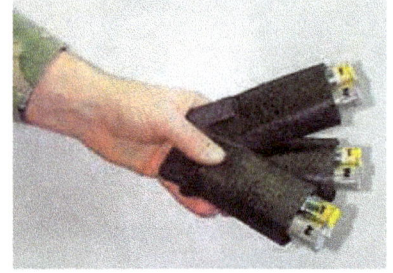

Mark 1 kits.

Chemical Agent Individual Protective Actions

Blister Agents

Characteristics
- Designed more to incapacitate
- Some also known as mustard agents
- May smell like garlic or have a fishy/musty odor
- Employed in liquids, or solids
- Destroys tissues, injures blood vessels, causes blisters
- Some violently irritate mucous membranes in eyes and nose
- Affects eyes, respiratory tract, and skin
- May be lethal if inhaled, ingested, or through skin absorption
- Incapacitation may last for days or weeks

Symptoms
- Symptoms may be immediate or take up to four hours to appear
- May cause stinging sensation upon contact
- Blisters any tissue it contacts
- Red, watering eyes
- Blurred vision
- Light sensitivity
- Blindness
- Sweaty groin and armpits are more susceptible to blister agents

Protection
- Wear IPE (MOPP 4), or as directed
- Avoid contaminated surfaces if possible
- Practice contamination avoidance and operations decon
- Decon skin with M291/M295 decon kits
- Seek medical attention as soon as possible after any exposure or as soon as symptoms appear

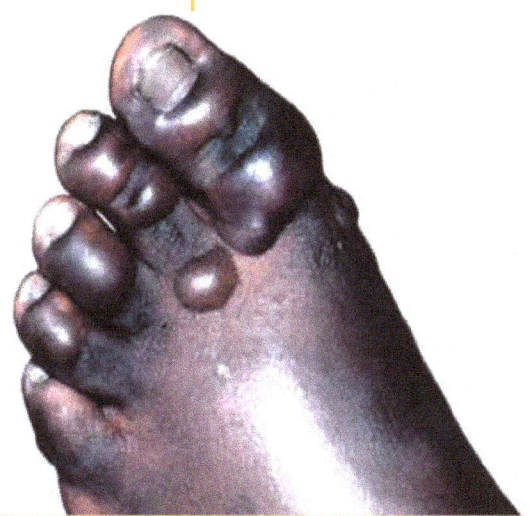

Toxic Industrial Material (TIM)

TIM hazards consist of Toxic Industrial Chemicals (TIC), Toxic Industrial Biologicals (TIB), and Toxic Industrial Radiologicals (TIR). TIM's may be manufactured, stored, distributed, or transported in close proximity to airbases. Most present a vapor (inhalation) hazard. They may also reduce the oxygen concentration below that required to support life.

Category	Type of Material	Primary Uses
Agriculture	Insecticides, Herbicides, Fertilizers	Agriculture, Vector Control
Industrial	Chemical and Radiological Materials	Manufacturing Processes, Cleaning, Water Treatment
Production and Research	Chemicals and Biological Materials	Laboratories, Storage Facilities
Radiological	Nuclear Fuel, Medical Sources	Nuclear Power Plants, Medical Facilities, Industrial Plants, Laboratories

Protection

The most important action is immediate evacuation outside the hazard's path (if feasible.) **The protective mask, ensemble, and military standard collective protection filters are not designed to provide protection from TIMs.** If evacuation is impractical, implement shelter-in-place procedures.

Shelter-In-Place

Ref: AFTTP(I) 3-2.46

Seek cover.

Shelter-in-place isn't the answer to every situation. However, it may be the only short-term practical solution to protect large populations in dormitories, workcenters, and office complexes following certain hazardous material (HAZMAT) incidents. Shelter-in-place is most effective when occupants pre-plan and practice contingency actions. Here are some shelter-in-place tips:

Outdoor Hazard While You're Outside a Building—an outdoor hazard release may result from an accident during storage, transport, fire, or the result of a malicious act.
- Take cover
- Notify others
- Don available protective equipment
- Report the event
- Perform self-aid and buddy care as needed
- Seek nearest building or safest area
- Shelter-in-place until otherwise directed
- Follow shelter or facility manager instructions

Notify others, take cover.

Outdoor Hazard While You're Inside a Building—to a very limited degree, buildings act as natural filters. In some cases, shelter-in-place can offer limited short-term protection against airborne hazards that originate outdoors. Purging a building after an airborne hazard has passed can eliminate hazards that have infiltrated the interior.
- Turn off HVAC and exhaust fan(s), fans, and combustion heaters
- Secure classified material

Turn off HVAC.

150 / Section 5 / Survive

Stay indoors.

- Move to a central safe room or area
- If directed, evacuate upwind or crosswind
- Notify unit control center
- Upon return, purge and ventilate buildings when directed:
  - Open operable windows and doors
  - Turn on smoke and exhaust fans
  - Turn on HVAC air handlers and fans

Outdoor Hazard While You're Inside an Expeditionary or Temporary Structure—may include tents, temporary buildings, trailers, or portable hard-wall shelters used by military forces in CONUS or OCONUS deployments. If the analysis of hazardous materials threat indicates an accidental or deliberate release could occur without warning:

Temporary structure.

- Operate HVAC systems, including window units, in the **closed or recirculation mode** at all times
- If a release warning is provided, follow the previous guidelines
- Aircrew (before or after taxiing) actions include closing hatches and windows and using oxygen masks (if available)
- Passengers might evacuate aircraft as required by the situation

Inside hazard while you're inside the building—an inside release could result from an industrial chemical spill or biological or radiological material release from supplies, equipment, or mail (as in the case where a contaminated letter affected a US post office.) Buildings generally inhibit the exchange of inside and outdoor air. An affected building could remain unusable without a significant rehabilitation effort. Many hazards produced by an inside release can be much more severe than a similar release outdoors.

- Turn off HVAC, exhaust fan(s), fans, and combustion heaters
- Report the incident to the Fire Department or Security Forces
- Close and seal doors and windows to contain the hazard
- Secure classified material
- Evacuate upwind or crosswind
- Notify unit control center

Turn off HVAC.

MCU-2 Series Protective Mask

Ref: TO 14P4-15-1

With a serviceable C2A1 filter canister installed, the MCU-2 Series is the first line of defense for your face, eyes, and respiratory tract from chemical and biological warfare agents, radioactive dust particles, and riot control agents (such as tear gas.)

Operational Considerations
- Do not over tighten the mask. Over tightening may actually cause leaks
- Check the mask for leaks every time you don it by performing a "leak" check
- Don the mask quickly–it should be donned and sealed before you take another breath
- The mask is a filter respirator–it doesn't supply or produce oxygen
- The mask is ineffective in environments with insufficient oxygen to support life
- The mask is ineffective in industrial chemical environments such as ammonia or chlorine spills, or within carbon monoxide atmospheres
- Don't loosen the head harness straps for comfort if you wear a hood over the outlet valve. If loosened, you could become unprotected against toxic agents or suffocate by carbon dioxide
- Don't remove your mask outdoors if you become overheated in cold weather until your head cools and any sweat has dried–frostbite may result
- Use buddy checks when possible

Second skin installed.

Properly store mask inside carrier.

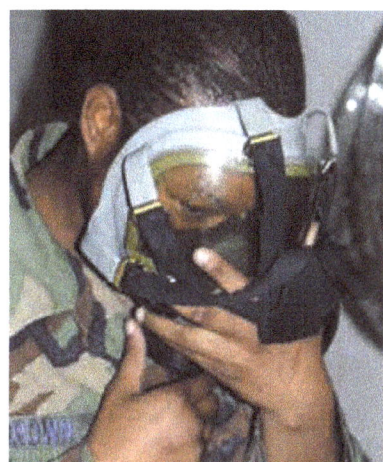

Place chin in chin cup.

Pull head harness over head.

MCU-2 Series–With the filter canister installed, head harness straps loose and inverted over the front of the mask, and the outsert removed, fit test the mask. Note: An unshaven face could prohibit a mask seal.

Warning: Women will remove hair clips, pins, etc., and let their hair hang freely before donning mask.

- Hold the outlet valve assembly in palm of one hand. Push hair back away from hairline. Place mask on face forcing chin cup very tightly against chin
- Keeping the hair out of the way, pull the head harness over the head using the quick don tab—the facepiece should come well up on the forehead but shouldn't extend over the hairline at any point
- Push mask as high on face as possible. Look down at nose to ensure mask is centered. Hold in this position with one hand until temple straps are tightened
- Adjust temple straps using small jerking pulls until the mask feels snug and both sides feel the same
- Ensure the headpad or skullcap is centered at the high point of rear of head. Adjust if necessary.
- With both hands, run a finger under each temple tab front-to-back to check for snugness and remove stray hair from sealing area

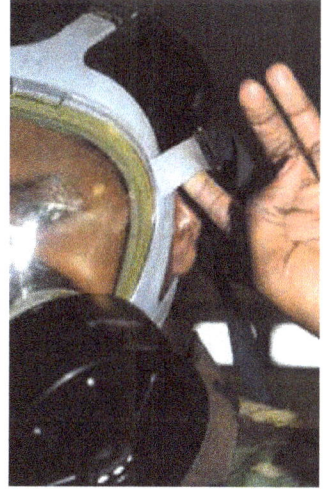

Check for leaks.

Tighten head harness.

Check seal.

- Grasp a neck strap in each hand and tighten with small jerking motions
- Grasp a forehead strap in each hand and tighten with small jerking motions
- Shake head quickly from side-to-side and up-and-down. Adjust mask straps as necessary
- The mask should be comfortable on the face with no straps cutting or pinching or so tight that the nosecup presses painfully on the nose
- Ensure the canister is sealed. Cover the canister inlet port and inhale until the lens deflects, then hold your breath. If lens stays deflected, this is a good indication of a proper fit. If it doesn't, readjust and recheck your mask until you get a proper seal
- You can now remove the mask. Loosen only the mask neck straps. Grasp mask by outlet valve assembly and remove by pulling down, outward, then up
- Shake or wipe out any accumulated moisture before storage

Don MCU-2 Series Mask While Wearing CPO

Note: Those who require vision correction should already be wearing MAG-1 prescription spectacles, or have an Advantage 1000 optical insert installed in your mask (as applicable)

- Stop breathing and close your eyes
- Remove your helmet
- Open the mask carrier
- Grasp and remove the mask from the carrier (don't grasp filter canister)
- Hold outlet valve assembly in palm of one hand. Using free hand, push forehead hair aside. Place mask on face, forcing chin-cup tightly against chin
- Grasp tab and pull head harness over your head centering the headpad at the back of your head—ensure your ears are between the temple and neck straps—make necessary strap adjustments for proper fit
- Block the outlet valve cover openings with your hand and forcefully exhale so air escapes past the edges of your facepiece
- Locate the filter canister, cover the inlet port, and inhale. The lens should collapse and stay collapsed while you hold your breath.
- If it does, the facepiece is sealed. If it doesn't, make necessary adjustments and recheck
- Open your eyes and resume normal breathing

Remove mask from carrier.

Quickly don mask.

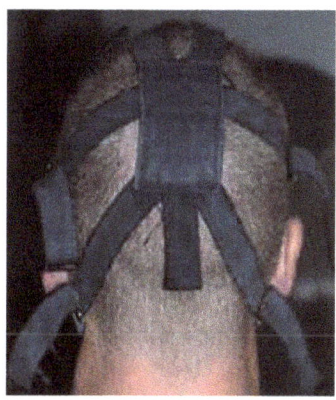
Center head harness.

- Pull hood over mask
- Close slide fastener completely and secure closure hook-and-pile fastener tape up as far as top of slide fastener
- Place edge of hood around edge of mask and secure hook-and-pile fastener tape
- Snap barrel locks together under chin. Squeeze barrel lock ends together. Pull both drawcord ends at the same time and slide barrel locks up to hood to maintain hood seal around the mask
- Have another person check hook seal around mask to ensure hood is positioned properly and skin is not exposed. Some discomfort may be experienced in the neck area of CPO coat due to the close fitting in the neck area
- Don your helmet and close the carrier

Pull hood over head.

Secure all closures.

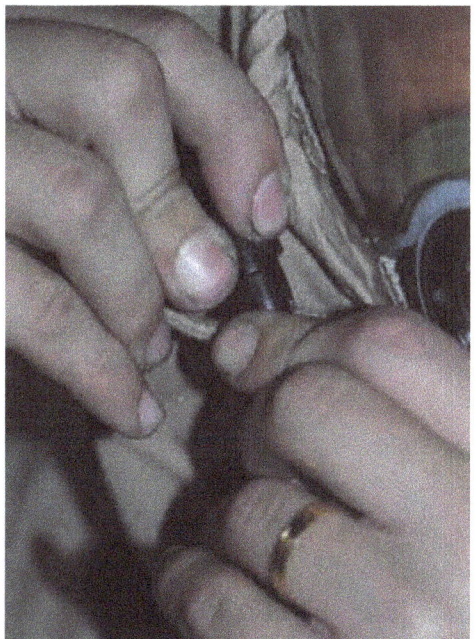

Loosen barrel locks.

Doff MCU-2 Series Mask While Wearing Uncontaminated CPO—

Warning: If you're contaminated or are in a contaminated environment, proceed to a CCA for mask removal instructions.

- Remove your helmet
- On CPO jacket, unfasten barrel locks, loosen hood drawcord, and pull hood from head so that the hood hangs behind neck and shoulders
- Loosen lower neck straps
- Grasp mask by outlet valve assembly and remove by pulling down, outward, and up over your head
- Shake or wipe any moisture or frost accumulations from inside of mask
- Properly stow mask in carrier
- Don your helmet

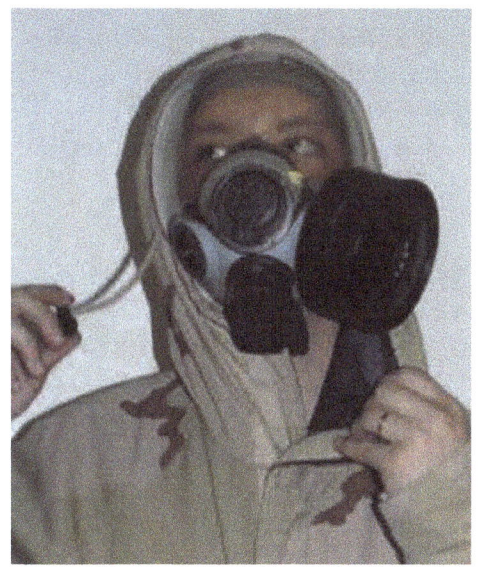

Open hood, pull back.

Remove mask, shake out moisture.

M45 Land Warrior Chemical-Biological Mask

Ref: TM 3-4240-348-10; TO 14P4-18-1

With a serviceable C2A1 filter canister installed, the M45 is the first line of defense for your face, eyes, and respiratory tract from chemical and biological warfare agents, radioactive dust particles, and riot control agents (such as tear gas).

Operational Considerations

- Only extra-small and large M45 masks are issued to hard-to-fit USAF personnel
- Do not over tighten the mask. Over tightening may actually cause leaks
- Check the mask for leaks every time you don it by performing a "leak" check
- Don the mask quickly—it should be donned and sealed before you take another breath
- The mask is a filter respirator; it doesn't supply or produce oxygen—**As such, it's ineffective in environments with insufficient oxygen to support life**
- The mask is **ineffective in industrial chemical environments** such as ammonia or chlorine spills, or within carbon monoxide atmospheres
- Don't loosen the head harness straps for comfort if you wear a hood over the outlet valve. If loosened, you could become unprotected against toxic agents or suffocate by carbon dioxide
- Don't remove your mask outdoors if you become overheated in cold weather until your head cools and any sweat has dried—frostbite may result
- Use buddy checks when possible

M45 with second skin installed.

M45 Fit—With the filter canister installed, head harness straps loose and inverted over the front of the mask, fit test the mask. Note: An unshaven face could prohibit a mask seal.

- Hold the outlet valve assembly in palm of one hand. Push hair back away from hairline, put chin in chin pocket, and press the mask snugly against your face
- Keeping the hair out of the way, pull the head harness over the head using the quick don tab—the facepiece should come well up on the forehead
- Adjust forehead straps so mask facepiece seats well up on your forehead, but not more than one-half inch into your hairline and within one inch of your ears
- Adjust temple and neck straps until the mask feels snug and both sides feel the same and don't cut into your ears
- Ensure your pupils are positioned above the center of the eyelens
- Ensure the nosecup seats comfortably on your nose
- Ensure the canister is sealed. Cover the canister inlet port and inhale until the mask collapses, then hold your breath. If the mask remains collapsed, this is a good indication of a proper fit. If it doesn't, readjust and recheck your mask until you get a proper seal
- You can now remove the mask. Loosen only the mask neck straps. Grasp mask by outlet valve assembly and remove by pulling down, outward, then up
- Shake or wipe out any accumulated moisture before storage

Chin in chin cup.

Head harness over head.

Check mask seal.

Don M45 Mask While Wearing CPO

- Stop breathing and close your eyes
- Remove your helmet
- If worn, take off your glasses
- Open the mask carrier
- Grasp and remove the mask from the carrier (don't grasp filter canister)
- Press chin in chin pocket, push hair back away from hairline, press mask snugly against your face
- Grasp tab and pull head harness over your head centering the headpad at the back of your head—ensure your ears are between the temple and neck straps
- Tighten both neck straps at the same time—pull each neck strap tab out approximately two inches to seat the mask
- Block the outlet valve cover openings with your hand and forcefully exhale so air escapes past the edges of your facepiece
- Locate the filter canister, cover the inlet port, and inhale. The facepiece should collapse against your face and stay collapsed while you hold your breath
- If it does, the facepiece is sealed. If it doesn't, make necessary adjustments and recheck
- Open your eyes and resume normal breathing

Remove from carrier.

Chin in chin cup. Pull head harness over head.

Tighten head harness.

Mask centered on head.

Perform leak test.

- Pull CPO hood over mask
- Close slide fastener completely and secure closure hook-and-pile fastener tape up as far as top of slide fastener

Pull hood over head and secure.

- Place edge of hood around edge of mask and secure hook-and-pile fastener tape
- Snap barrel locks together under chin. Squeeze barrel lock ends together. Pull both drawcord ends at the same time and slide barrel locks up to hood to maintain hood seal around the mask
- Have another person check hook seal around mask to ensure hood is positioned properly and skin is not exposed. Some discomfort may be experienced in the neck area of CPO coat due to the close fitting in the neck area
- Don your helmet and close the carrier

Close carrier.

Loosen hood fasteners.

Doff M45 Mask While Wearing Uncontaminated CPO—Warning: If you're contaminated or are in a contaminated environment, proceed to a CCA for mask removal instructions

- Remove your helmet
- On CPO jacket, unfasten barrel locks, loosen hood drawcord, and pull hood from head so that the hood hangs behind neck and shoulders
- Loosen lower neck straps

Pull hood over head.

- Grasp mask by outlet valve assembly and remove by pulling down, outward, and up over your head
- Be careful of low temperatures and wind chill factors in cold climates
- Shake or wipe any moisture or frost accumulations from inside of mask
- Don your helmet and stow mask in carrier

Pull mask out and up.

Remove and shake out moisture.

Canisters and Filters

Ref: TO 14P4-1-151; TO 14P4-15-1; TO 14P4-18-1

Warning: Filter canisters will not afford protection from industrial chemicals, ammonia, or carbon monoxide, or in areas with insufficient oxygen to support life.

A serviceable C2A1 filter canister installed on a serviceable M45 or MCU-2 Series mask creates an effective first line of defense for your face, eyes, and respiratory tract from chemical and biological warfare agents, radioactive dust particles, and riot control agents (such as tear gas.) You must install a serviceable canister on your mask when the threat of attack is possible and prior to entry into a toxic chemical or biological agent environment.

cross section

Replace Canisters and Filters

- When directed by higher authority or there's clear indication of imminent use of Chem/Bio agents
- Within fifteen days after any exposure to Chem/Bio agents (except blood agents)
- As soon as it is safe to do so when exposed to blood agents
- As soon as it is safe to do so when mechanically damaged (i.e., breaks or cuts in material or edge of seal, a bent or split connector, etc.)
- If filter has been immersed in water or wetted in any way
- If you experience excessive breathing resistance (clogged filter/canister element will increase breathing resistance but will not impair the ability of the filter to remove agents)

Service Life

Once removed from the factory sealed package:
- 52 weeks—Cold humid and warm moderate climate
- 39 weeks—Hot dry climate
- 10 weeks—Hot humid climate

Document DD Form 1574

- Date canister removed from the sealed package
- Canister lot number

Mask Second Skin

Ref: TO 14P4-15-1; TM 3-4240-348-10; TO 14P4-18-1

In a chemical warfare environment, you're protected by a combination of the agent-resistant facepiece, second skin, and hood. Although all three components protect you against agents in vapor form, the second skin and hood provide increased liquid agent protection against a penetrating liquid agent. It's designed to interface with the CPO suits. The second skin is made of agent resistant rubber and fits over the facepiece of your mask. The second skin covers exposed exterior portions of the mask's facepiece.

Precautions:
- Ensure the second skin is installed on your mask prior to entry into a potential chemical warfare environment
- Second skin cannot be changed in a contaminated environment
- Replace the second skin if it shows signs of cracks, tears, or splits
- Don't use second skin without the eyelens outsert(s) installed
- Avoid over stretching holes in the second skin. Use caution when pulling second skin over flanges of outlet valve and side voicemitter ring
- Don't damage outlet valve disk while stretching second skin over the outlet valve body
- When installing canister, make sure second skin does not get pulled down inside the threaded area
- When using a sharp instrument to remove a contaminated second skin, be careful to only cut the second skin and not the mask or straps

Second skin cannot be changed in a contaminated environment.

Second Skin Installation:
- Remove canister from facepiece
- Remove detachable microphone (if equipped)
- Remove eyelens outsert(s)
- Remove drink tube from receptacle
- Remove outlet valve cover
- Remove head harness temple straps from mask
- Orient second skin over mask
- Place second skin on top of mask
- Pull drink tube through lower center hole on second skin
- Stretch lower center hole over outlet valve body… position so it's beneath the drink tube
- Stretch second skin over side voicemitter retaining ring (if installed)
- Stretch sides and top over lens opening(s)
- Pull temple straps through slots in second skin and reattach head harness
- Place thumbs at bottom of the front voicemitter and work second skin around retaining ring
- Adjust second skin as needed to ensure as much mask is covered as possible around voicemitter and inlet valve
- Reinstall eyelens outsert(s) ensuring second skin eyelens opening(s) are covered
- Reinstall outlet valve cover and replace drink tube into receptacle
- Reinstall canister
- Reinstall detachable microphone (if equipped)

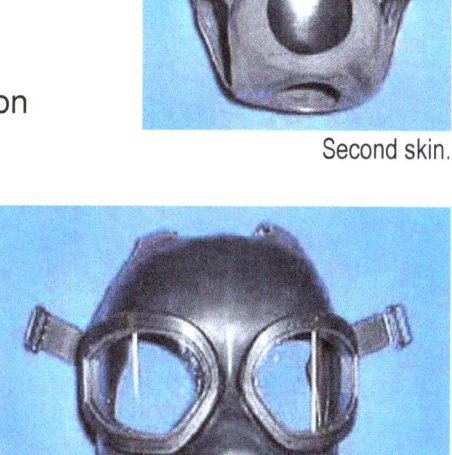

Second skin.

Facepiece.

M50 Joint Service General Purpose Field Mask

Ref: TM 14P4-20-1

The M50 Joint Service General Purpose Field Mask, is designed to provide 24 hours continuous head-eye-respiratory Chemical/Biological (CB), radiological particulates, and Toxic Industrial Chemical (TIC) protection.

The M50 components reduce the overall profile of the mask and to improve integration with future warfighter systems. There are three M50 sizes: small, medium, and large. Masks are equipped with a Mask and Equipment Carrier Bag, Sunlight Outsert, Waterproofing Bag, Canteen Cap, and Operator Cards. The mask uses twin filters positioned on the facepiece to protect against CBRN threats. The facepiece assembly has serial number bar coding and Airman readable lot and serial number markings.

M50 Components

Equipment Carrier Bag.

Mask Carrier.

Sunlight Outsert.

Operator Cards.

Canteen Cap.

Waterproofing Bag.

M50 Operator Cards

Refer to the Operator Cards included with the M50 for a parts and mask inspection check list, as well as information on donning and doffing the mask.

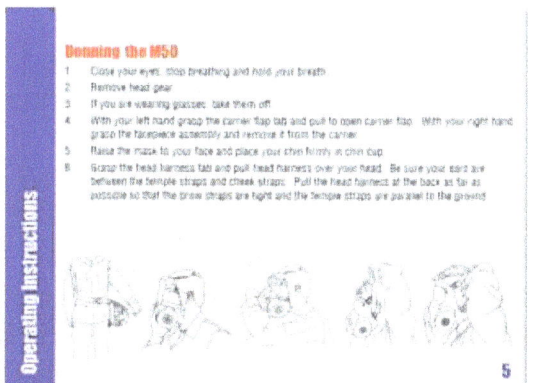

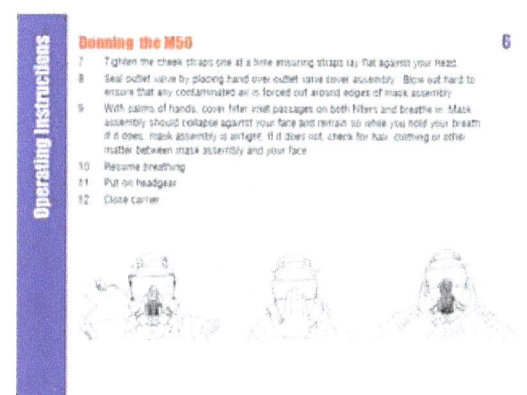

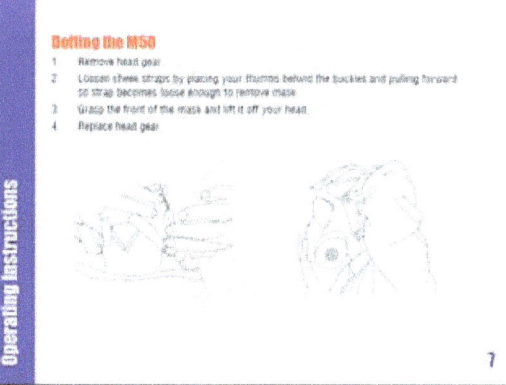

AFPAM 10-100 / 1 March 2009

168 / Section 5 / Survive

Drinking Through the Mask

Ref: TO 14P4-15-1; TM 3-4240-348-10; TO 14P4-18-1

Maintaining proper hydration and rest discipline helps to offset the adverse effects of thermal build-up, dehydration, and associated stress factors. To drink through your mask, you must have a serviceable M1 canteen cap installed on your canteen. Follow the directions below.

Warning—Do not connect the drink tube to your canteen until all mating surfaces have been checked and are free of contamination. First, decon your canteen and mask's drink tube with an M291 or M295 decon kit if necessary. Take care not to break the mask seal while pressing on the outlet valve cover or using the drinking system.

NOTE: Liquids other than water may leave residue in tube. Sugars in some liquids can block the tube and decay, causing illness. Only use water unless otherwise approved.

- Decontaminate the M1 canteen cap and drink tube coupling before use in suspected contaminated environment
- If you're wearing a hood, uncover the outlet valve cover to access the drink tube
- Steady your mask and remove the drink tube coupling from the outlet valve cover
- Use buddy system to drink if buddy is available

Use buddy system.

- Push on the outlet valve cover and grasp the internal drink tube between your teeth
- Remove your canteen from its carrier and flip open the M1 cap lid
- Blow through the internal drink tube while coupling the external drink tube into the M1 cap until it seats (you should feel some resistance. If resistance is not felt, your drinking system is leaking. Do not drink! If system leaks, pinch and hold drink tube and seek help.)
- If system is sealed, invert the canteen above the voicemitter, and drink
- After several swallows, stop sucking and return the canteen to the upright position. Air should replace the water you drank from the canteen through the drink tube. If necessary, blow into the drink tube to return the canteen to its original shape. Repeat the drinking procedure until finished
- Water may leak into the mask if the drink tube slips out of your mouth while the canteen is inverted
- Disconnect the drink tube from the canteen by blowing into the drink tube while twisting and pulling the coupling from the canteen
- Return the drink tube coupling back into its socket
- Close canteen lid
- Return canteen to carrier
- Replace hood over outlet valve cover (if necessary)

Carefully connect drinking tube.

Invert canteen to drink.

Immediate.

Operational.

Thorough.

Levels of Chemical Decontamination

Ref: AFTTP(I) 3-2.60

Level	Purpose	Who	What	When	How
Immediate	Minimize casualties, save lives, and help limit contamination exposure and spread	Individuals	Skin, personal clothing and equipment, frequently touched surfaces	As soon as contamination is suspected or detected	M291 and M295
Operational	Limit contamination exposure and spread, helps to sustain operations by providing temporary and, in some cases, long-term relief from wearing IPE	Individuals, crews, teams, units	Parts of essential operational equipment, work areas, vehicles, and material	When operations require and resources permit	M295 and 5% bleach
Thorough	Reduces or eliminates the need for wearing IPE	Units or wings, with or without external support	Personnel (CCA), equipment, material, vehicles, aircraft, work areas, terrain	When required for MOPP reduction; when operations, manning, and resources permit; required for total reconstitution and return to unrestricted use	Contact UCC for guidance

M291 Skin Decontamination Kit

Ref: TO 11D1-1-131

Operational Use

- Capable of decontaminating biological and liquid agents from the surface of skin, clothing, masks, gloves, personal equipment, and weapons
- Wallet-sized kit contains six packaged pads containing nontoxic decontaminant
- Proved to be more than 90% effective in removing biological agents from the skin
- Six pads sufficient for three personal decontaminations
- Operates in ranges from -50°F to 120°F

Inspection

- Inspect kit for loose black powder
- If no loose powder present, kit is serviceable
- If powder detected, inspect packets for leaks
- Discard leaking packets
- Replace bad packets
- Reinsert packets into pouch; ensure tear line is at bottom
- Request additional kit if less than four packets
- Use kit until all packets are used

M291 Packets

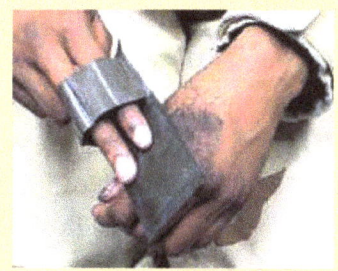

M291 Pad

M291/M295 Instructions For Use

- Remove decon packet
- Tear open packet and remove decon pad/mitt
- Discard empty packet
- Unfold decon pad/mitt
- M291—Insert fingers into loop
- M295—Grasp non pad side of decon mitt with one gloved hand, insert decontaminated gloved hand into mitt, tighten wristband on glove

MORE

M295 Individual Equipment Decontamination Kit
Ref: TO 11D1-3-11-1

Operational Use

- For operational decon and/or self-aid/buddy care
- Accomplish decon prior to agent sorption (seconds to minutes)
- Used at ground crew CCAs to remove/minimize contact transfer hazards
- Used for immediate decon of mask, OG, equipment
- Used to decon weapons and tools

M295 Decon Kit Components

- Carrying pouch containing four individual decon packets
- Four packets sufficient for two complete individual equipment decon operations
- Contains four decon mitts filled with decon powder
- Kit is expendable
- Discard packets and pouch after use
- Treat used mitts as contaminated waste

CONTINUED

- Decontaminate individual equipment or exposed skin by rubbing with pad/mitt
- M295–Decontaminate gloved hand that was holding equipment
- Discard pad/mitt
- If more contamination is present, repeat decon with another mitt

M295 Packet.

M295 Mitt.

M291/M295 WARNING
- Keep decon powder out of eyes, cuts, and wounds
- Use water to wash powder out of eyes, cuts, and wounds
- Avoid inhalation of decon powder

Casualty Collection

Ref: AFH 36-2218, Vol 1, Vol 2; AFI 10-404

- Casualties are usually moved to a centralized, safe-point for emergency treatment and forwarding, if necessary
- The casualty collection point (CCP) is staffed as needed by medical and base personnel. The CCP's mission is to evaluate wounded for return to duty, reinforce Self-Aid & Buddy Care (SABC) as needed to stabilize casualties, and/or transport wounded to a deployed medical facility for further care
- When moving casualties, ensure that they are moved feet first
- The CCP may be at the Expeditionary Medical Support Facility, tent, building, an ambulance at a disaster site, or simply a spot on the ground—Shelter is preferable, but not essential
- CCP location and use depends on the contingency operation, threat situation, and available medical and support personnel
- You may be tasked to assist the medical staff at the CCP in casualty care management
- Upon arrival at your deployed location, familiarize yourself with the local casualty care protocols and locations
- Use the buddy system to transport human remains to a point identified by Mortuary Affairs

Perform SABC.

Transport casualty to CCP.

Casualty Care in a CBRN Contaminated Environment

Ref: AFMAN 10-2602

- Place mask on casualty
- Perform SABC measures
- Inject antidote if nerve agent symptoms are present—use casualty's auto-injectors, not yours!
- Report casualty to UCC—DO NOT transmit personal information over unsecure net
- Decon casualty and their equipment with M295 or M291 kits
- Transport casualty to unit CCP
  - Follow route directed by UCC for safe roads and Split-MOPP operations
  - Ambulances do not run during attacks

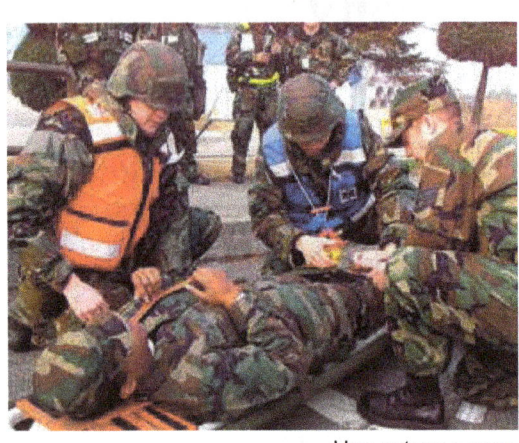

Use extreme care.

Basic Lifesaving Steps

Ref: AFH 36-2218, Vol 1, Vol 2

Use extreme care when treating injuries in a contaminated environment—different rules may apply!

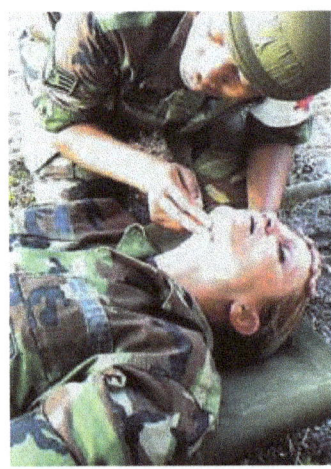

Head tilt, chin lift.

Immediate Steps
When a person is injured:
- Establish an open **Airway** (If possible neck injury, ensure airway opened using the jaw thrust maneuver, do not turn head)
- Ensure **Breathing**
- Stop bleeding to support **Circulation**
- Prevent further **Disability**
  - Immobilize neck injuries
  - Place dressings over open wound
  - Splint obvious limb deformities
- Minimize further **Exposure** to adverse weather

A	Airway
B	Breathing
C	Circulation
D	Disability
E	Exposure

Shock

Symptoms:
- Confusion
- Sweaty but cool skin (clammy skin)
- Breathing shallow, labored, and rapid
- Weak and rapid pulse

Treatment:
- Keep airway open
- If unconscious, place on side in recovery position and monitor airway
- Keep the person calm, warm, and comfortable
- Elevate lower extremities
- Seek medical attention immediately
- Do not give food or drink

Elevate lower extremities.

Abdominal Wound

Treatment:
- If organs are outside body, gently pick them up and place them on top of abdomen... do not replace or push organs into the body
- Cover exposed organs with moist clean dressing
- Secure with bandages
- If legs are not fractured bend knees to relieve pressure

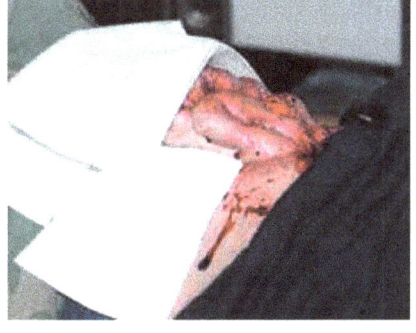

Place organs on abdomen.

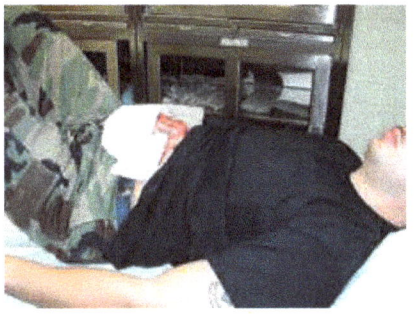

Secure with bandages.

Always check and treat for shock

Bleeding

Symptom: Obvious external bleeding
Treatment:

Conventional:

1. Apply direct pressure with hand: use a dressing if available
2. Elevate the extremity if no fractures are suspected
3. Use pressure points with elevation to control bleeding
4. Tourniquet as a last resort to stop bleeding. Use to save life at possible loss of limb
5. Consider using QuikClot if available

Care Under Fire:

1. Return fire as directed or required before providing medical treatment
2. If the casualty can function, direct to return fire, move to cover, and administer self-aid
3. If casualty is unable to follow above instructions and you cannot assist, tell casualty to "play dead" until enemy fire is suppressed
4. If the casualty has life-threatening bleeding from a limb, apply a tourniquet FIRST to the limb or amputation. If bleeding is in a location where a tourniquet cannot be applied (Armpit or Groin), consider QuikClot in conjunction with direct pressure

Consider QuikClot.

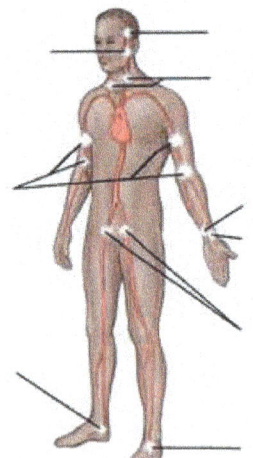

Pressure points.

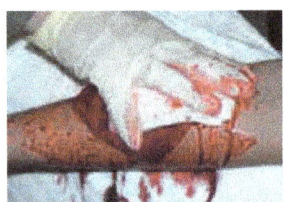

Apply direct pressure.

Always check and treat for shock

How to Apply a Tourniquet

Used as the last resort to stop bleeding. Use to save life at possible loss of limb.

1. Place one inch wide constricting band around arm or leg to stop severe bleeding
2. DO NOT use wire or shoestrings
3. Place band 2-4 inches above injury if possible
4. Tighten band enough to stop bleeding and no more
5. Once in place do not loosen or remove
6. Leave tourniquet area exposed for quick visual reference
7. Mark time and letter "T" on casualty's forehead (ink or blood)
8. Do not remove a tourniquet once applied

Use tourniquet as last resort.

NOTES:
- **Do not remove old dressings. Add more dressing over old, if needed**
- **Do not remove a tourniquet once applied**
- **Review the external packaging for QuikClot indications/contraindications**
- **Combat Application Tourniquet (CAT) and QuikClot are in AF Individual First Aid Kits**

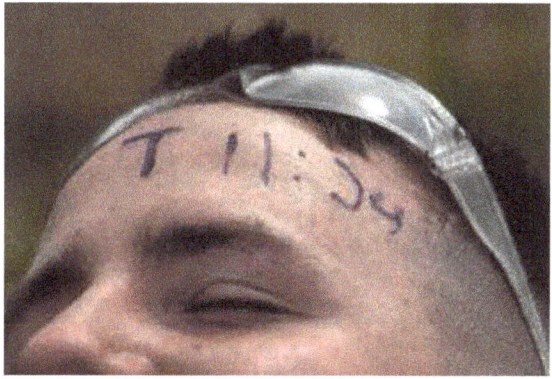
Mark time and letter "T" on casualty's forehead.

Always check and treat for shock

Eye Injury

Symptom:
- Obvious pain or injury

Treatment:
- DO NOT remove any impaled objects
- Dress around object to secure it
- Apply bandage lightly to BOTH eyes
- Do not leave casualty unattended

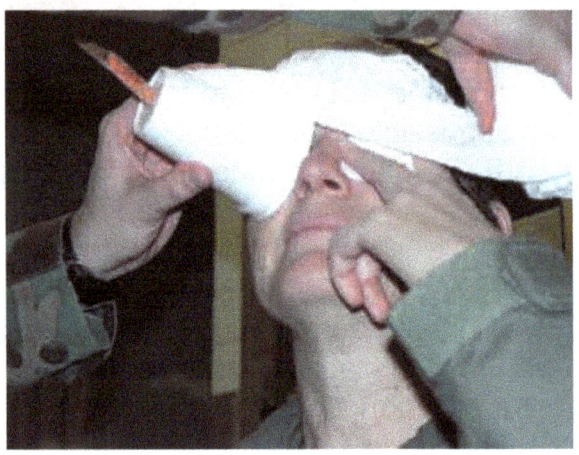
Cover both eyes.

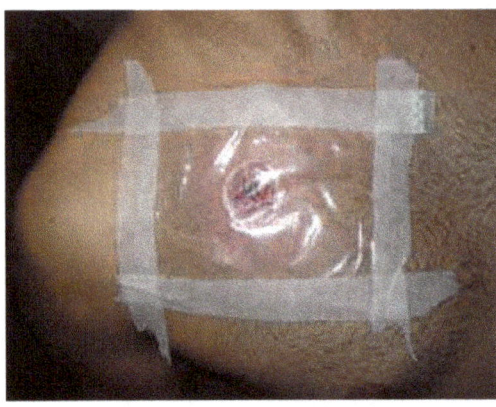
Make an airtight seal over wound. Tape down all four sides.

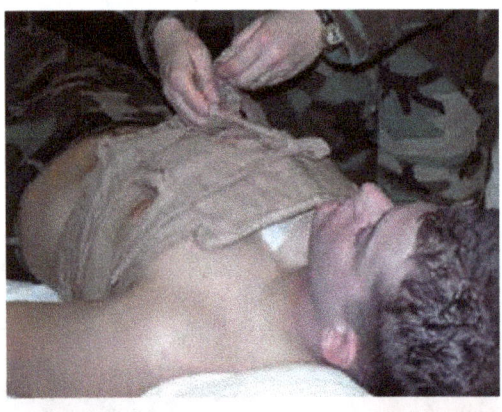

Common Injuries

Ref: AFH 36-2218, Vol 1, Vol 2

Sucking Chest Wound

Symptoms:
- Sucking noise from chest
- Frothy red blood from wound
- Difficulty breathing

Treatment:
- Look for entry and exit wound
- Cover holes with airtight seal (plastic, tin foil, ID card)
- Tape down all four sides
- Allow casualty to assume position for easiest breathing, preferably on affected side

Always check and treat for shock

Fractures

Symptoms:
- Deformity, bruising
- Tenderness over a specific part of body
- Swelling and discoloration

Treatment:
- DO NOT straighten limb
- If in doubt, splint injury-where they lie if possible
- Splint joints above and below injury
- Remove clothing from injured area
- Remove rings from fingers, if possible
- Check pulse below injury-away from heart to determine if blood flow is restricted

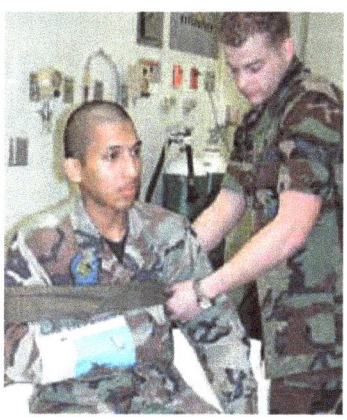

Do not straighten limb.

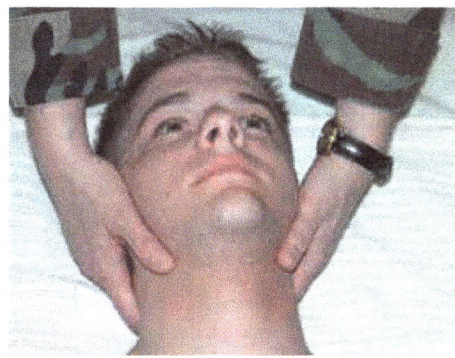

Maintain immobilization until completely secured.

Spinal/Neck/Head Injury

Symptom:
- Lack of feeling and/or control anywhere below neck, drainage of fluid or blood from ear, nose or mouth

Treatment:
- If conscious, caution casualty not to move
- Continuously monitor and check airway without turning head
- Immobilize the head and neck

If Casualty Must Be Moved

- Use hard surface for litter (door, cut lumber, other)
- Use as many people as needed to place casualty on litter
- One person must immobilize the head and neck
- Ensure casualty's limbs are secured at the chest and thigh regions
- Turn whole body together, as a unit

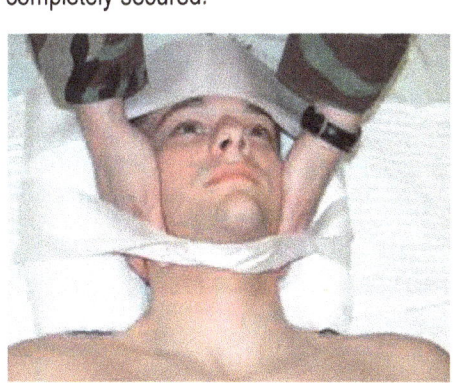

Do NOT Bend Spinal Cord or Rotate Head and Neck

Combating Heat Illness and Cold Injury

Ref: AFMAN 10-2602; AFPAM 48-151

Airmen should focus on the key indicators (see table) when deciding the appropriate action to take. Heat related illnesses can occur during strenuous activity at almost any Heat Stress condition. Heatstroke is a life threatening medical emergency that needs to be identified and treated immediately. Death may result from brain, kidney, liver, heart and muscle damage.

SEE Page 216, Quick Reference, Work/rest Cycles

	Dehydration	Heat Exhaustion	Heat Stroke
Key Indicators Mental State	Conscious, may be dizzy	Conscious, may be dizzy	Suden collapse, unusual behavior, altered mental state
Body Temperature	Normal	Normal	Hot, elevated
Action	Sit down in shade/cool area. Provide water. Observe	Sit down in shade/cool area. Provide water. Observe	Call 911 immediately. SABC. Cool Victim
Other Symptoms	Headache, Dry Mouth, Loss of Skin Turgor (remains elevated when pinched)	Weakness, Headache, Dry Mouth, Nausea, Muscle Cramps, Muscle Spasms	Red Face/Skin, Strong Rapid Pulse, Wet or Dry Skin, Most likely sweating in younger individuals

Exertional heatstroke occurs in young, active healthy individuals, progresses rapidly, and sweating is usually present, with the skin wet to touch. If at any time an Airman who is involved in strenuous activity in a hot and humid environment loses conciousness, begins to have an altered mental state, behave abnormally, or has an elevated body temperature (hot to touch), call for immediate professional emergency medical services (911).

There are additional symptoms and effects from heat related illnesses Airmen may want to be aware of, but the "key indicators" let you know when you need to call 911 for immediate professional emergency medical services.

Dehydration

Ref: AFMAN 32-4005

Symptoms
- Dizzy
- Headache
- Dry mouth
- Loss of Skin turgor (skin remains elevated when pinched)

Treatment
- Provide water

Note: If you're urinating, and it's light yellow, that's a good indicator that you're hydrated.

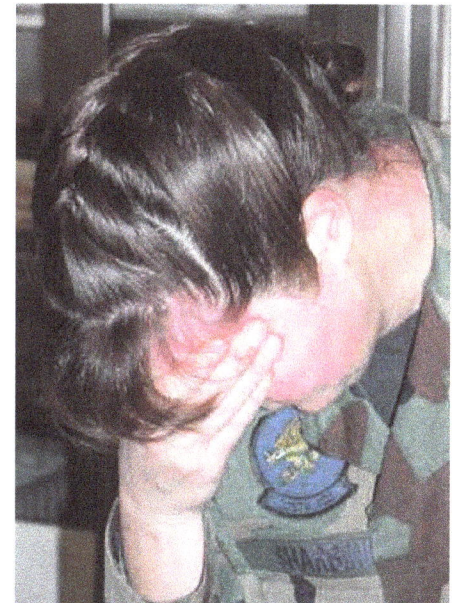
Dizziness, headache.

Heat Exhaustion

Ref: AFH 36-2218 V1, V2

Early Symptoms
- Dizziness/weakness
- Headache
- Dry Mouth
- Nausea
- Muscle Cramps
- Spasms, usually in muscles or arms results from strenuous work or exercise
- Profuse Sweating
- Loss of salt in the body
- Normal body temperature

Actions
- Remove from work or training
- Allow casualty to rest in shade or cool area
- Provide sips of water
- If symptoms do not improve in 15-30 minutes, transport to medical facility
- If signs or symptoms worsen call ambulance (see immediate actions)

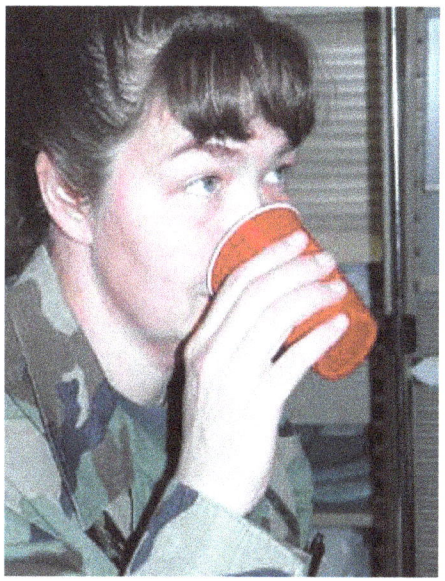
Give sips of water.

Late Signs and Symptoms
- Weak and/or rapid pulse
- Confusion, unresponsive, or coma
- Loss of bowel or bladder control
- Convulsions
- Cramps in abdomen or limbs
- Pale face
- Dizziness/faintness/weakness
- Nausea or vomiting
- Profuse sweating or moist, cool skin
- Weak pulse
- Normal body temperature

Treatment:
- Treat for shock
- Lay person down in cool area
- Loosen/open clothing
- Cool body by sprinkling with cool water or fanning (not to point of shivering)
- Give victim cool water to drink if conscious
- Seek medical attention

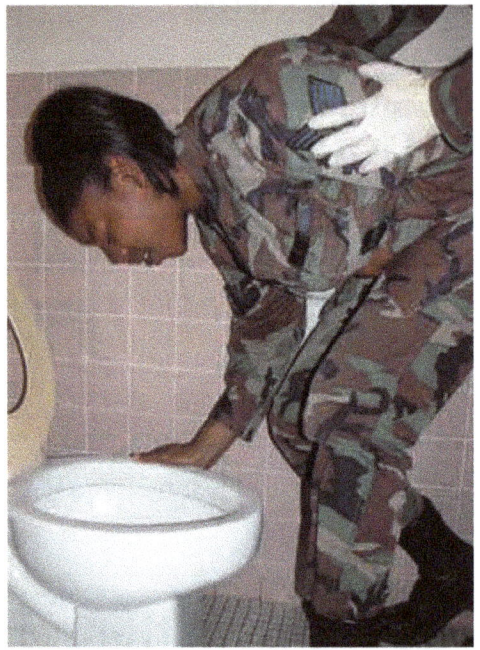

Nausea or vomiting.

Always check and treat for shock

Heat Stroke
Ref: AFH 36-2218 V1, V2

Symptoms
- Headache
- Dizziness
- Red face/skin
- Strong, rapid pulse
- Confusion and disorientation
- Hot dry skin or sweating
- High body temperature (hot to touch)

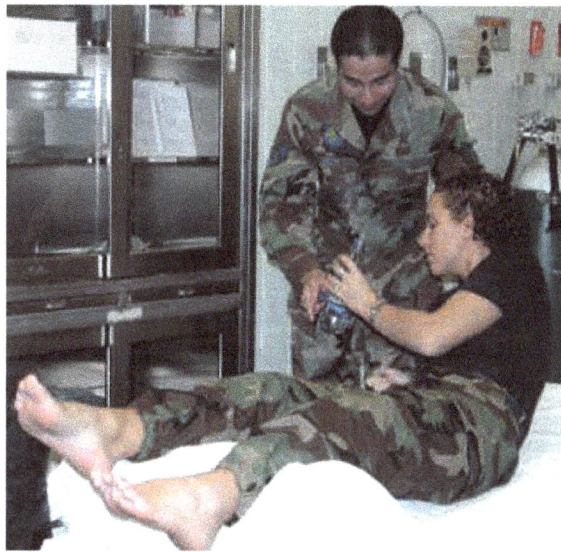
Give sips of water.

Immediate Actions
- Emergency—call 911/ local number to request medical assistance, or radio for ambulance immediately for transport to the medical treatment area. During combat, transport victim to CCP via unit assets
- Lay person down in shade or cool area with feet elevated, until help arrives
- Give sips of water if casualty is conscious
- If skin is hot and dry to touch, remove clothing; pour water over person and fan. If casualty begins shivering stop fanning process. When shivering stops resume fanning

Transport to CCP.

Treatment
- Lay person in cool area
- Loosen/open clothing
- Cool body by sprinkling with cool water or fanning (not to point of shivering)
- Give cool water to drink if conscious—add two teaspoons of salt to one canteen if available
- Seek immediate medical attention
- Treat for shock

Always check and treat for shock

Heat Injuries

Ref: AFH 36-2218 V1, V2

Burns
- Burns may be from heat (thermal), electrical, chemical, or radiation. Treatment is based on depth, size, and severity (termed degree of burn)
- Always treat for shock and seek medical advice

Thermal/Partial Thickness (First and Second Degree)
Symptoms:
- Skin reddens (sunburn-like), blisters, painful

Treatment:
- Stop the burning process
- Apply cool water to affected area
- DO NOT break blisters
- Apply clean dry dressing to affected area

Thermal/Full Thickness (Third Degree)
Symptoms:
- Charred or whitish looking skin
- May burn clear to the bone
- Burned area not painful but area around burn very painful

Treatment:
- Stop the burning process
- Do not remove clothing adhered to burned area
- Cover with or apply clean dry dressing to affected area

Electrical Burns
- Ensure power is off
- Look for entry and exit wound
- Treat burned area

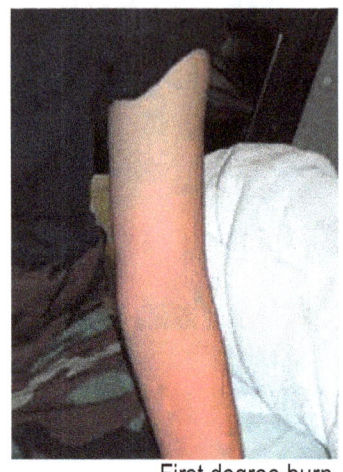

First degree burn.

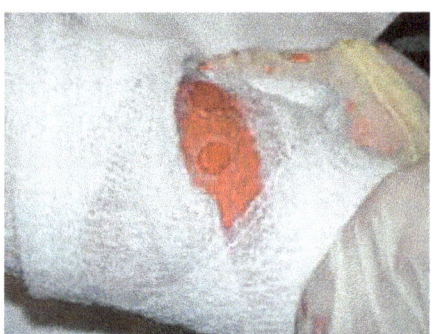

Second degree.

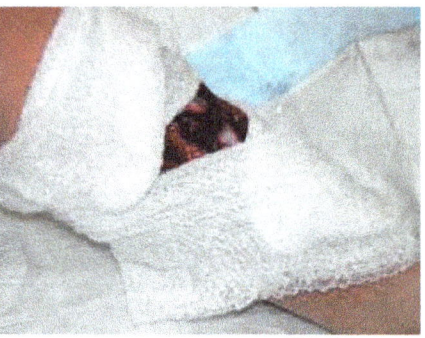

Third degree.

Chemical Burns
- Flush with large amount of water
- Flush eyes for at least 20 minutes
- Brush off visible contaminates
- Keep phosphorous burns covered with a wet dressing (prevents air from activating the phosphorous)
- Fingers have a tendency to swell, ensure that rings/jewelry are removed immediately

Flush eyes.

Cold Injuries
Ref: AFH 36-2218, V2

Hypothermia
Symptoms:
- Body is cold under clothing
- May appear confused
- May appear dead

Treatment:
- Move to a warm place
- Remove wet clothing
- Put on warm clothes or wrap with dry blanket
- Do NOT rub body parts
- Do NOT give or consume alcohol

Wrap casualty in blanket.

Frostbite
Symptoms:
- Skin has white or waxy appearance
- Skin feels hard to touch

Treatment:
- Move to warm place
- Re-warm affected area in warm water 104-108° F (40°C) for 15-30 minutes (NOT hot water)
- Cover with several layers of clothing
- Do NOT rub affected area
- Seek medical attention immediately

SEE Page 197, Quick Reference, **Wind Chill Chart**

Slowly re-warm areas.

Emergency Life-Saving Equipment

Ref: AFH 36-2218, V2

The key to self-aid and buddy care is improvising when you don't have the equipment you need, use the casualty's gear.

Shirts = Dressings/Bandages

Belts, Ties = Tourniquets, Bandages

Towels, Sheets = Dressings/Bandages

Socks, Flight cap = Dressings/Bandages

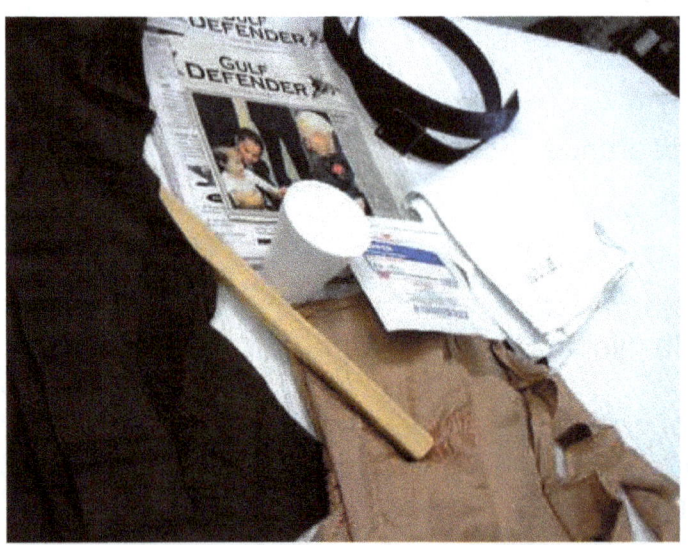
Expedient equipment.

Sticks or Tree Limbs = Splints

Handling Human Remains

Ref: AFI 34-242

Ensure that you treat human remains with dignity. Use the buddy system to transport human remains to a point identified by Mortuary Affairs.

Protect Yourself First
- Wear gloves when handling remains
- DO NOT endanger yourself to retrieve remains
- Wear CBRN protective gear if you suspect/confirm the remains are contaminated

Protect yourself first.

Secure Available Identification Information
- DO NOT remove any identification information from remains (dog tags, ID cards)
- DO NOT remove any personal effects from remains (pictures, jewelry, money)

Treat with dignity.

DO NOT Transport to the Casualty Collection Point (CCP)
- Use available transportation and pass information up your chain of command

Use available transportation.

Rights as a Prisoner of War

Ref: Geneva Conventions

As a member of a military force, you must understand that you might be captured by a hostile force and held captive as a POW. However, the Third Geneva Convention provides special protections for you in the event you're captured. Your ID card is your Geneva Convention card. Do not remove the computer chip from CAC ID during combat—the card doesn't contain any information electronically that's not already shown in print.

The Convention States:

- If captured, you may be **disarmed**, **searched**, and **guarded** but you must be **humanely treated** without distinction based upon race, color, gender, religious belief, or other arbitrary reason
- As a prisoner, you must **not be humiliated** or degraded and must **be protected** against all acts of violence, insults, public curiosity, and reprisals of all kind
- All prisoners must **be treated alike** with privileges only extended because of poor health, advanced age, military rank, or professional qualifications. Medical personnel and chaplains are not POWs, but rather "retained personnel" and must be allowed to tend to prisoners. Gender-female POWs must be provided any special care required by their gender.

- POWs should be promptly, safely, and humanely evacuated from battle area
- When questioned, you must give your **name, age, rank**, and **service number** but you do not have to give any other information. Although you may be questioned, you may not be harmed, tortured, or threatened in any way
- As soon as possible, but not later than a week after reaching a POW camp, you must be allowed to send a "**Capture Card**"
- This Geneva Convention postcard informs your next-of-kin of your whereabouts and state of health
- Completion of this card does not violate the Code of Conduct
- POWs, with the exception of officers, may be forced to work
- You may never be forced to do military work or work that is dangerous, unhealthy, or degrading
- You must be paid for all work performed
- Officers may voluntarily work
- NCOs can only be required to perform supervisory work

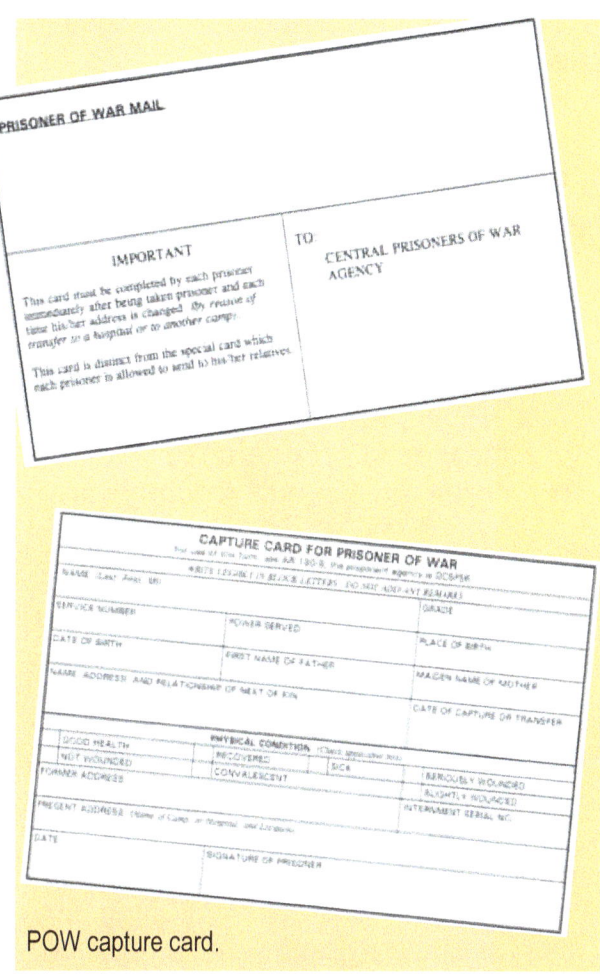

POW capture card.

Complaints

- The text of the Geneva Convention must be posted in each camp in a language you and all other POWs understand
- You have the right to complain to representatives of a Protecting Power (the neutral State responsible for safeguarding your interests) or to delegates of the International Committee of the Red Cross

Discipline

- Military discipline continues in a POW camp and includes saluting high ranking enemy officers and the camp commander, regardless of rank
- The Uniform Code of Military Justice applies to you while a prisoner
- You must obey the senior US POW regardless of service
- You are **subject to the laws** of the Detaining Power (enemy) for offenses committed during captivity or before capture but not for having fought against the enemy before capture
- If tried by the Detaining Power, you **must be given** notice of the charges, provided counsel and an interpreter, and be allowed to call witnesses in your defense
- If convicted, you still **retain your rights** as a POW

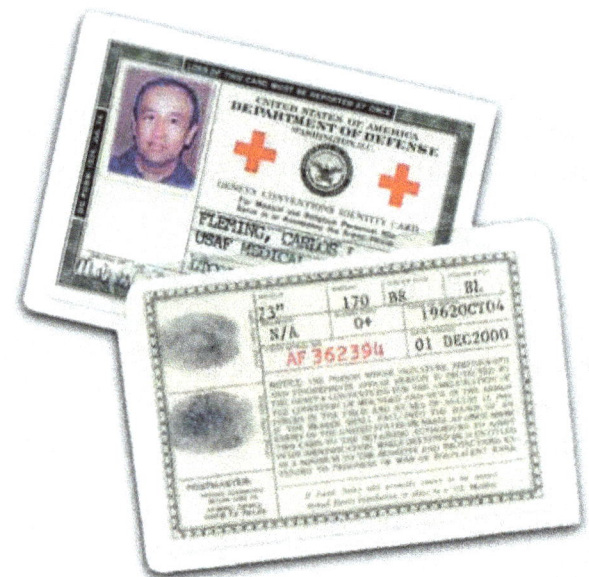

Geneva Conventions identity card.

Medical personnel and chaplains are non-combatants and have certain rights as a result of their status. This card identifies such personnel. In addition to carrying this card, they also wear a distinctive Geneva Conventions armband.

The Code of Conduct

As a member of the US Armed Forces, you are protecting your nation. It is your duty to oppose all enemies of the United States whether in combat or as a captive in a POW facility. The Code of Conduct is a guide for your proper behavior. This code is the result of the heroic lives, experiences, and deeds of Americans from the Revolutionary War through our more recent conflicts.

Code of Conduct

ARTICLE I I am an American, fighting in the forces which guard my country and our way of life. I am prepared to give up my life in their defense.

ARTICLE II I will never surrender of my own free will. If in command, I will never surrender the members of my command while they still have the means to resist.

ARTICLE III If I am captured I will continue to resist by all means available. I will make every effort to escape and aid others to escape. I will accept neither parole nor special favors from the enemy.

ARTICLE IV If I become a prisoner of war, I will keep faith with my fellow prisoners. I will give no information or take part in any action which might be harmful to my comrades. If I am senior, I will take command. If not, I will obey the lawful order of those appointed over me and will back them up in every way.

ARTICLE V When questioned, should I become a prisoner of war, I am required to give name, rank, service number, and date of birth. I will evade answering further questions to the utmost of my ability. I will make no oral or written statements disloyal to my country and its allies or harmful to their cause.

ARTICLE VI I will never forget that I am an American, fighting for freedom, responsible for my actions, and dedicated to the principles which made my country free. I will trust in my God and in the United States of America.

AFPAM 10-100 / 1 March 2009

192 / Section 5 / Survive

GEN NORTON A. SCHWARTZ
AIR FORCE CHIEF OF STAFF

Section 6
Quick Reference

Access to most technical orders and technical references used in this manual can be found on the AF Portal at www.my.af.mil

Accurate communication is essential to effective communication.

Phonetic Alphabet / Numbers

Letter	Word
A	ALPHA
B	BRAVO
C	CHARLIE
D	DELTA
E	ECHO
F	FOXTROT
G	GOLF
H	HOTEL
I	INDIA
J	JULIET
K	KILO
L	LIMA
M	MIKE
N	NOVEMBER
O	OSCAR
P	PAPA
Q	QUEBEC
R	ROMEO
S	SIERRA
T	TANGO
U	UNIFORM
V	VICTOR
W	WHISKEY
X	XRAY
Y	YANKEE
Z	ZULU

Number	Word	Pronunciation
1	ONE	
2	TWO	
3	THREE	(TREE)
4	FOUR	(FOW-er)
5	FIVE	(FIFE)
6	SIX	
7	SEVEN	(SEV-en)
8	EIGHT	(AIT)
9	NINE	(NIN-er)
10	TEN	(TIN)
11	ELEVEN	(E LAV-en)
12	TWELVE	(TWELL)
13	THIRTEEN	(THIRD TEEN)
14	FOURTEEN	(FOR TEEN)
15	FIFTEEN	(FIFT TEEN)
16	SIXTEEN	(SIX TEEN)
17	SEVENTEEN	(SEV-en TEEN)
18	EIGHTEEN	(AIT TEEN)
19	NINETEEN	(NIN TEEN)
20	TWENTY	(TWIN TEE)
30	THIRTY	(THIRD TEE)
40	FORTY	(FOUR TEE)
50	FIFTY	(FIFE TEE)
60	SIXTY	(SIX TEE)
70	SEVENTY	(SEV EN TEE)
80	EIGHTY	(AIT TEE)
90	NINETY	(NIN TEE)
100	HUNDRED	(HUN DRED)
1000	THOUSAND	(THAL SUN)
1,000,000	MILLION	(MIL YEN)

Radio Communications Procedure Words (PROWORDS)

PROWORDS	MEANING
ACKNOWLEDGE	Let me know you received and understood this message.
AFFIRMATIVE	Yes; permission granted; or that is correct.
ALL AFTER	Everything which follows.
BREAK*	Indicates the separation of text from other message portions.
DISREGARD	This transmission is in error–disregard it. NOTE: Don't use this PROWORD to cancel completely transmitted messages.
GO AHEAD	Proceed with your message.
I READ BACK	The following is my response to your instructions to read back.
I SAY AGAIN	I am repeating the transmission or portion indicated.
I SPELL	I shall spell the word phonetically.
NEGATIVE	No; permission is not granted; or that is not correct.
OUT	This is the end of my transmission to you and no answer is required or expected. NOTE: This PROWORD is always preceded by the user's call sign.
OVER*	This is the end of my transmission and a response is necessary. Go ahead and transmit your response. NOTE: This PROWORD is normally used only in tactical communications.
PREPARE TO COPY	This lets the individual receiving your message to prepare to take down the information you are about to pass.
READ BACK*	Repeat all of the specified part of this message back to me exactly as received.

RELAY TO (OR FOR)	Transmit this message to all addresses or to the address designation immediately following this PROWORD.
ROGER	I have received your last transmission satisfactorily.
SAY AGAIN	Repeat all or the following part of your last transmission. NOTE: Never use the word "repeat." This term is used to place indirect weapons fire onto the enemy.
STAND BY	Wait for further instructions or information.
THAT IS CORRECT	You are correct or what you have transmitted is correct.
THIS IS	The transmission is from whose call sign immediately follows.
UNKNOWN STATION	The call sign I am attempting to contact is unknown. NOTE: Previously known as "last calling."
VERIFY	Confirm entire message (or portion indicated) with the sender. If original message (or portion indicated) is incorrect, send correct version.
Wait*	One must pause for a few seconds.
Wait-out*	Resume communications.
Wilco	Will comply.
Word after*	Word after.
Word before*	Word before.

* For tactical radio transmissions only.

WIND CHILL CHART

wind (mph) / **temperature °F**

wind \ temp	40	35	30	25	20	15	10	5	0	-5	-10	-15	-20	-25	-30	-35	-40	-45
Calm	40	35	30	25	20	15	10	5	0	-5	-10	-15	-20	-25	-30	-35	-40	-45
5	36	31	25	19	13	7	1	-5	-11	-16	-22	-28	-34	-40	-46	-52	-57	-63
10	34	27	21	15	9	3	-4	-10	-16	-22	-28	-35	-41	-47	-53	-59	-66	-72
15	32	25	19	13	6	0	-7	-13	-19	-26	-32	-39	-45	-51	-58	-64	-71	-77
20	30	24	17	11	4	-2	-9	-15	-22	-29	-35	-42	-48	-55	-61	-68	-74	-81
25	29	23	16	9	3	-4	-11	-17	-24	-31	-37	-44	-51	-58	-64	-71	-78	-84
30	28	22	15	8	1	-5	-12	-19	-26	-33	-39	-46	-53	-60	-67	-73	-80	-87
35	28	21	14	7	0	-7	-14	-21	-27	-34	-41	-48	-55	-62	-69	-76	-82	-89
40	27	20	13	6	-1	-8	-15	-22	-29	-36	-43	-50	-57	-64	-71	-78	-84	-91
45	26	19	12	5	-2	-9	-16	-23	-30	-37	-44	-51	-58	-65	-72	-79	-86	-93
50	26	19	12	4	-3	-10	-17	-24	-31	-38	-45	-52	-60	-67	-74	-81	-88	-95
55	25	18	11	4	-3	-11	-18	-25	-32	-39	-46	-54	-61	-68	-75	-82	-89	-97
60	25	17	10	3	-4	-11	-19	-26	-33	-40	-48	-55	-62	-69	-76	-84	-91	-98

Frostbite occurs in 15 minutes or less!

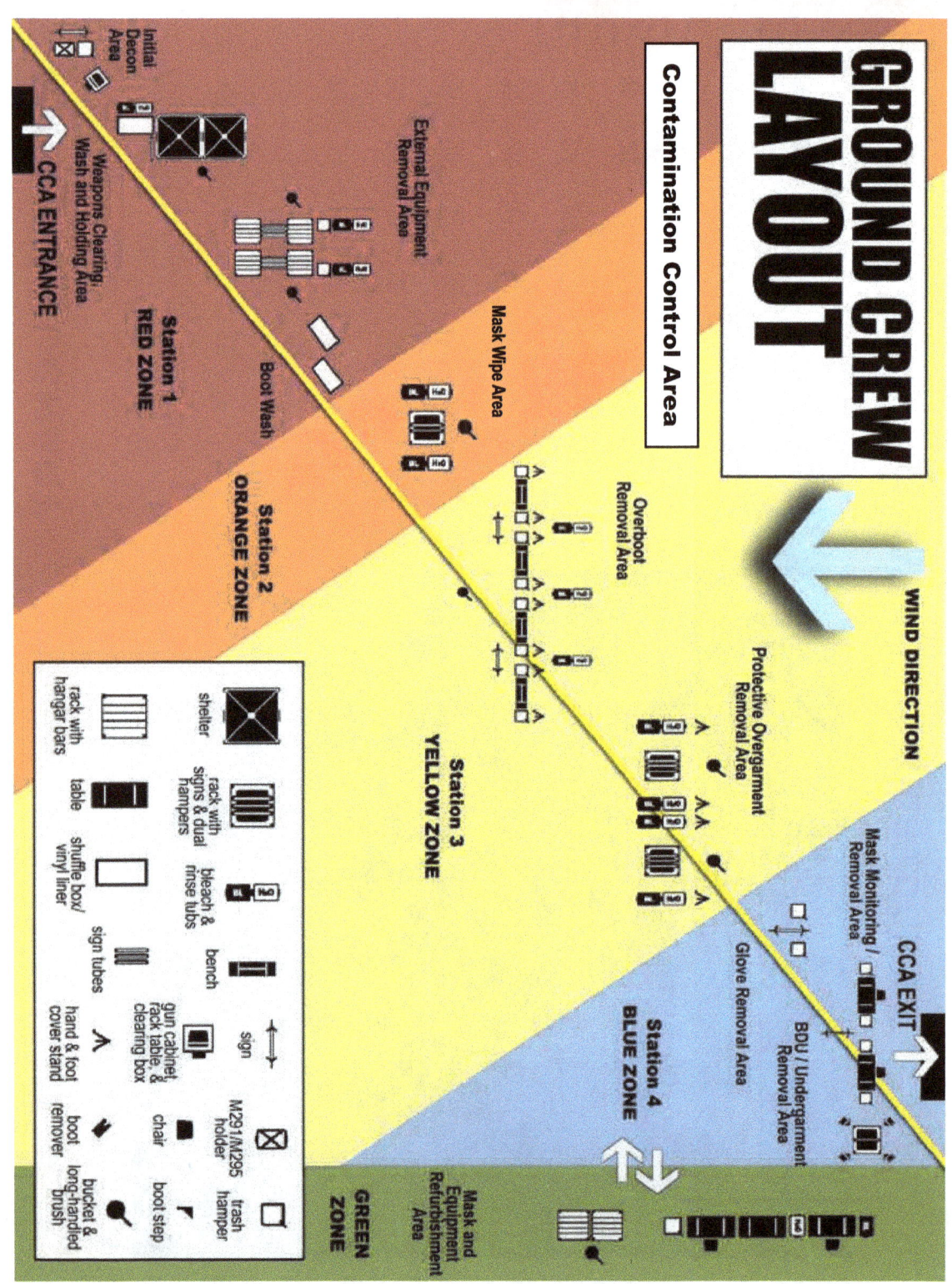

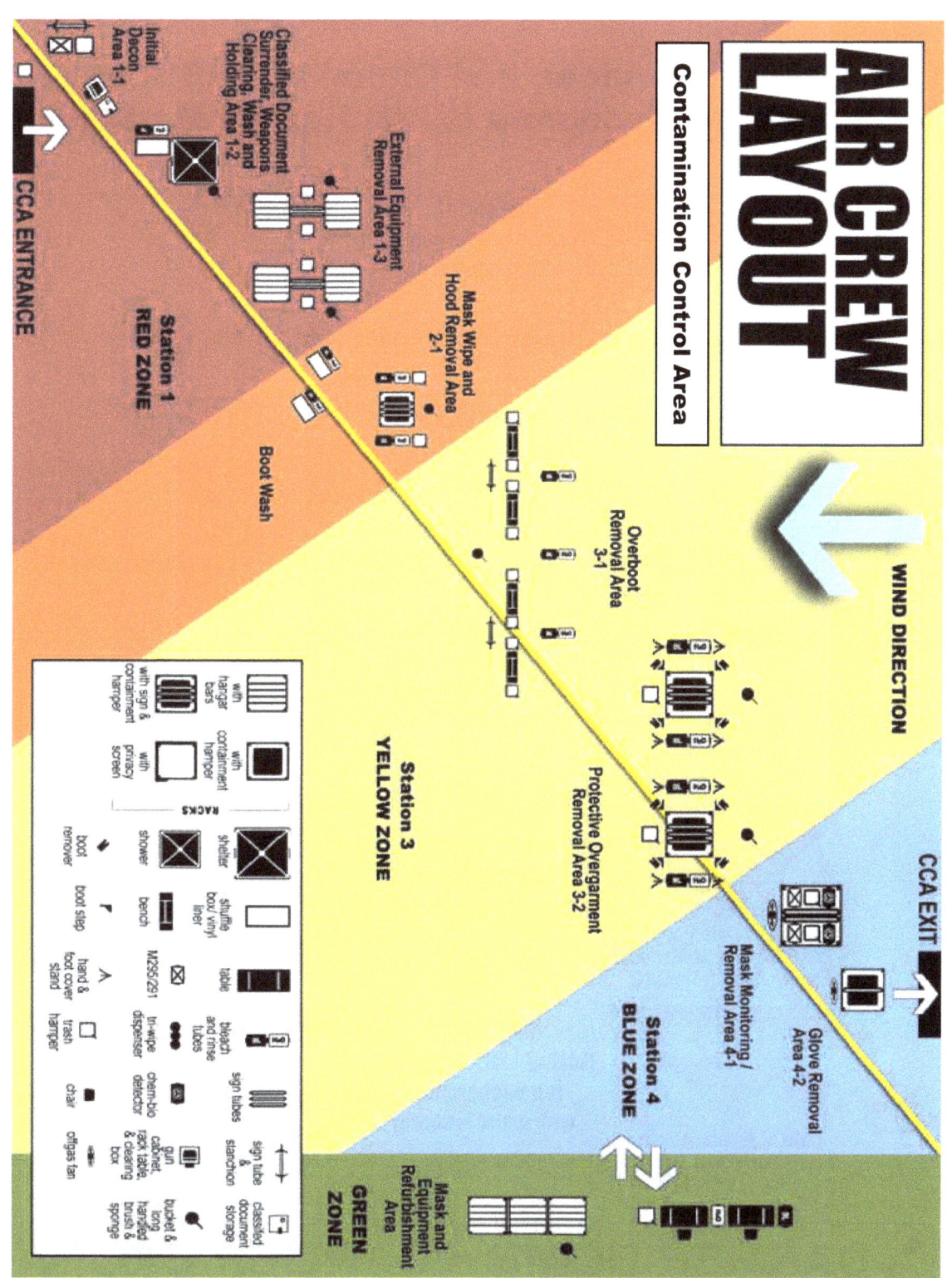

Nuclear, Biological, and Chemical (NBC) and Unexploded Ordnance (UXO) Hazard Markers

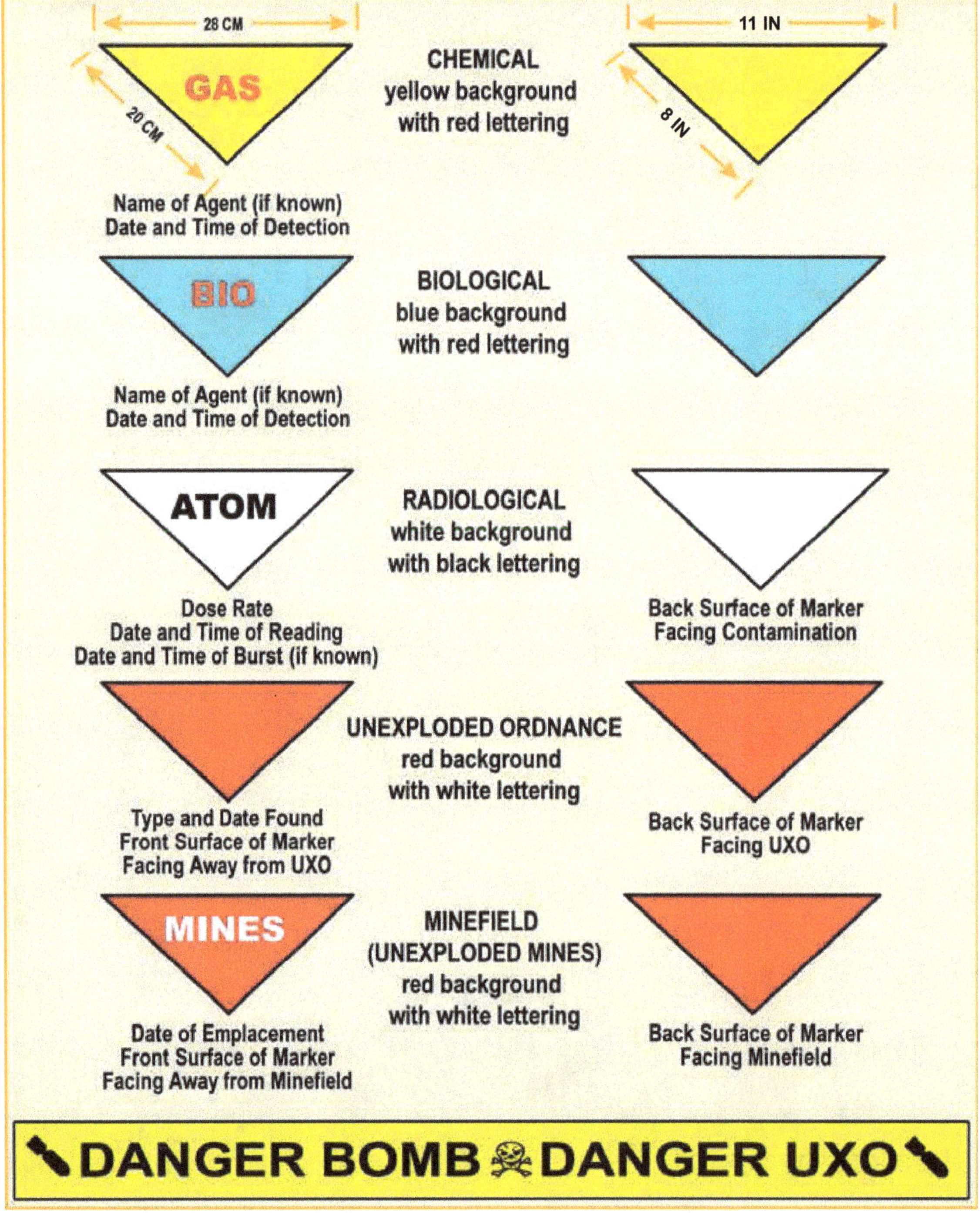

CHEMICAL — yellow background with red lettering
- 28 CM / 20 CM (11 IN / 8 IN)
- Marker labeled "GAS"
- Name of Agent (if known), Date and Time of Detection

BIOLOGICAL — blue background with red lettering
- Marker labeled "BIO"
- Name of Agent (if known), Date and Time of Detection

RADIOLOGICAL — white background with black lettering
- Marker labeled "ATOM"
- Dose Rate, Date and Time of Reading, Date and Time of Burst (if known)
- Back Surface of Marker Facing Contamination

UNEXPLODED ORDNANCE — red background with white lettering
- Type and Date Found, Front Surface of Marker Facing Away from UXO
- Back Surface of Marker Facing UXO

MINEFIELD (UNEXPLODED MINES) — red background with white lettering
- Marker labeled "MINES"
- Date of Emplacement, Front Surface of Marker Facing Away from Minefield
- Back Surface of Marker Facing Minefield

DANGER BOMB ☠ DANGER UXO

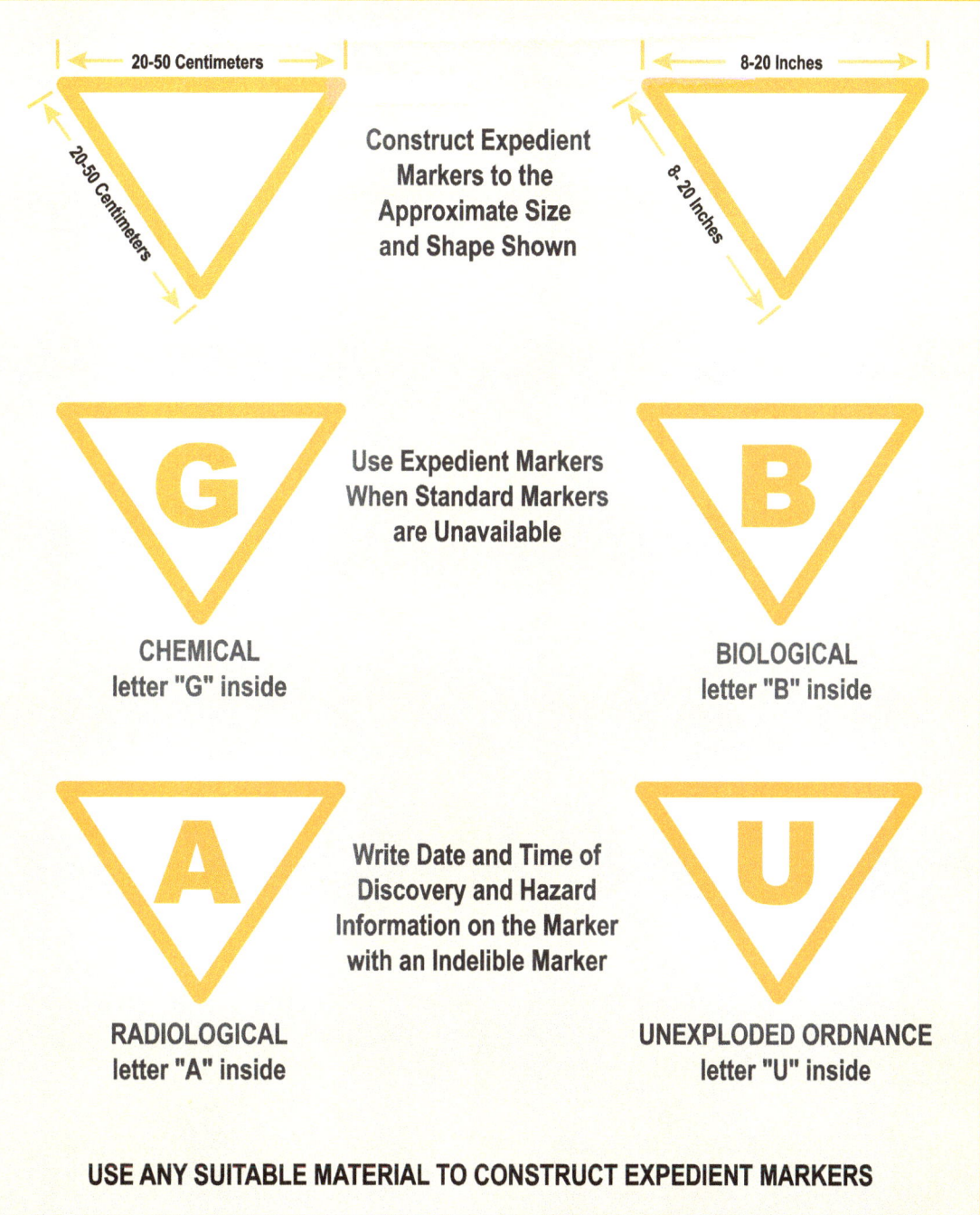

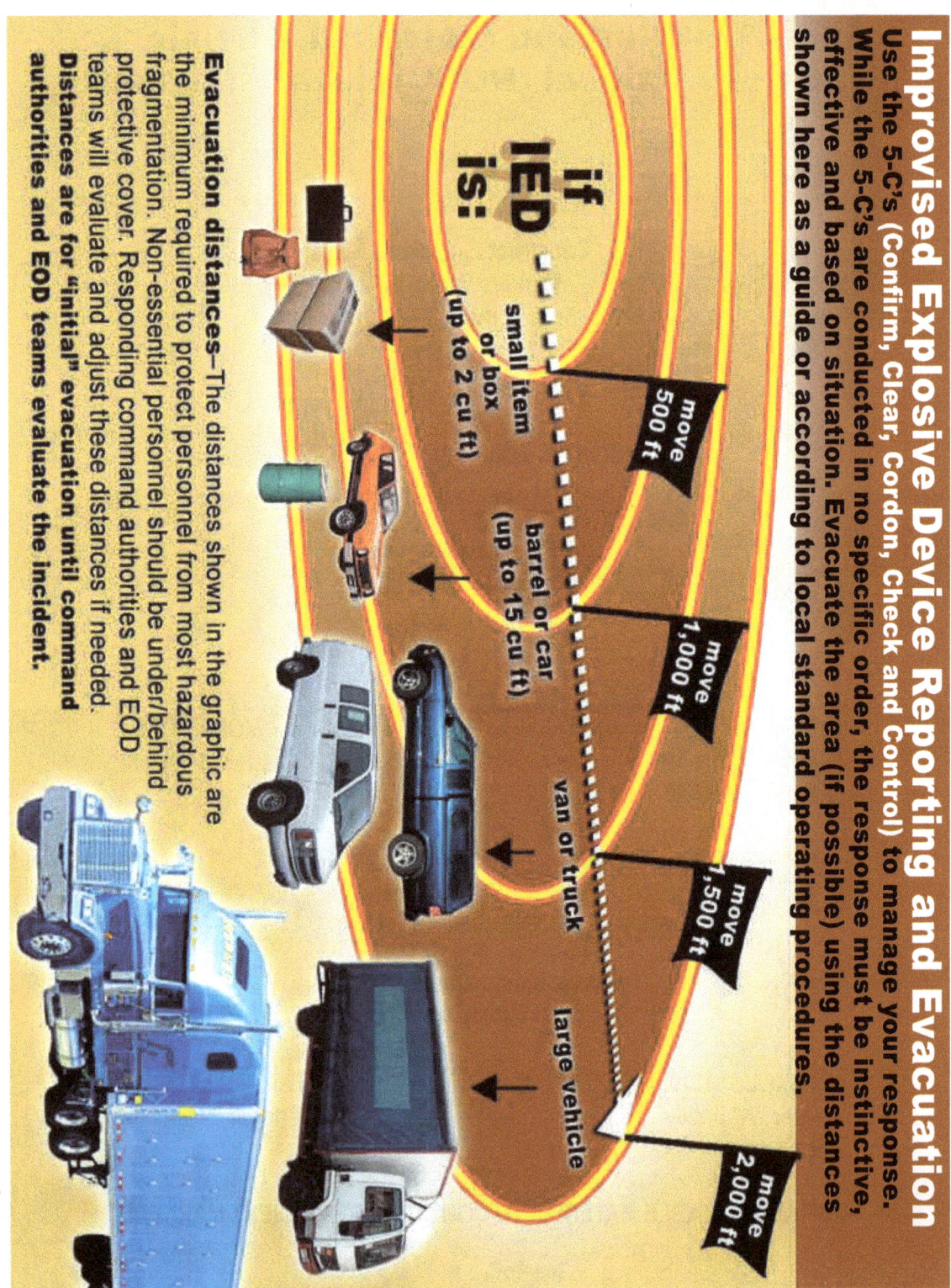

Improvised Explosive Device Reporting and Evacuation

Use the 5-C's (**C**onfirm, **C**lear, **C**ordon, **C**heck and **C**ontrol) to manage your response. While the 5-C's are conducted in no specific order, the response must be instinctive, effective and based on situation. Evacuate the area (if possible) using the distances shown here as a guide or according to local standard operating procedures.

if IED is:

- small item or box (up to 2 cu ft) — move 500 ft
- barrel or car (up to 15 cu ft) — move 1,000 ft
- van or truck — move 1,500 ft
- large vehicle — move 2,000 ft

Evacuation distances—The distances shown in the graphic are the minimum required to protect personnel from most hazardous fragmentation. Non-essential personnel should be under/behind protective cover. Responding command authorities and EOD teams will evaluate and adjust these distances if needed. Distances are for "initial" evacuation until command authorities and EOD teams evaluate the incident.

Serviceable Tag-Materiel, DD Form 1574

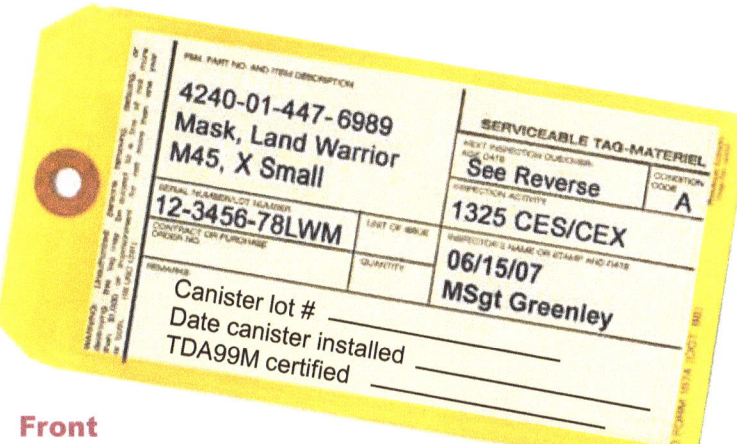

Masks will be cleaned and inspected:
- Use technical orders shown on the Quick Reference pages that follow for specific masks (pp.204-213)
- Obtain technical orders from your mask issue point
- Upon issue and every six months after initial issue date during peacetime
- Prior to deployment and every seven days during contingency operations.
- Before long term storage (30 days or more)
- Prior to turn-in to supply
- After completion of each training contingency/exercise

Front
- Stock number
- Mask type
- Size
- Mask lot number
- Inspection activity
- Inspector's name and date
- Fill-in remarks section when serviceable C2 series canister is Installed
    - Canister lot number
    - Date canister installed
    - TDA99M or JSMLT certified MMYY

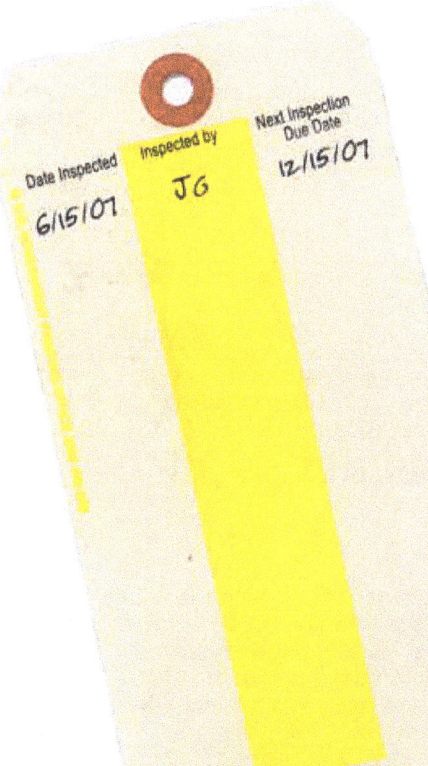

Rear
- Date inspected
- Inspected by
- Next inspection due date

MCU-2 Series Mask Inspection Ref: TO 14P4-15-1

ITEM	INSPECT FOR	CORRECTIVE ACTION
Facepiece	Cracks, tears, or deterioration and separation between silicone, rubber, and the metal parts.	Condemn Mask
Face seal	Cracks or tears. Run finger over seal to inspect for nicks or surface irregularities. Face seal must be soft, smooth, and pliable.	Condemn Mask
Forehead, Temple, and Neck Tabs	Nicks or rips, along edges, or where buckles connect. Run a finger around edges to check for discrepancies.	Condemn Mask
Buckles	Bends, cracks or looseness where molded into the facepiece tabs. Pull on head harness straps. Make sure the buckles hold the strap tight.	Condemn Mask
Head Harness or Skull Cap	Tears, surface dirt, or mildew. Pull straps to make sure they have not lost their elasticity.	Replace if straps are torn, broken, or have lost their elasticity.
Side Voicemitter Retaining Ring	Corrosion or looseness.	Replace if corroded. Tighten if loose.
Side Voicemitter	Dents, punctures, or cracks. The four pins in the center face toward the outside of mask.	Replace if dented, punctured, or cracked. Remove and correctly reinstall if four pins are not facing outwards.
Side Voicemitter Gasket	Cracks and cuts	Install a new side voicemitter gasket, if unserviceable, (e.g. cut, distorted or damaged)
Front Voicemitter Retaining Ring	Tightness using the tips of two fingers on the flat part of the ring WARNING: Do not attempt in any way to loosen front voicemitter ring during check for tightness.	Repair mask
Front Voicemitter	Punctures or cracks. (Damaged microphone connector assembly MCU-2 Series).	Repair mask
Outlet Valve Cover	Cracks, rips and general cleanliness inside and out.	Replace if cracked, ripped or if it will not seat firmly on outlet valve body. Wipe away any dirt or moisture on cover with a soft, dry, clean clot
Outlet Valve Disc and Valve Disc Body	Curls, nicks, rips, dirt or moisture. Turn disc to make sure it is not stuck to valve seat. Make sure outlet valve disc with supportive screen has been installed. Push cover back on outlet valve. Make sure cover is seated firmly.	Replace if curled, nicked, ripped, cannot be cleaned, or will not seat properly. Replace outlet valve disc with supportive screen, if required. Wipe away any dirt or moisture with a soft, dry, clean cloth.
Disbonding	Lift nose cup from around flange of the outlet valve assembly. Check for disbonding of silicone facepiece to metal outlet valve assembly.	Condemn mask if disbonding has occurred.

Component	Inspection	Action
Nosecup	Cracks or cuts, and that it is seated in outlet valve flange and securely held around the front voicemitter.	Condemn Mask if the nosecup is cracked, cut or loose at the voicemitter. If nosecup is not sealed around the outlet valve flange, push the nosecup back over the flange.
Valve Disc	Inspect for proper installation of valve seat or separation from the nosecup. Make sure valve discs are not cut or torn. Turn the disc with the tip of finger to make sure disc are not stuck on valve seats.	Replace valve discs that are curled, or torn.
External Drinking Tube	Cracked, cut or deteriorated rubber. Dented or cracked coupling. Loose on feed through pipe or at metal coupling. Check for stuck valve by performing drink tube leak check	Replace
Internal Drinking Tube	Cracks, cuts, and to see if it is lose on the feed-through pipe	Replace if cracked, cut or loose
Drink Tube Assembly	Perform drink tube leak test	Replace if required
Inlet Valve Disc	Curls or tears. Turn disc to make sure it is not stuck to valve seat. Make sure disc is properly installed on Air Deflector Post	Replace if curled or torn, install valve disc behind valve disc retaining ring.
Lens	Punctured lens. Stains or scratches that prevents normal vision. Any separation between the mask lens and facepiece	Condemn Mask
Canister	Cracks, dents, or holes around the seams, dirt clogging the air intake and for damaged threads. Any signs of loose particles in filter when shaken	Replace if cracked or dented on a seam, dented deeper than a 1/4 inch, if it has holes, threads are damaged, or air intake is clogged with dirt. Replace filter if signs of loose particles are present.
Carrier	Cleanliness, damage, excessive wear, missing straps or fasteners	Repair if possible or replace
Waterproofing bag	Damage	Replace if required
Outsert	Stains or scratches that prevents normal vision. Cracks, missing clips, or rubber straps	Replace the rubber strap if broken or missing.
Front Voicemitter/Micmitter Assembly	Broken, missing, damaged, loose, corroded, dirty, etc.	Repair mask
Body, Inlet Valve	Cracks, tears or deterioration, surface irregularities and dirt	Clean if dirty, replace if worn or cracked.

M45 Mask Inspection Ref: TO 14P4-18-1

ITEM	PROCEDURE	NOT FULLY MISSION CAPABLE IF:
Canister	Check that canister is securely attached to facepiece.	Filter canister cannot be securely attached to the facepiece.
Mask	Run finger under inner lip to make sure folded material doesn't stick together.	Inside surfaces are damaged or cannot be separated.
Internal Drink Tube and Microphone Assembly	Check that internal drink tube and microphone assembly (if issued) are present and securely attached to outlet valve housings.	Internal drink tube or microphone assembly are missing or loose
Nosecup Assembly	a. Check that nosecup is attached to front voicemitter and outlet valve housing. b. Run finger along inner lip of nosecup to ensure it is not sticking. c. Check that nosecup is not stuck to inside of facepiece. d. Check that nosecup valve disks are present and seated on nosecup valve seats, rotate discs to be sure they are not stuck, curled, or torn.	a. Nosecup is pulled away from voicemitter/outlet valve housing. b. Inside surfaces are damaged or cannot be separated. c. Nosecup cannot be separated from facepiece. d. Nosecup valve disks are missing or not seated on valve of nosecup valve seats. Disks are stuck, curled, or torn.
Inlet Valve Assembly	a. Fold back left side of nosecup to fully expose inlet valve assembly. Check that inlet valve disk is present and positions in the slot on the cage and post assembly. Check cage for cracks. b. Check inlet valve disk for tears and curls. Make sure disk lies flat c. Rotate inlet valve disk and cage and post assembly with finger. Make sure it lies flat and doesn't stick.	a. Inlet valve disk is missing or not positioned on the cage and post assembly. Cage is cracked, missing or not positioned on inlet valve gasket. b. Inlet valve disk has cuts, tears, curls or does not seal against inlet valve gasket. c. Inlet valve sticks.
Vision Correction Inserts	Ensure inserts are attached to facepiece (if issued.)	Inserts will not attach to facepiece.
Outserts	Check that outserts are installed and securely attached to facepiece.	Outserts are missing or will not attach securely to facepiece.
Microphone Cable	Check to see that microphone cable is attached securely to the receptacle on the facepiece (if issued.)	Microphone cable cannot be attached securely to facepiece, or cable is cut or cracked.
Second Skin	Check that second skin is present and properly installed.	Second skin is missing or installed incorrectly.
Outlet Valve Disk and Outlet Valve Cover	a. Grasp tab, pull and stretch bottom portion of outlet valve cover over the barb. Check that outlet valve disk is present and not curled, distorted, or dirty. b. With finger, rotate outlet valve disk to ensure it is not sticking. Replace outlet valve cover.	a. Outlet valve disk is missing, curled, distorted, or dirty. b. Outlet valve disk is sticking and cannot be rotated.

Item	Procedure	Not Fully Mission Capable If:
External Drink Tube	Check that external drink tube is present and securely attached.	External drink tube is missing or loose.
Waterproof Bag	a. Check waterproof bag for cracks, tears, holes or brittleness. b. Check that rubber bands are in bag and are not sticky, broken or brittle.	a. Waterproof bag is torn, has holes, or is brittle. b. Rubber bands are missing, or are sticky, broken, or brittle.
Mask	Don mask and check mask for leaks.	Mask leaks

AFTER USE

ITEM	PROCEDURE	NOT FULLY MISSION CAPABLE IF:
Canister	a. Check canister intake for clogs. b. Check canister replacement criteria.	a. Canister intake is clogged. b. Canister is expired.
Microphone Cable	a. Check microphone cable for cuts, cracks and bent pins (if issued.) b. Check that microphone cable is attached to the receptacle in the facepiece.	a. Microphone cable is cut, cracked or has bent pins. b. Microphone cable will not securely attach to the facepiece.
Second Skin	Inspect second skin for cracks, tears, and splits.	Second skin is cracked, torn or split.
External Drink Tube	a. Check external drink tube for cuts, cracks or holes. b. Check external drink tube for tight connection to the outlet valve housing and quick disconnect coupling.	a. External drink tube is missing, or has cuts, cracks or holes. b. External drink tube connection to outlet valve housing or quick disconnect coupling is loose.
Outlet Valve Disk and Outlet Valve Cover	a. Grasp tab, pull and lift bottom of outlet valve cover over barb. Check cover for cuts, holes, and tears. b. Check that outlet valve disk is seated and not curled, torn, dirty, punctured, or distorted. Rotate disk to ensure it is not sticking. c. Wipe moisture from outlet valve and seat with cheesecloth. d. Check outlet valve seat for dirt, nicks, or cracks. Smooth outlet valve disk so it lies flat on seat. e. Check that barb is not broken or cracked. f. Wipe moisture and dirt from outlet valve cover with cheesecloth and check for cuts, tears or holes. Reinstall cover.	a. Outlet valve cover is cut, torn, or punctured. b. Outlet valve disk is curled, sticking, punctured, dirty, distorted, torn, or will not seat. c. Outlet valve disk or seat cannot be cleaned. d. Outlet valve seat is nicked or cracked, or disk will not seat properly. e. Barb is cracked or broken. f. Outlet valve cover is cut, torn, has holes, or will not seat firmly over outlet valve.

WARNING: Do not use paper to remove moisture from outlet valve cover, outlet valve disk, or outlet valve seat. Paper may break up and lodge in outlet valve area causing leakage.

continued... M45 Mask Inspection Ref: TO 14P4-18-1

ITEM	PROCEDURE	NOT FULLY MISSION CAPABLE IF:
Voicemitters	Check front and side voicemitters for dirt, cracks, punctures or obstructions.	Voicemitters are dirty or damaged.
Head Harness	a. Check buckles for bends, cracks, or corrosion. Pull on head harness straps to ensure buckles hold straps. b. Put on facepiece and check head harness for loss of elasticity. c. Check for dirt. Check each strap for cuts, tears, missing parts or deterioration such as mildew or fraying.	a. Buckles are missing, broken, or will not hold straps. b. Head harness will not hold mask firmly against face. c. Head harness is dirty, cut, torn, frayed, has missing parts or is deteriorated.
Facepiece	Inspect facepiece for dirt, holes, tears and splits. Look closely at the inside of the facepiece where it touches your skin.	Mask has holes, tears, splits, or soft spots that allow air to enter.
Internal Drink Tube	a. Check internal drink tube for cuts, cracks or holes. b. Ensure that internal drink tube opening is oriented so you can drink with the mask on.	a. Internal drink tube has cuts, cracks or holes. b. Internal drink tube is oriented so that you cannot grasp it with your mouth.
Inlet Valve Assembly	a. Fold back left side of nosecup to fully expose inlet valve assembly. Check that inlet valve disk is present and properly positioned on cage and post assembly. b. Check inlet valve disk for tears, curls or dirt. Make sure inlet valve disk lies flat. c. From outside the mask, blow on inlet valve disk to ensure it isn't sticking. d. Check inlet valve cage and post assembly for distortion.	a. Inlet valve disk is missing or not positioned on the cage and post assembly. b. Inlet valve disk has tears, curls, or does not seat against inlet valve gasket. c. Inlet valve disk sticks. d. Inlet valve cage and post is damaged or won't rotate freely.
Nosecup	a. Check that nosecup is not pulled away from back of outlet valve housing and front voicemitter. b. Check that nosecup and nosecup valve seats are free of dirt. Check nosecup for cracks, cuts, tears and holes. Look at inside of nosecup inner lip where it touches your skin. c. Rotate nosecup valve disks to ensure they are not sticking. Check that valve disks are not dirty, curled or torn.	a. Nosecup is pulled away from back of outlet valve housing and front voicemitter. b. Nosecup is dirty, cracked, cut or has holes. Nosecup valve seats are dirty. c. Nosecup valve disks are torn, missing, dirty, or stuck to nosecup.

AFTER USE

Vision Correction Inserts	Inspect vision correction inserts (if issued) for loose or broken lenses, and frames that will not attach to facepiece.	Loose, broken or missing lens or frame. Insert frame disconnected from facepiece.
Outserts, Eyelens and Eyerings	a. Remove outserts by grasping tab and pulling away from mask. Check outserts for cracks, scratches or discoloration that affects vision. b. Check eyelens for cracks, scratches, dirt or stains that affect vision c. Check eyerings for cracks. Install outserts onto eyerings by snapping front edge into place first.	a. Outserts are broken, distorted, or discolored. b. Eyelenses are cracked, scratched or stained enough to affect vision. c. Eyerings are cracked.
Carrier	a. Empty carrier and check for dirt, tears, holes or missing buckles, d-rings, straps, strap hooks and hardware. Check seams for broken stitches. b. Ensure hook and pile fasteners hold carrier flap securely. Stow your mask.	a. Carrier is torn, seam stitching is loose, or buckles, d-rings, straps, or strap hooks are missing. b. Carrier flap will not stay closed.

M50 Mask Inspection
Ref: TO 14P4-20-1

ITEM	INSPECT FOR	NOT FULLY MISSION CAPABLE IF:
Mask Carrier	a. Fraying, tears or rips and damage to hook and pile fasteners. b. Visually inspect carrier waist strap, leg strap, and MOLLE attachment panel for fraying, tears or rips and damaged or missing hardware. c. Check for mildew, solvents, or abrasive materials that might harm mask assembly. Check seams for broken stitches.	a. Severely frayed, torn, or ripped or there is damage to the hook and pile fasteners b. Waist strap, leg strap or MOLLE attachment panel are severely frayed, torn, or ripped or attaching hardware is damaged or missing. c. Mildew, solvents, or abrasive materials are present. Seams are broken or stitching is loose.
Bag, Individual Equipment Carrier	a. Visually inspect bag for fraying, tears or rips. Inspect slide fastener and snaps for damage. b. Visually inspect AAL item hold-down straps in interior of bag for fraying, tears or rips. Ensure hold-down straps are secured to bag. c. Check for mildew, solvents, or abrasive materials that might harm AAL items. Check seams for broken stitches.	a. Severely frayed, torn, or ripped. Slide fastener or snaps damaged. b. Severely frayed, torn, or ripped or not secured to bag. c. Mildew, solvents, or abrasive materials are present. Seams are broken or stitching is loose.

Facepiece Assembly Exterior	a. Check to see that the following components are present:
	  Facepiece assembly with eyelens.
	  Head Harness buckles.
	  Head Harness.
	  Filters mounts, left and right with inlet disk valves, self-sealing disk valves and filter mount air deflectors.
	  Front module main body with outlet disk valve, drink tube lever, external drink tube and drink coupler.
	  Cover assembly, outlet valve with communications port cover.
	b. Visually inspect Serial Number and Lot on filter mount to ensure they are readable.
	c. Visually inspect Bar Code on filter mount for damage.
		a. Any components are missing or damaged.
		b. Not readable.
		c. Bar Code damaged.

Facepiece Assembly	a. Inspect facepiece assembly for holes, tears, and splits. Look closely at edges of mask assembly. Inspect for soft or sticky spots. Inspect for stiff areas that crumble when rubbed between fingers and for cracks that expand when rubber is stretched.	a. There are tears or holes in the facepiece. Facepiece has soft or sticky spots that allow air to enter mask assembly or stiff areas that crumble when rubbed between fingers and cracks that expand when rubber is stretched.

Component	Inspection Procedure	Defect Criteria
Facepiece Assembly (continued)	b. Visually inspect eyelens for cracks, cuts, scratches, or stains that affect vision. c. Pull head harness brow strap slots, head harness buckles and facepiece beard and visually inspect for rubber deterioration. d. Visually inspect bonding around the eyelens. e. Visually inspect head harness pivoting and ladder lock buckles for damage.	b. The eyelens is cracked or is scratched so as to impair vision. c. There are signs of rubber deterioration. d. Bonding around eyelens is not secure or appears to be coming loose. e. Buckles are broken or missing.
Head Harness	a. Visually inspect skullcap and stitching, head harness straps and brow strap covers. b. Inspect head harness for loss of elasticity. c. Pull on head harness straps and make sure buckles hold straps tight.	a. Skullcap is cut, ripped, or torn; stitching is loose or coming apart; brow strap covers are damaged. b. Head harness will not hold mask assembly firmly against face. c. Buckles will not hold straps.
Cover Assembly, Outlet Valve	a. Remove cover assembly, outlet valve and visually inspect for breaks or other damage. b. Inspect communications port cover for damage and ensure front cover baffle is in place and secure.	a. Cover is broken, cracked or otherwise damaged. b. Front cover baffle is damaged, loose, or missing.
Front Module	a. Remove cover assembly, outlet valve and visually inspect front module main body, communications port, drink tube lever, external drink tube, drink tube coupler and drink coupler receptacle for damage and/or missing parts. b. Remove outlet disk valve and visually inspect for damage or deterioration. c. Inspect valve seat and valve mounting post for damage. d. Turn drink tube lever upward to open drink system shut-off valve. Check drinking system by blowing into internal drink tube. Some resistance should be felt.	a. Front module main body is loose; communications port, drink tube lever, external drink tube and drink coupler are damaged or missing and/or drink coupler receptacle is damaged. b. Outlet disk valve is damaged and/or shows signs of deterioration. c. Valve seat is damaged and/or valve mounting post is broken. d. There in no resistance when blowing into the internal drink tube. Drink tube lever is hard to rotate or will not rotate.
Filter Mounts Left and Right	a. Remove primary filters from filter mounts and visually inspect filter mounts for tight fit and damage. b. Remove self-sealing disk valves and visually inspect for damage or deterioration. c. Inspect self-sealing valve seat and valve mounting post for damage. Remove filter mount air deflectors and Inlet valves from filter mounts inside the facepiece and visually inspect for damage or deterioration. Inspect inlet valve seat and valve mounting post for damage. (continued on next page)	a. Filter mounts left or right are loose or damaged. b. Self-sealing disk valve is damaged and/or shows signs of deterioration. c. Valve seats are damaged and/or valve mounting posts are broken. Filter mount air deflectors are damaged or show signs of deterioration. (continued on next page)

continued... M50 Mask Inspection Ref: TO 14P4-20-1

ITEM	INSPECT FOR	NOT FULLY MISSION CAPABLE IF:
Filter Mounts Left and Right	d. Reinstall inlet valves and filter mount air deflectors. Reinstall self-sealing disk valves and inspect for proper operation by pressing down firmly on center of valve. Disk valve should pop open and then close when pressure is removed. e. Install primary filters and check self-sealing disk valves for proper function.	d. Self-sealing disk valve does not operate properly. e. Self-sealing disk valves do not function properly.
Facepiece Assembly Interior	a. Check to see that the following components are present: Internal drink tube. Nosecup. Inlet disk valves, left and right. Filter mounts air deflectors.	a. Any components are missing or damaged.
Chin Cup and Beard	a. Visually inspect chin cup and beard for tears, holes, and signs of deterioration or other damage.	a. Chin cup or beard is torn, has holes or other damage and/or shows signs of deterioration.
Nosecup	a. Gently pull back chin cup and visually inspect nosecup for tears, holes, signs of deterioration or other damage.	a. Nosecup is torn, has holes or other damage and/or shows signs of deterioration.
Inlet Disk Valves, Left and Right	a. Gently pull back chin cup and pull filter mount air deflector away from filter mount clamp ring, left or right to expose inlet disk valve. Inspect the air deflectors for damage or deterioration. Remove inlet disk valve and visually inspect for damage and/or deterioration. b. Inspect valve seat and valve mounting post for damage. c. Reinstall inlet valves and air deflectors. Ensure filter mount air deflectors mount snugly over filter mount clamp rings, left and right.	a. Air deflectors are damaged or show signs of deterioration. Inlet disk valve is damaged and/or shows signs of deterioration. b. Valve seat is damaged and/or valve mounting post is broken. c. Air deflectors will not mount snugly over filter mount clamp rings, left and right.
Internal Drink Tube	a. Visually inspect internal drink tube for damage, and signs of deterioration. b. Ensure internal drink tube moves from stowed position to drink position by rotating the drink tube lever on the front module main body upward.	a. Internal drink tube is damaged or shows signs of deterioration. b. Drink tube does not move.
Primary NBC Filters	a. Remove and install primary NBC filters to check for proper attachment to filter mount. b. Check that primary filter seal is present.	a. Primary NBC filters do not properly attach to filter mount assemblies. b. Primary filter seal is missing.

Primary NBC Filters	c. Visually inspect primary filters for cracks, dents, or holes. Inspect air passages to ensure filter is not clogged with dirt. d. Visually inspect primary filters for alignment markings. e. Visually inspect primary filter base landing connectors and connector surface on filter mount assemblies for damage. f. Visually inspect primary filter self-sealing valve actuator for damage. g. Shake primary filters and listen for signs of loose absorbent particles. h. Inspect Primary NBC Filter Service Life Indicator. i. Visually inspect for filter Lot number.	c. Primary filter is cracked, dented, or damaged on a seam and/or filter air passages are clogged with dirt. d. Alignment markings worn or damaged. e. Primary filter base landing connectors are broken or otherwise damaged or filter mount assembly surface is damaged. f. Primary filter self-sealing valve actuator is damaged. g. Loose particles rattle or dust falls out when filter canister is shaken. h. Service Life Indicator color is dark blue. i. Filter Lot number not readable.
Sunlight Outsert	a. Inspect outsert lens for cracks, chips, or discoloration that affects vision. Inspect outsert-connecting points for tears, looseness, or cracks.	a. Outsert is broken, distorted, or discolored enough to impair vision. Connecting points are torn, cracked, or loose.
Cap, Water Canteen	a. Inspect canteen cap for dirt, damage and tight connection with drink coupler. b. Inspect canteen cap for missing, damaged, or deteriorating drink tube coupler "O" ring and internal canteen seal. c. Inspect drink tube coupler protective lid for damage and deterioration.	a. Canteen cap is damaged or does not make tight connection with drink coupler. b. "O" ring or canteen seal are missing, damaged, or show signs of deterioration. c. Drink tube coupler protective lid is damaged or shows signs of deterioration.
Facepiece Assembly Function	a. Don the M50 facepiece assembly with primary filters. b. Check to see that you are able to drink while wearing the mask. c. Check to see that you can see through the eyelens and outsert. d. Check for excessive breathing resistance.	a. Check the M50 facepiece assembly for leaks. Facepiece fails to seal. b. Unable to drink while wearing the mask. c. Unable to see through the eyelens or outsert. d. There is excessive breathing resistance.
Waterproof Bag	a. Inspect waterproof bag for cracks, tears, holes, and/or brittleness.	a. Waterproof bag is torn, has holes, or is brittle.

Chemical Protective Overgarment (CPO) and Accessory Inspection Checklist
Ref: TO 14P3-1-141

Caution: Do not remove overgarments (OG) from factory vacuum-sealed bags specifically for inspection.

ITEM	INSPECT FOR	CORRECTIVE ACTION
CPO Factory Bag	a. General Cleanliness b. Holes or tears c. Loss of vacuum seal (puffy bag) d. Labels	a. If dirty, wipe clean. b. If present, inspect visible fabric under hole or tear for damage and cleanliness. If undamaged and clean, seal hole or tear with high quality adhesive tape (e.g. common duct tape). When taping of the factory bag is impractical, place the CPO in the original factory bag, in a clear plastic bag and seal with tape. c. Tests have shown that loss of vacuum seal alone does not impact OG serviceability. Inspect for holes, tears, etc., if found, repair. d. Packages that have surveillance information labels in danger of falling off, remove the outer clear plastic bag and using an indelible marker, clearly print on the nylon foil package at a minimum, the following information: Contract number, last four digits of NSN, manufacture date, surveillance marking number and the garment size. Reseal foil package in the outer clear plastic bag.
Coat and Trouser	a. Signs of wetting (i.e. stains, deterioration, etc.) b. Holes or tears c. Cleanliness d. Fasteners proper operation e. Shelf life manufactured date	a. If present, condemn the item. Use for training or dispose of it b. If present, Use for training or dispose of it c. If dirty, wipe clean with a dry cloth d. Broken or torn fasteners that cannot be secured, will be condemned. Use for training or dispose of it e. If expired, condemn the CPO. Use for training or dispose of it
Protective Gloves	a. Factory bag cleanliness b. Holes or tears c. Glove material dry rot, brittleness, holes or tears d. Shelf life/manufacture date	a. If dirty, wipe clean b. If present, inspect glove material c. If present, condemn the item. Use for training or dispose of it d. If expired, condemn the item. Use for training or dispose of it

Glove Inserts	a. Factory bag cleanliness b. Holes or tears c. Cotton material condition	a. If dirty, wipe clean b. If present, inspect cotton material c. Dispose of inserts which are damaged to the point where they cannot be comfortably worn
Footwear cover	a. Factory bag cleanliness b. Factory Bag holes or tears c. Footwear cover material dry rot, brittleness, holes or tears d. Footwear cover material oily residue ("slimed" overboot) on unopened/unused overboots e. Laces and elastic fasteners (GVO/BVO) breaks f. Shelf life manufacture date	a. If dirty, wipe clean. b. If present, inspect footwear cover material and laces. c. If present, condemn the item. Use for training or dispose of it. d. If present, suspend the item. Submit a product deficiency report IAW AFTO 00-35D-54. DSCP will authorize one-for-one replacement. e. Replace the laces or elastic fasteners. f. If expired condemn the item. Use for training or dispose of it.

Quick MOPP

Aircrew

MOPP Level	Field Gear	Overgarment	Mask/Hood	Gloves	Footwear/Overcape
0	Worn	Carried	Carried	Carried	Carried
1	Worn	Worn	Carried	Carried	Carried
2	Worn	Worn	Carried	Carried	Carried
3	Carried	Worn	Worn	Carried	Carried
4	Carried	Worn	Worn	Worn	As Required

Groundcrew

MOPP Level	Field Gear	Overgarment	Footwear	Mask/Hood	Gloves
0	Worn	Carried	Carried	Carried	Carried
1	Worn	Worn	Carried	Carried	Carried
2	Worn	Worn	Worn	Carried	Carried
3	Worn	Worn	Worn	Worn	Carried
4	Worn	Worn	Worn	Worn	Worn

Work Rest Cycles and Fluid Replacement Guidelines

Heat Category	WBGT[1] Index (°F)	Light (Easy) Work		Moderate Work		Hard (Heavy) Work	
		Work/Rest[2]	Water Intake[3] (Qt/Hour)	Work/Rest[2]	Water Intake[3] (Qt/Hour)	Work/Rest[2]	Water Intake[3] (Qt/Hour)
1	78-81.9	NL[4]	1/2	NL	3/4	40/20 min	3/4
2	82-84.9	NL	1/2	50/10min	3/4	30/30 min	1
3	85-87.9	NL	3/4	40/20min	3/4	30/30min	1
4	88-89.9	NL	3/4	30/30min	3/4	20/40min	1
5	>90	50/10mm	1	20/40min	1	10/50min	1

Notes:
1. If wearing MOPP Level 4, add 10°F to Wet Bulb Globe Temperature (WBGT). If wearing personal body armor in humid climates, add 5°F to WBGT.
2. Rest means minimal physical activity (sitting or standing), accomplished in shade if possible.
3. **Caution:** Daily fluid intake should not exceed 12 quarts. Hourly fluid intake should not exceed 1 quart. The work/rest time and fluid replacement volumes will sustain performance and hydration for at least 4 hours of work in the specified work category. Individual water needs will vary = 1/4 quart hour.
4. NL = no limit to work time per hour.

Work Intensities of Military Tasks

Light (Easy) Work
- Weapons maintenance
- Walking on hard surface at 2.5 mph, with <30 pound load
- Marksmanship training
- Tower operations
- Operations NCOs/officers
- Pilot ground activities
- Command post and unit control center activities

Moderate Work
- Walking on loose sand at 2.5 mph, with no load
- Walking on hard surface at 3.5 mph <40 pound load
- Calisthenics
- Patrolling
- Individual movement techniques such as low/high crawl
- Refueling
- Avionics shop
- Aircraft maintenance
- Unit post attack reconnaissance

Heavy (Hard) Work
- Walking on hard surface at 3.5 mph, with >40 pound load
- Walking on loose sand at 2.5 mph, with any load
- Armament crew
- Heavy aircraft repair
- Specialized teams such as CBRN reconnaissance, search and recovery, rapid runway repair, CCA, fire protection, decontamination, medical, damage assessment and repair, and EOD

Square Grid Matrix

Outside border letter/number combinations identify anticipated response symbol

	1	2	3	4	5	6	7	8	
H	T	7	Z	E	C	N	I	V	H
G	9	A	4	1	J	A	G	I	G
F	N	L	M	8	Y	E	Q	E	F
E	E	L	K	A	R	H	N	L	E
D	U	E	Y	S	R	6	2	S	D
C	E	N	E	7	E	A	X	K	C
B	C	P	O	3	T	6	P	I	B
A	M	R	I	E	R	E	I	R	A
	1	2	3	4	5	6	7	8	

Given E2 or 2E. Answer = L

Given D8 or 8D. Answer = S

Very secure method that's often used during MOPP conditions when visual identity is difficult

AFPAM 10-100 / 1 March 2009

AFPAM 10-100 / 1 March 2009

218 / Section 6 / Quick Reference

Reading a Grid Map Ref AFJMAN 24-306

- Grid maps help you find and report locations
- Grid maps contain intersecting horizontal and vertical lines that form square box grids
- Grid numbers run left-to-right
- Grid letters run bottom-to-top
- The combined grid number and letter is the grid coordinate
- Grid maps are read "right-up"
- **This is grid coordinate 2-B**
- Identify grids using a number and letter combination (in that order)
- Write it as shown here or say grid coordinate "two, bravo"

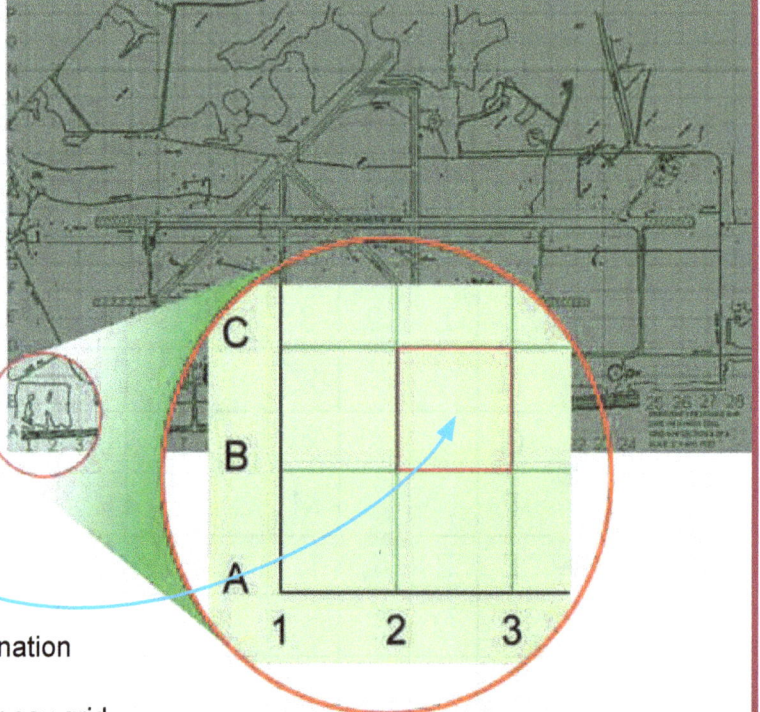

- For improved accuracy, grid squares are further subdivided into 10 evenly spaced blocks
- **This example shows grid coordinate 2.2-B.5**
- Write it as shown here or say grid coordinate "two point two - bravo point five"

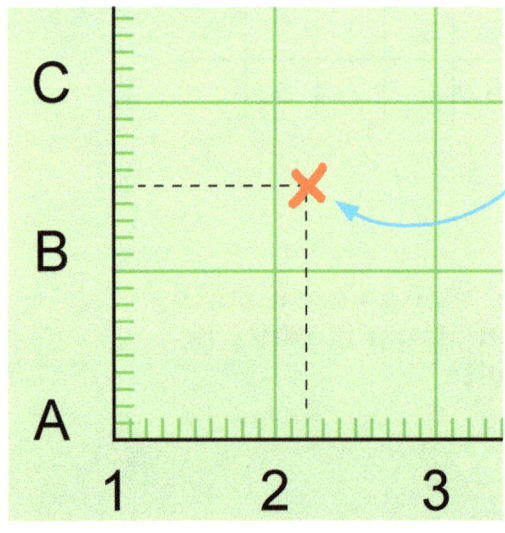

NOTE: Sub-blocks may or may not be marked on your map. If they're not, use your best judgment to identify the coordinate you want to plot within a grid square.

Chemical Warfare: Four Major Categories of Agents Ref: AFTTP(I) 3-2.55

Category	Agent	General Symptoms	Personal Protection
Nerve and Blister agents present the most significant hazards to an air base because of their high toxicity at low-levels of exposure.			
Nerve	VX GA (Tabun) GB (Sarin) GD (Soman) GF (Cylcosarin)	Designed to attack the nervous system–runny nose, tightness of the chest, breathing difficulty, eye pain, dimness of vision, pinpointing of pupils, drooling, excessive sweating, nausea, vomiting, diarrhea, cramps, twitching of large muscle groups, headache, confusion, drowsiness, involuntary defecation and urination, cessation of breathing, loss of consciousness, coma and death.	MOPP-4 when operating in proximity of either a liquid or vapor hazard. All clothing should be immediately decontaminated after coming into contact with liquid agent.
Blister	H & HD (Distilled Mustard) L (Lewisite) CX (Phosgene Oxime)	Primary hazard is to incapacitate, but it can be lethal in high enough doses–tearing, conjunctivitis, ulceration of exposed eye surfaces, lung inflammation accompanied by fluid accumulation in irritated tissues, impairment of respiratory gas exchange, blistering action on the skin.	MOPP-4 when operating in proximity of either a liquid or vapor hazard. All clothing should be immediately decontaminated after coming into contact with liquid agent.
Blood and Choking agents do not produce long-term threats to an air base. However, unprotected exposure to high enough quantities of these agents can cause death.			
Blood	AC (Hydrogen Cyanide) CK (Cyanogen Chloride) SA (Arsine)	Headache, dizziness, and nausea, which can progress to coma, convulsions, and cessation of breathing.	MOPP-4 when operating in proximity of either a liquid or vapor hazard.
Choking	CG (Phosgene) DP (Diphosgene)	Coughing, choking, and tightness of the chest as well as occasional nausea, vomiting, headache, and tearing. Difficulty in breathing and a diminished lung oxygen exchange become evident as fluids accumulate in lungs.	MOPP-4 when operating in proximity of either a liquid or vapor hazard.

Acronyms Used in This Manual

ADC	Area Defense Counsel (US military public defender)
AFOSI	Air Force Office of Special Investigations
AFTTP	Air Force Tactics, Techniques and Procedures
ATNAA	Antidote treatment, nerve agent, auto injector
BDOC	Base Defense Operations Center
BDU	Battle Dress Uniform
C2	command and control
CANA	convulscant antidote for nerve agent
CAT	crisis action team, combat application tourniquet
CBRN	Caribbean Basin Radar Network; chemical, biological,
CBRNE	chemical, biological, radiological, nuclear, and high yield
CCA	contamination control area;
CCP	casualty collection point
CHA	contact hazard area
CLP	cleaner, lubricant, and preservative
COA	course of action
CPO	chemical protective overgarment
DEET	N,N-Diethyl-meta-Toluamide (insect repellent)
DFP	defensive fighting position
ECC	Emergency Communications Center
EMP	electromagnetic pulse
EOC	early operational capability; emergency operations center
EOD	explosive ordnance disposal
EOR	Explosive Ordnance Reconnaissance
EPW	enemy prisoner of war
ESF	Economic Support Fund; emergency support function
FP	force protection
FPCON	Force Protection Condition
HAS	hardened air shelter
HAZMAT	hazardous materials

HVAC	heating, ventilation, and air conditioning
IBD	integrated base defense
IED	improvised explosive device
IPE	Individual Protective Equipment
JA	judge advocate
JFIRE	Joint Fire Integrated Response Ensemble
LAW	light anti tank weapon; lubricating oil, arctic weapons
LOAC	law of armed conflict
LSA	lubricating oil weapons semi-fluid
MOPP	mission-oriented protective posture
MULO	Multipurpose Lightweight Overboot
MWD	military working dog
NBC	nuclear, biological, and chemical
NBCC	nuclear, biological, chemical, and conventional
OCONUS	outside the continental United States
OG	overgarment
OPSEC	operations security
OPSTEMPO	Operations Tempo
OPTEMPO	Operating/Operations Tempo
OSI	Office of Special Investigations
PA	physician assistant; probability of arrival; public affairs
PAR	Post Attack Reconnaissance
PDA	Preliminary Damage Assessment, personal digital assistant
PDF	Personnel Deployment Function
POA	Power of Attorney
RDD	radiological dispersal device; required delivery date
ROE	rules of engagement
RST	Readiness Support Team
RST	religious support team
SABC	Self Aid Buddy Care
SALUTE	size, activity, location, unit, time, equipment
SOFA	status-of-forces agreement
SSCRA	Soldiers and Sailors Civil Relief Act

TFA	toxic free area
TIC	target information center; toxic industrial chemicals
TIM	toxic industrial material
TIR	toxic industrial radiologicals
UCC	Unit Control Center
UCMJ	Uniform Code of Military Justice
UGR	Unitized Group Ration
USERRA	Uniformed Services Employment and Re-employment Rights Act
UXO	unexploded explosive ordnance; unexploded ordnance
VHA	Vapor hazard area

Index

AFOSI ....9, 14, 36 ,37, 54, 68, CR27
Alarm Black 124
Alarm Blue...........................18, 88, 89
Alarm Green 73, 74
Alarm Yellow........................75, 76
Alarm Red............................18, 74, 88, 89
Ambush 40, 97
Animals................................44, 141
Anthrax 142
Arrival Actions.....................34, 36
Atropine 145, 146, CR12
Autoinjector.........................145, 146, CR10, CR12
Biological 158, 163, 166, 171
Blackout...............................37, 58, 59
Blister Agent 133, 136, 147, 219
BVO 215
C2 Canister.........................19, 23, 65, 203
Camouflage 58, 59, 61
Cargo Pallet........................36, 53, 64, 103, 116
Chem/Bio............................57, 58, 113, 125, 163, CR1
CCA 22, 37, 74, 131, 132, 157, 161, 170, 216
CCP 173, 174, 183, 187, CR1, CR17
Chaplain 4, 34, 46
Cold 5, 28, 42, 146, 152, 158, 162, 163, 180, 185
Communications..................35, 37, 67, 75, 97, 195, 196, 210, 211
COMSEC.............................67
Contaminated Waste 37, 51, 52, 62, 64, 74, 94, 113, 125, 172
Contamination Avoidance.....37, 51, 62, 64, 73-76, 124, 144, 147
Convoy 40, 96, 97

Cordon................................71, 80, 129, 143, CR3
CPO 19, 20, 21, 22, 24, 25-27, 155, 156, 157, 160, 161, 164, 214
Decon 31, 51, 63, 73, 74, 94-95, 113, 132, 144, 147, 168, 171, 172, CR17
DEET 44
Defectors 85
DFP 60, 61
Diazepam 146, CR11, CR12
Dispersal............................37, 58, 66, 73, 139
Drinking through Mask.........168
EOD....................................34, 128, 129, 216
EPW 12, 85, 86
Finance...............................2, 4, 9, 34
Fire 25, 26, 34, 36, 37, 47, 48, 49, 50, 51, 55, 56, 60, 61, 88, 96, 97, 99, 102, 104, 105, 106, 107, 108, 115, 118, 119, 120, 149, 151, 176, 196, 216, CR1, CR16, CR18, CR25, CR26, CR27
Flags...................................18, 87, 88, 89, 124
Flares..................................93
FPCON 8, 17, 34, 36, 65, 88
Geneva Convention..............85, 188, 189
Grid Map.............................218
GVO....................................215
HAZMAT 149
Heat....................................27, 29, 42, 48, 49, 55, 56, 95, 137, 138, 180, 181, 183, 184, 216, CR8

Term	Pages
Human Remains	173, 187
HVAC	62, 75, 149, 150, 151, CR14, CR15, CR16
Hydration	36, 168, 216
Hygiene	5, 43, 140, 142
IBD	78, 79
IED	38, 39, 40, 41, 69, 97
Insects	44, 50, 51
IPE	8, 19, 23, 28, 29, 35, 36, 42, 57, 73, 74, 75, 85, 90, 95, 108, 131, 144, 145, 147, 170
JFIRE	19, 24, 25, 26, 27
Legal	2, 3, 4, 9, 16, 35
LOAC	10, 11, 12, 16
M16	111, CR25
M295	28, 51, 94, 113, 125, 147, 168, 170, 171, 172, 174
M45 Mask	19, 20, 158, 159, 160, 161, 163, 206, 208
M8	19, 28, 31, 51, 60, 62, 62, 63, 64, 73, 74, 94, 124, 125, 133, 134, 135, CR1
M9 Pistol	111, 115, 116, 122, CR26
M9 Paper (Tape)	19, 22, 24, 28, 31, 36, 51, 74, 125, 136
Mark 1 Kit	146, CR12
Marking	22, 23, 36, 52, 94, 125, 214
MCU-2 Series Mask	19, 20, 152, 153, 155, 157, 163, 204
Media	13, 14
Medical	4, 8, 9, 12, 34, 35, 37, 42, 43, 44, 46, 65, 131, 140, 141, 143, 144, 145, 147, 148, 173, 175, 176, 180, 181, 182, 183, 184, 185, 188, 190, 216, CR11, CR18, CR20, CR27
Mobility Bag	8, 34, 35
MOPP 0	73-76
MOPP 1	24, 75
MOPP 2	75
MOPP 3	75
MOPP 4	27, 31, 75, 84, 89, 124, 144, 147, 219
MOPP Options	29
MULO	21
NBC	28, 52, 89, 95, 125, 212, 213
Nerve Agent	28, 36, 133, 144, 145, 146, 174
Nuclear	23, 55, 56, 137, 138, 139, CR8
OPSEC	14, 92
Permethrin	44
Public Affairs	14, 15
Plague	142
POW	188, 189, 190, 191
PROWORDS	195
Readiness	8
Recon	124
Roadblock	97
ROE	10, 89
SABC	37, 74, 124, 173, 174, 180, CR1, CR9, CR13
Safety	31, 32, 34, 36, 47, 50, 93, 119, 120, 145, CR10, CR12, CR26
S-A-L-U-T-E	83, 89, 91, 96, 97, CR1
Search	72, 85, 216
Security Forces	36, 37, 54, 67, 68, 72, 80, 82, 84, 85, 88, 89, 151, CR16, CR27

Second Skin 19, 36, 152, 158, 164, 165, 206, 207
Services 3, 23, 34, 35, 37, 53, 66, 76, 141, 180, CR16
Shelter 37, 66, 74, 75, 76, 87, 90, 94, 124, 124, 128, 131, 137, 148, 149, 173, CR8, CR13, CR14, CR15, CR16, CR27
Smallpox 142
Split-MOPP 30, 66, 73, 87, 88, 174
Supply 4, 5, 35, 44, 152, 158, 203
Take Cover 88, 94, 149, CR13
Tent 37, 48, 50, 173
Terrorist 17, 38, 68, 71, 141
TFA 132
Threat 8, 17, 28, 30, 38, 41, 57, 58, 59, 60, 64, 67, 68, 70, 73, 78-80, 142, 143, 150, 163, 173
TIM 148
UCC 25, 26, 30, 31, 37, 66, 68, 73, 74, 82, 83, 86, 89, 94-97, 124, 125, 127, 129, 133, 170, 174, CR1-3, CR14, CR16, CR17, CR27
UCMJ 16
UXO 36, 74, 124, 126-128, 129, CR1, CR2, CR3, CR4, CR5-7
Waste 37, 50, 51, 52, 62, 64, 74, 94, 125, 172

NOTES  #2 pencil works best

NOTES

CRITICAL

NOTES

#2 pencil works best

Important Phone Numbers and Quick Reference

	Phone #	Building #
UCC		
Alternate UCC		
ICC		
Command Post		
EOC		
Work Center		
Security Forces		
AFOSI		
Fire, 911 or different		
Casualty Collection Point		
Medical Clinic		
My Shelter		
Alternate Shelter		
Billeting		

Bed # _____

Radio Call Signs–My Call Sign: _____
_____
_____

Dining Facility: Phone # _____ Bldg # _____
Operating Hours: Breakfast _____
              Lunch _____
              Dinner _____
              Midnight _____

CRITICAL

PHONE

M9 Jammed

CRITICAL

- Reload weapon
- Select Semi
- Fire

M9 Procedures:
(If weapon fails to fire)
- Ensure decocking /safety lever is in the fire position (up)
- Smack upward on bottom of magazine to ensure it is fully seated
- Rack the slide to the rear and release
- Fire

M9 Remedial Action Procedures:
(If above actions do not correct problem)
- Remove magazine
- Eject chambered round
- Insert new magazine
- Rack slide to rear and release to chamber new round
- Attempt to fire
- If pistol still does not fire, replace ammunition

M16A2 Procedures:
(If the weapon fails to fire)
- **S**lap upward on bottom of magazine to ensure magazine is fully seated
- **P**ull charging handle to rear
- **O**bserve to see if a round or cartridge casing was ejected and chamber/receiver area are clear (proceed to remedial action if chamber isn't clear)
- **R**elease charging handle (allow bolt to slam forward)
- **T**ap forward assist button to ensure bolt is fully forward
- **S**hoot

M16A2 Remedial Action:
(If above actions do not correct problem, or an obstruction is found)
- Clear weapon
- Check again for jammed cartridge case. NOTE: Inspect closely... a ruptured cartridge case can be difficult to see
- If cartridge case is detected, use a cleaning rod to remove

M16 Jammed

CRITICAL

die cut around tab

24 Common Injury

CRITICAL

Fracture Symptoms:
- Deformity, bruising
- Tenderness over specific part of body
- Swelling/discoloration

Treatment:
- DO NOT straighten limb
- If in doubt, splint injury where they lie (if possible)
- Splint joints above and below injury
- Remove clothing from injured area
- Remove rings from fingers (if possible)
- Check pulse below injury–away from heart to determine if blood flow is restricted

Eye Injury Treatment:
- DO NOT remove impaled objects
- Secure objects with clean dressing
- Apply bandage lightly to BOTH eyes
- DO NOT leave casualty unattended

Chest Wound Symptoms:
- Sucking noise from chest
- Frothy red blood from wound

Treatment:
- Look for entry and exit wound
- Cover holes with airtight seal (tin foil, ID card)
- Tape down seal on 4 sides
- Let casualty assume position for easiest breathing (preferably on affected side)

CRITICAL

Common Injury

22 Common Injury

CRITICAL

Common Injury Treatment

Spinal/Neck/Head Injury Symptoms:
- Lack of feeling and/or control anywhere below neck, drainage of fluid or blood from ear, nose, or mouth

Treatment:
- If conscious, caution casualty not to move
- Continuously monitor and check airway without turning casualty's head
- Immobilize head and neck
- If casualty must be moved:
  - Use hard surface for litter (door, cut lumber, other)
  - Use as many people as needed to place casualty on litter
  - Immobilize head and neck
- Ensure casualty's limbs are secured at chest and thigh regions
- Turn/rotate whole body as a unit

DO NOT Bend Spinal Cord
DO NOT Rotate Head and Neck

Abdominal Wound Treatment:
- If organs are outside body, gently pick them up and place them on top of abdomen—do not replace or push organs into body
- Cover exposed organs with moist clean dressing
- Secure with bandages
- If legs are not fractured bend knees to relieve pressure

Abdominal Wound

CRITICAL

Shock

CRITICAL

Shock Symptoms:
- Confusion
- Sweaty but cool skin (clammy skin)
- Shallow, labored-and-rapid breath
- Weak-rapid pulse

Shock Treatment:
- Keep airway open
- If unconscious, place on side in recovery position, monitor airway
- Keep person calm, warm, and comfortable
- Elevate lower extremities
- Seek medical attention
- Do not give food or drink

How to Apply a Tourniquet:

1. Place one inch wide constricting band around arm or leg
2. DO NOT use wire or shoestrings
3. Place band 2-4 inches above injury
4. Tighten band only enough to stop bleeding
5. Do not loosen or remove
6. Leave tourniquet area exposed
7. Mark time and letter "T" on casualty's forehead (ink or blood)

NOTES:

- Do not remove old dressings; add more dressing over old if needed
- Do not remove a tourniquet once applied at risk of losing limb

CRITICAL

Tourniquet

18 Control Bleeding

CRITICAL

Conventional:
1. Apply direct pressure with hand: use a dressing if available
2. Elevate the extremity if no fractures are suspected
3. Use pressure points with elevation to control bleeding
4. Use tourniquet as last resort
5. Consider using QuikClot

Care Under Fire:
1. Return fire then provide medical treatment
2. **Functioning Casualty:**
   A) Return fire
   B) Move to cover
   C) Administer self-aid
3. **Non-Functioning Casualty:**
   A) Do Not move until enemy fire is suppressed
4. Life-threatening bleeding from a limb - apply a tourniquet
5. Life-threatening bleeding from another location (Armpit or Groin) - consider QuikClot and direct pressure

Lifesaving Steps

Perform Self-Aid and Buddy Care
- Open **Airway** (possible neck injury, use jaw thrust maneuver, DO NOT turn head)
- Ensure **Breathing**
- Support **Circulation** (stop bleeding) immobilize neck injuries
- Prevent further **Disability** (place dressings over open wounds and splint obvious limb deformities)
- Minimize further **Exposure** to adverse weather

For Chemical Environment Casualty
- Place mask on casualty
- Decon casualty as needed using casualty's decon kits
- Report casualty to UCC
- Ambulances DO NOT run during/following attacks
- Follow UCC instructions for transport to CCP
- Watch for chemical agent symptoms

CRITICAL

Life Saving

16 Shelter In-Place

CRITICAL

Inside hazard while you're inside the building (same as outdoor hazard while you're outside a building plus...)
- Turn off:
  - HVAC
  - Fans and exhaust fan(s)
  - Combustion heaters
- Report incident to Fire Services or Security Forces
- Close and seal doors and windows to contain hazard
- Secure classified material
- Evacuate upwind or crosswind
- Notify UCC

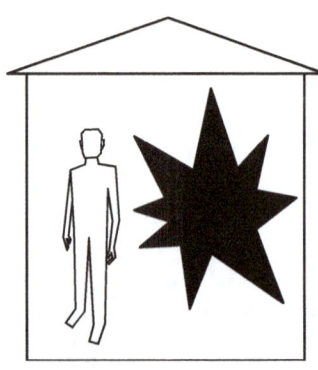

Outdoor Hazard While You're Inside an Expeditionary or Temporary Structure
- Operate HVAC systems including window units in closed or recirculation mode
- If a release warning is provided, follow previous guidelines

If you're aboard an aircraft:
- Aircrew actions (before or after taxiing) include closing hatches, windows, and using oxygen masks (if available)
- Passengers might evacuate aircraft as required by situation

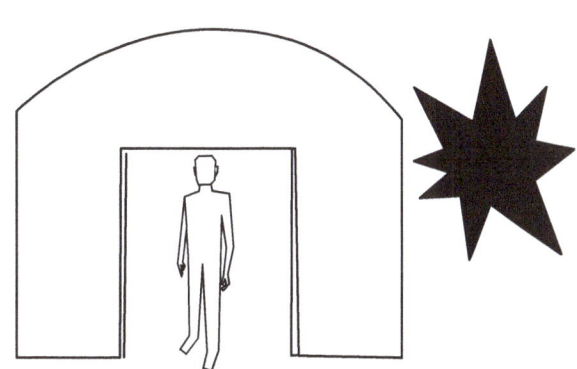

Shelter In-Place

CRITICAL

14 Shelter In-Place

CRITICAL

Outdoor Hazard While You're Inside a Building (same as outdoor hazard while you're outside a building plus...)

- Turn off:
  - HVAC
  - Fans and exhaust fan(s)
  - Combustion heaters
- Secure classified material
- Move to a central safe room or area or evacuate upwind or crosswind (if directed)
- Notify UCC after hazard passes
- Purge and ventilate buildings when directed:
  - Open windows and doors
  - Turn-on smoke and exhaust fans
  - Turn-on HVAC air handlers and fans

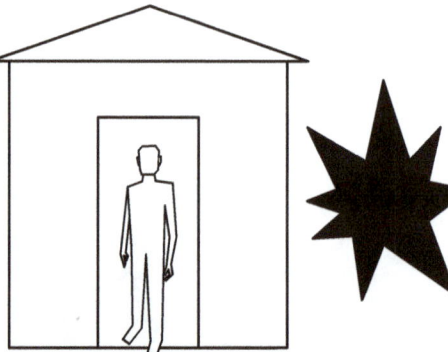

Shelter In-Place Actions

Outdoor Hazard While You're Outside a Building
- Take cover
- Notify others
- Don protective equipment
- Report the hazard
- Perform SABC
- Seek nearest building or safest area
- Shelter-in-place until otherwise directed
- Follow shelter or facility manager instructions

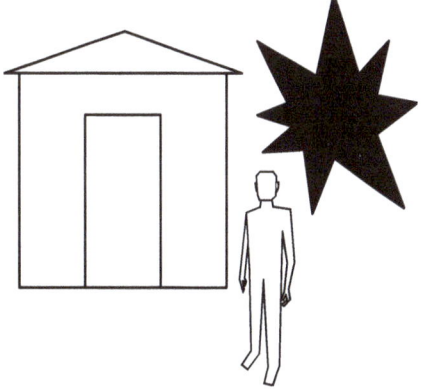

Shelter In-Place

CRITICAL

[12] Nerve Agent

CRITICAL

WARNING: DO NOT use more than three ATNAA. Use Diazepam ONLY after all three ATNAA have been administered.

Mark 1 kit:
1. Remove one atropine autoinjector
2. Remove safety cap
3. Place needle end of injector on injector site
4. Press firmly until needle triggers
5. Hold In place for 10 seconds
6. Remove injector
7. Follow steps 2-6 with one 2-PAM chloride autoinjector (large injector)
8. Bend needles to form a hook
9. Hang injectors from your or casualty's pocket

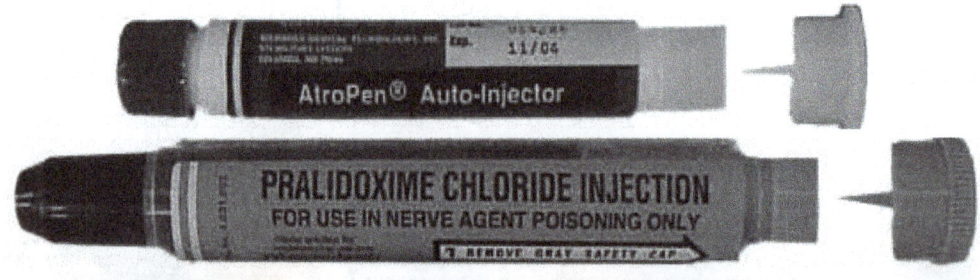

6. Remove injector
7. Bend needle to form a hook
8. Hang injector from your or casualty's pocket

WARNING: DO NOT inject second ATNAA if within 5-10 minutes:
- Heart beats very quickly
- Mouth becomes dry

MILD SYMPTOMS: If mild symptoms persist AFTER 10-15 MINUTES, inject second ATNAA (use buddy) seek medical help

SEVERE SYMPTOMS: Administer ALL THREE ATNAA followed by Diazepam injector to prevent convulsions–DO NOT WAIT between injecting ATNAA

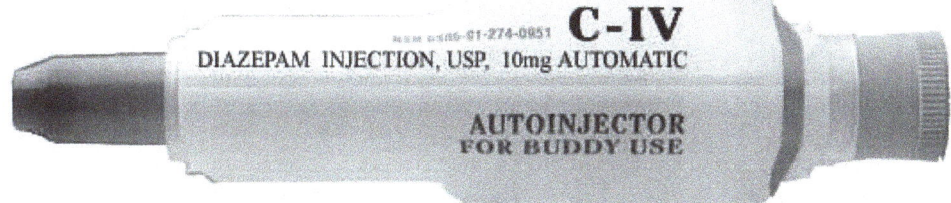

CRITICAL

Nerve Agent

10 Nerve Agent

CRITICAL

NERVE AGENT POISONING AND ANTIDOTE

Self Administer or Administer for Casualty (Use casualty's antidote on casualty–not yours!)

1. Don mask (place mask on casualty)
2. Observe for SYMPTOMS
   - Dimming vision
   - Pinpoint pupils
   - Unconsciousness
   - Muscles twitching
   - Sweating
   - Runny nose
   - Diarrhea
   - Seizures

When Symptoms are Present:

1. Remove one ATNAA autoinjector

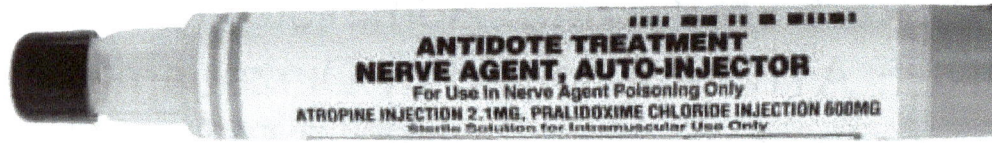

2. Remove safety cap
3. Place needle end of injector on injector site
4. Press firmly until needle triggers
5. Hold In place for 10 seconds

FOLLOW-ON ACTIONS

- Stay under cover until directed otherwise
- Perform SABC
- Perform post-attack recon when released
- Decon yourself
  - Brush dust/fallout off clothing
  - Blot away with adhesive tape
  - Rinse exposed skin
- Limit radiation exposure by using:
  - Time
  - Distance
  - Shielding

⁸ NUC Attack

CRITICAL

Nuclear Attack/ Radioactive Individual Protective Actions

INITIAL ACTIONS

Advanced warning:
- Find shelter that provides greatest protection
- Use window barriers and shielding to improve protection
- Upon seeing nuclear flash, seek protection from blast wave, heat, and flying debris

If a detonation occurs without warning:
- Drop to a prone position
- Cover eyes and face
- DO NOT move until initial and any reflected blast waves pass

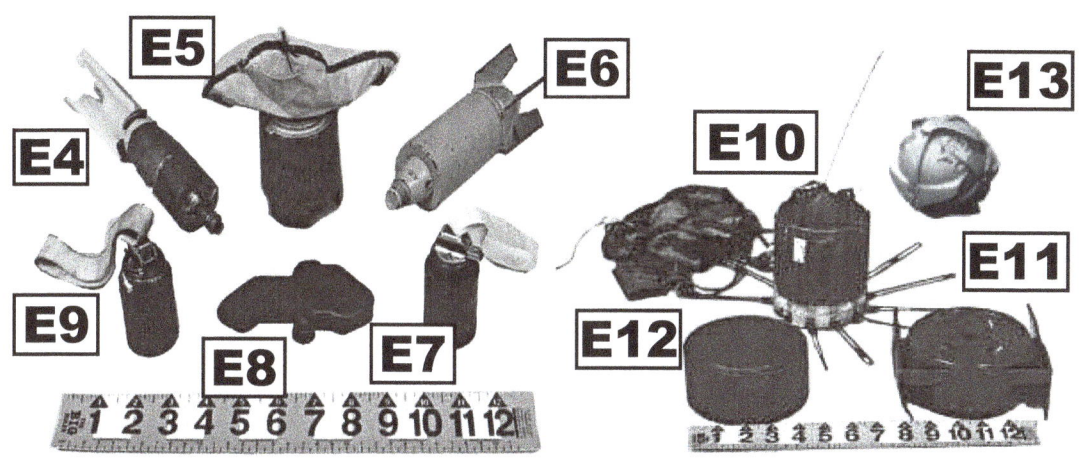

Class F: Rocket Propelled Grenades, Grenades

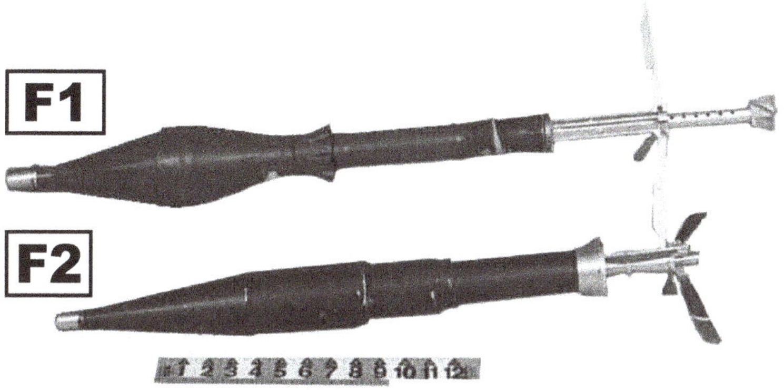

RPGs

GRENADES

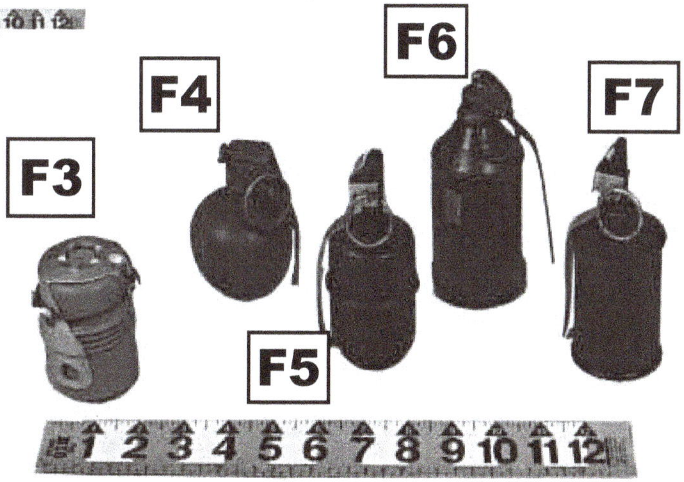

UXO Chart 7

CRITICAL
die cut around tab

⁶ UXO Chart

CRITICAL

MORTARS

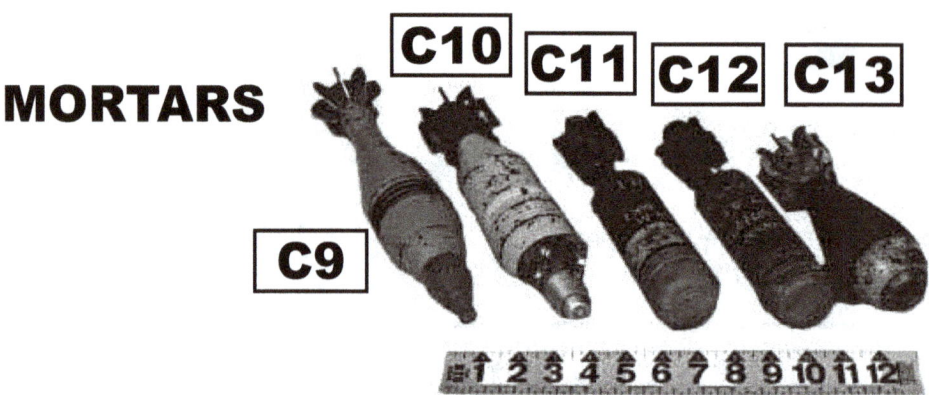

Class D: Landmines

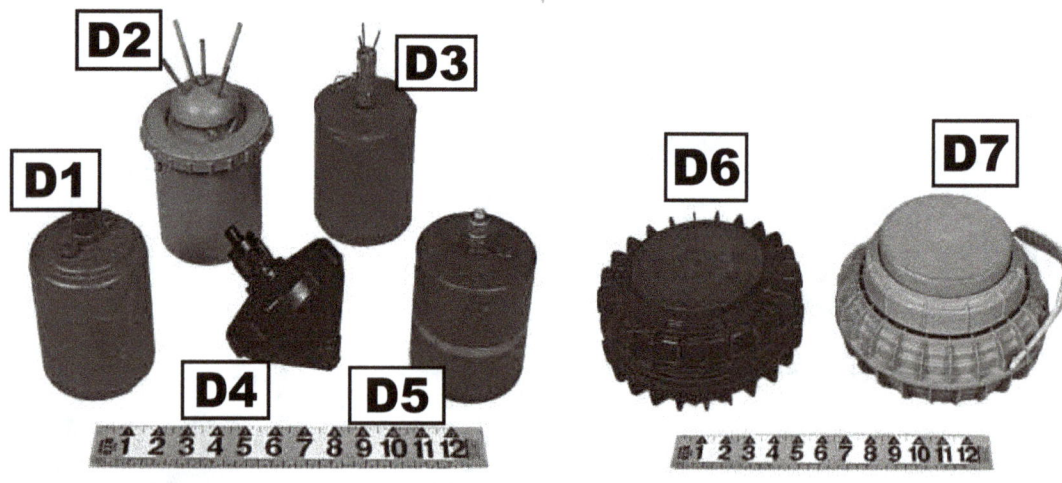

Class E: Bomblets

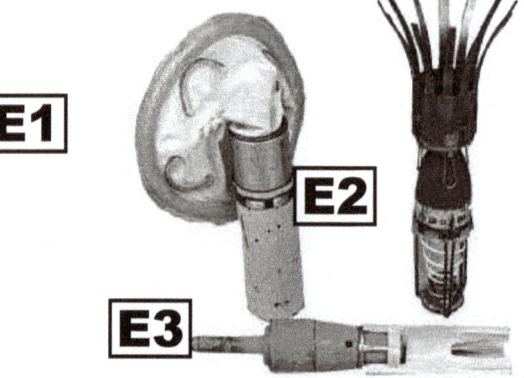

Class B: Rockets, Missiles

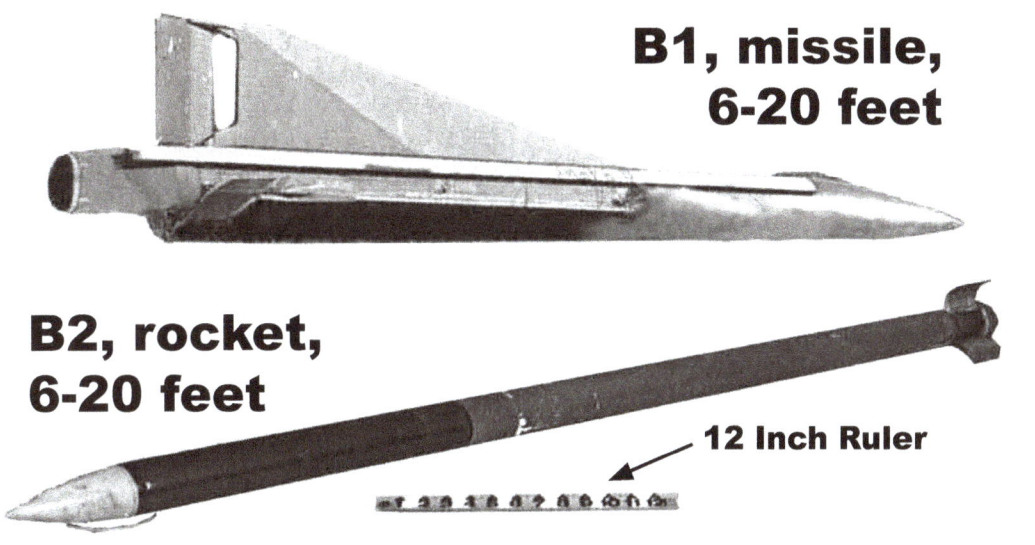

B1, missile, 6-20 feet

B2, rocket, 6-20 feet

12 Inch Ruler

Class C: Projectiles, Mortars

PROJECTILES

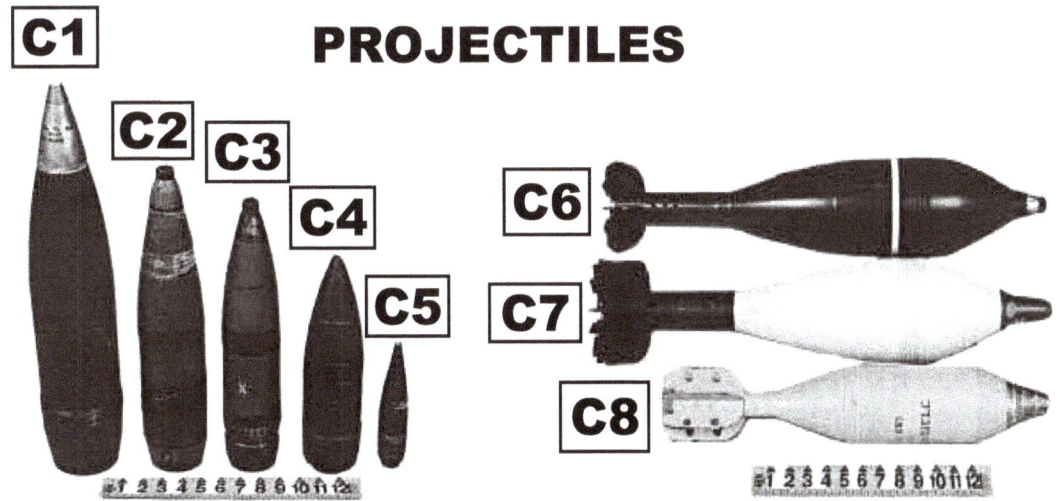

 UXO Chart

CRITICAL

Class A: Large Bombs

A1, Bomb, 3-8 ft

A2, bomb, 3-8 feet

A3, bomb, 3-8 feet

A4, bomb, 5-6 feet

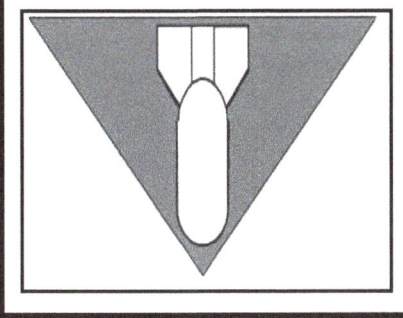

USAF Unexploded Ordnance (UXO) Recognition and Reporting Chart

Report to UCC or EOC
- Location, cordon size, how UXO is marked, and distance between UXO and marker
- Class or shape (i.e. Bravo 1)
- UXO features
- UXO condition (leaking? intact? broken?)
- Other information

BLOCK APPROACH AVENUES

UCC / EOC

CRITICAL

² UXO Survey

CRITICAL

UXO Survey
Follow UXO 5-C's - Confirm, Clear, Cordon, Check and Control.

 DO NOT...
- Touch or attempt to extinguish
- Move closer
- Transmit handheld radio within 25 ft
- Transmit vehicle radio within 100 ft

 DO...
- Approach from UPWIND or CROSSWIND
- Recognize by CLASS, SHAPE, SIZE
- Remember FEATURES, COLORS, MARKINGS
- Mark UXO
- Depart UPWIND or CROSSWIND
- Mark or barricade approach routes
- Report to UCC when safe

Post-Attack Actions

- S-A-L-U-T-E (ground attack)
- SABC self/buddy
- Decon self/buddy
- Listen for Chem/Bio alarms
- Listen for people who need help
- Survey:
  - Damage/fires
  - Facilities
  - Vehicles
  - Equipment
  - Aircraft
  - Routes
  - M8 Paper
- Survey area for UXO–mark UXO
- Report to UCC
  - UXO location(s)
  - Damage/fire(s)
  - M8 Paper
  - Casualties
- Transport casualties to CCP
- Fight fires
- Maintain UCC contact
- Request help if needed
- Continue mission

Read M8 Paper with white light only!

CRITICAL

Critical Information Checklist

Post Attack Actions 1

UXO Survey 2

USAF Unexploded Ordnance (UXO)
   Recognition and Reporting Chart ... 3

Nuclear Attack/Radioactive
   Individual Protective Actions 8

Nerve Agent Poisoning and Antidote 10

Shelter In-Place Actions 13

Lifesaving Steps 17

Bleeding Control 18

Tourniquet 19

Shock 20

Abdominal Wound 21

Common Injury Treatment 22

Spinal/Neck/Head Injury 22

Eye Injury 23

Chest Wound 23

Fracture 24

M16 Jammed 25

M9 Jammed 26

Important Phone Numbers
   and Quick Reference 27

www.ingramcontent.com/pod-product-compliance
Lightning Source LLC
Chambersburg PA
CBHW080535170426
43195CB00016B/2568